EFFECTIVE INTERVIEWING OF CHILDREN

A Comprehensive Guide for Counselors and Human Service Workers

Michael L. Zwiers, M.Ed.

Patrick J. Morrissette, Ph.D., NCC, LCPC

USA	Publishing Office:	ACCELERATED DEVELOPMENT
		A member of the Taylor & Francis Group
		325 Chestnut Street
		Philadelphia, PA 19106
		Tel: (215) 625-8900
		Fax: (215) 625-2940
	Distribution Center:	ACCELERATED DEVELOPMENT
		A member of the Taylor & Francis Group
		47 Runway Road, Suite G
		Levittown, PA 19057-4700
		Tel: (215) 269-0400
		Fax: (215) 269-0363
UK		ACCELERATED DEVELOPMENT
		A member of the Taylor & Francis Group
		1 Gunpowder Square
		London EC4A 3DE
		Tel: +44 171 583 0490
		Fax: +44 171 583 0581

EFFECTIVE INTERVIEWING OF CHILDREN: A Comprehensive Guide for Counselors and Human Service Workers

2 3 4 5 6 7 8 9 0

Printed by Edwards Brothers, Ann Arbor, MI, 1999.
Cover design by Nancy Abbott.

A CIP catalog record for this book is available from the British Library.

∞ The paper in this publication meets the requirements of the ANSI Standard Z39.48-1984 (Permanence of Paper).

Library of Congress Cataloging-in-Publication Data

Zwiers, Michael L.
    Effective interviewing of children : a comprehensive guide for counselors and human service workers / Michael L. Zwiers, Patrick J. Morrissette
        p. cm.
    Includes bibliographical references and index.
    ISBN 1-56032-741-3 (pbk. : alk. paper)
    1. Interviewing. 2. Children—Interviews. I. Morrissette, Patrick, J.
II. Title.
BF637.I5Z85   1999
158'.39'083—dc21

                                    98-43084
                                            CIP

ISBN: 1-56032-741-3

To the children in my life. You invited me into your world and revealed to me, bit by bit, all I know about interviewing. You taught me about inquiring, about pacing, about leading and following and turn-taking, but mostly about listening and observing, the heart of any interview. *MLZ*

To Eleanor Dyck (Miss Ellie) for her loving concern for children, their well-being, and happiness. *PJM*

CONTENTS

CHAPTER 3
THE PRACTICE OF THE INTERVIEW 49

CHAPTER 4
LANGUAGE OF THE INTERVIEW 69

CHAPTER 5
DEALING WITH UNIQUE CHILDREN AND CIRCUMSTANCES 93

PREFACE

This comprehensive text focuses on multiple aspects of the child-focused interview. The ultimate goals are to help both novice and seasoned professionals become knowledgeable about salient (and often overlooked) issues regarding child-focused interviews and to emphasize skills that are required for effective interviewing of children. When interviewing children, professionals need to consider carefully the biases and influences they might bring to the interview, then treat each child as a unique entity (within the broad parameters of age-based development) to be approached with a respectful and open attitude. Effective interviewing involves more than casual conversations with children and requires specific skills, knowledge of growth and developmental issues, and awareness of various methods of data collection and analysis. Until recently, minimal emphasis has been accorded to these elements.

Children are generally referred to professionals for assessment or therapeutic purposes. In addition, they are recruited as research participants or informants in legal and criminal investigations. Interviews comprise the majority of these interactions. Often, interviews are completed according to designated goals with little consideration given to the manner in which they are conducted. For example, psychiatrists conduct clinical diagnostic interviews, psychologists collect data using structured and semi-structured formats, teachers and child-care workers assess communications and elicit indicators of developmental understanding, counselors utilize empathy, police officers and social workers elicit information without using leading questions or probes, and researchers design interview protocols to collect and analyze data. In most cases, practical skills are acquired through observation of practicing professionals and are rarely articulated to developing professionals.

This book represents a synthesis of literature from various related fields pertaining to children and the interview process. Many of the techniques and suggestions offered within this text are based on extensive experience working with children in a myriad of contexts. As emphasized in this text, interviewing involves more than obtaining pertinent knowledge. Effective interviewing is couched in a relationship consisting of two or more people. As such, professionals must attend to personal needs, beliefs, and values that guide their interactions with children.

Because excellent resources are available to help professionals conduct child sexual abuse interviews and to interview children as witnesses in legal cases, no attempt has been made to replicate that work here.

Terms Used in this Book

Individuals who engage in child-focused interviews are referred to as professionals in this book. All individuals who have the task of interviewing children are accorded equal status and meaning.

From time to time the authors refer to themselves (MLZ or PJM) in presenting case studies or examples.

ACKNOWLEDGMENTS

The best way to find things out is not to ask questions at all. If you fire off a question, it is like firing off a gun—bang it goes, and everything takes flight and runs for shelter. But, if you sit quite still and pretend not to be looking, all the little facts will come and peck around your feet, situations will venture forth from thickets, and intentions will creep out and sun themselves on a stone; and, if you are very patient, you will see and understand a great deal more than a man with a gun does.

Elsepth Huxley (1982)
The Flame Tree of Thicka

This book has had a very humble beginning. Several years ago, huddled over a piece of paper at the University of Alberta, we haphazardly mapped out an outline for a potential article pertaining to the child-focused interview. Enthusiastic about our idea, we decided to delve deeper into the subject and were surprised to learn that very little literature regarding the interviewing of children was available to professionals. In a short period of time, our idea grew from a single article to a series of chapters that eventually evolved into this text. Although it seems like just yesterday that we were jotting down our ideas, a tremendous amount of time and energy has gone into what was once a small idea.

Words of thanks are due to those who helped with this book, including our friends and families and those colleagues who reviewed the manuscript and provided feedback and suggestions. Without them, this book would not have been possible.

We are especially grateful to Joe Hollis and his staff, who remained supportive and enthusiastic about our work. Joe unselfishly shared his expertise and wisdom throughout this project.

CHAPTER 1

CHILD VARIABLES

To conduct effective interviews, one must recognize developmental trends across the span of childhood and adolescence, as well as individual differences between children of similar ages. Children are so varied and unique that it hardly seems possible to identify the many ways in which they may differ from one another, as well as from adults. Professionals cannot know every difference, but they can begin to sensitize themselves to some important developmental differences. La Greca (1983) suggested that interviews are critical means of establishing rapport with, obtaining information from, and understanding the distinctive viewpoints of different children. Although some universal elements (e.g., respect, pacing) transcend the interview process regardless of the population, child-focused interviews require specific, unique knowledge and skills. In short, professionals must be prepared for the territory that they are about to explore.

The interview is a context wherein information about children can be obtained. Consequently, there is a need to be knowledgeable about developmental trends, socialization, self-awareness, memory, recall, deception, and suggestibility. Furthermore, knowledge regarding child witness issues (White, 1990) is important to those who investigate child sexual abuse. A working knowledge of developmental psychopathology (including internalizing and externalizing problems) and family dynamics is often useful.

This chapter reviews issues pertaining to the use of children's self-reports in the process of interviewing. Such reports are important when documenting histories; exploring inner thoughts, perceptions, and conceptions; or when making decisions. Effective interviewing involves a mixture of informal and structured communication acts between children and professionals. When children are carefully oriented to the interview process to determine operational developmental levels and to monitor ongoing interactions, information may be collected and interpreted appropriately. If ample time is devoted to the process, results should include fruitful and valid data collection and reliable decision-making based on the interview findings.

WHY INTERVIEW CHILDREN?

Children bring a great deal to the interview situation and can be unique and important sources of data. Children's ability to reflect, recall, and report on what they experience or observe however, may be questioned or under-valued. Consequently, rich and vital information remains uncovered because it is assumed that children are unable to articulate experiences or that child-generated information is faulty. As a result, professionals fail to pursue inquiry.

Children can be reliable reporters about their own personal experiences (Herjanic, Herjanic, Brown, & Wheatt, 1975; Hodges, 1993; Reynolds, 1993; Walco, Cassidy, & Schechter, 1994). Although Reynolds (1993) concluded that children are generally reliable reporters about themselves, he tempered this finding with the recognition that children will naturally present a range of skills in reporting their own behaviors, feelings, beliefs, and emotional states. Some children will be better equipped than others to respond to the questions of professionals.

Since children are constantly growing and developing, the influence of developmental concerns on their lives and daily functioning are important considerations. Such information can help in creating a physical and psychological environment that is conducive to children's self-disclosure. Being knowledgeable about developmental differences among children can assist professionals in making informed decisions about how to interview them sensitively and responsively. Professionals interested in factors that contribute to problematic behavior need to be aware of source contributors to later problems, as well as of potential mediating and moderating variables. Such information is emerging in the literature in the area of developmental psychopathology.

NARRATIVES AND OBSERVATIONS

Gaining the perspective of children is often a challenge; therefore, substantial data must often be inferred from observations. With children who have developed verbal skills and are prepared to share information, personal narratives can provide reliable information. However, when conversing with children, the content and the manner of their speech—their communicative intentions and interactional patterns—need to be monitored. For many children, having adults ask their opinion and inquire about their thoughts may be a highly unusual social-cultural event for which they may not have a communication map to follow. If they do respond, they may do so half-heartedly because they do not expect to be listened to with sincere interest. Children may also find it unusual to be asked to reflect on what they think or what they have experienced. Barker (1990) contended that interviewing children poses a number of challenges including: (a) children have cognitive and linguistic abilities that differ from the professional's, who may inadvertently talk either above or below a child's level; (b) children often come to an interview not of their own volition but because they have been volunteered or coerced; (c) children are familiar with being questioned about misdeeds and not for other purposes, and this leads to suspicion or uncooperativeness; (d) many children arrive misinformed regarding the intentions or methods, or both, of the interview; (e) children may have misconceptions about the role of the professional conducting the interviewing; and (f) children may actually present with some form of communication disorder. In light of these factors, a flexible interviewing approach is needed wherein the unique needs of children are recognized and appreciated. Children generally respond poorly to rigid interview settings and methods. While it may be more convenient and comfortable to follow predetermined interview formats, the best interests of children must be maintained. Despite these potential barriers to communication, valuable information can be obtained from children.

THE ROLE OF DEVELOPMENT IN THE INTERVIEW PROCESS

Developmental psychology suggests that children change and grow over time, beginning from the moment of conception. This foundational belief has implications for professionals who strive to understand what is best, or at least appropriate, for children at particular ages. To be cognizant of children's needs and abilities, it is essential to understand what is developmentally appropriate and what to expect. Although child development issues may be obvious to some professionals, many remain unaware of them. For example, unrealistic expectations may exist concerning a child's ability to sit in a chair or remain on task for an extended period of time. Without relevant knowledge and experience, an interviewer may misinterpret a normal developmental need to get up and move around as hyperactivity. Or, conversely, overactive behavior may be perceived as normal. Such erroneous assumptions can have major implications for children and their families.

Children can be assessed over extended periods of time. In some cases, complete assessments can last as long as several days. Typically however, children are assessed over the course of an extended day. Sometimes children are seen for one to two hours before being moved along to the next specialist. Justification of this demanding interview schedule is based on the notion that a change is as good as a break. Unfortunately, such thinking completely ignores children's developmental needs. Some suggest that school-age children are accustomed to attending school for a full day, and therefore, a day-long assessment is no different than a regular day of work at school. Once again, such thinking is both naive and problematic. Teachers know that the morning is the most productive time in the day, a time when young children are typically able to concentrate best. Afternoons are usually set aside for less demanding activities. In addition, a good deal of school time is lost to transitions between activities, so that children are really not expected to concentrate intensely for longer than 30 to 60 minutes at one time. If the goal is to collect valid data, then circumstances surrounding data collection should be conducive to helping children perform at optimum levels.

A thorough understanding of developmental pathways and trends can help in designing and implementing effective interactions with children. Moreover, the areas of cognitive, social, emotional, and physical development warrant careful consideration. In the final analysis, although developmental information can be helpful, an idiographic evaluation must be made of the extent to which that information applies to each child (Yuille, Hunter, Joffe, & Zaparnik, 1993). More specifically, while awareness of developmental norms may be helpful, children are not homogeneous; they differ in intelligence, language, memory, attention, social skills, and general emotional maturity (Morgan, 1995). Psychological phenomena have been found to vary with age (e.g., specific behavioral constituents of childhood depression), and attention should be rendered to developmental changes in comprehension and information processing as well as to social-cognitive perceptions of self and others (Flanery, 1990).

In addition to regular development, Yuille et al. (1993) have taken the position that professionals should be familiar with developmental psychopathology, or disordered behavior and functioning. Information is readily available in this growing field (e.g., Luthar, Burach, Cicchetti, & Weise, 1997; Rolf,

Masten, Cicchetti, Nuechterlein, & Weintraub, 1990). Knowledge of developmental psychopathology should include an awareness of behavior within the total psychological context of children; their active role in developing skills; their modes and means of solving problems to achieve goals; their flexibility in applying differing solutions and patterns; and recurrent or interlinking patterns of stability and change. Without such information, a professional may overlook serious childhood problems or inadvertently reinforce them, or both. For example, a growing concern regarding sibling abuse requires professionals to be familiar with what is a normal or abnormal interactional pattern. The problem of sibling abuse is particularly prevalent in families where violent behavior between siblings is considered healthy behavior. In other words, such behavior is seen to prepare children, particularly males, for the real world. When children do report excessive force or even injury, their concerns may be perceived as whining behavior, and they may be sent back to settle their disputes. There have been circumstances where professionals have dismissed serious violent behavior toward siblings as normal sibling rivalry.

Although much of what is believed about children's cognitive abilities and development has emerged from the pioneering work of Jean Piaget, his general findings have been challenged based on a lack of meaningful contexts for research questions and tasks, and on a methodological reliance on children's ability to verbalize their understanding (e.g., Astington, 1993; Donaldson, 1978; Dunn & Kendrick, 1982; Hughes & Baker, 1990; Siegal, 1991). Certainly, Piaget's broad-based stages of development no longer stand up to close scrutiny. In a similar vein, the work of Kohlberg (1969) has been questioned for its reliance on adult-biased moral concerns (Damon, 1977), as well as its gender bias toward males (Gilligan, 1982).

Another oft-quoted developmental theorist is Erickson (1963), whose developmental stages, while intuitively appealing, have never been empirically validated. Such shortcomings are not restricted to theorists like Piaget, Kohlberg, and Erickson; the developmental literature is rife with examples of ecologically and methodologically weak research. Results from recent investigations that utilize more appropriate methodology demonstrate that children are much more capable and competent in their reasoning and cognitive functioning than previously suspected (e.g., Harris, 1989; Perner, 1991; Stipek, Recchia, & McClintic, 1992; Wellman, 1990). These mixed findings suggest that task situations (e.g., experimental conditions) can lead to differing and misleading developmental pictures of children's abilities.

In spite of the problems that exist with the developmental literature, there is a tendency to revert to outdated roots rather than to take the time to determine what relevant current literature exists. Even recently published text-books continue to reference Piaget as more than a historical footnote. For example, Merrell (1994) raised some concerns about Piagetian stage theory, and then proceeded to describe in some detail those same stages (along with Erickson's and Kohlberg's), offering no contradictory modern research findings. Professionals need to be critical consumers of research that may misrepresent or at least underestimate children's capabilities. For some, the idea of challenging a paradigm that they have enthusiastically embraced prompts a sense of insecurity and disloyalty. For others, the challenge of integrating the available literature across a range of developmental areas is overwhelming; yet it is necessary.

Based on the developmental literature, broad individual assessments of children can be made prior to interviews. To determine general functioning, Morgan (1995) suggested that assessments include the ability to tell dates and times, a sense of measurement, numerical skills, causal relationships, and empathic perspective-taking. A traditional mental status exam will provide a brief assessment of all significant areas of functioning (e.g., American Academy of Child and Adolescent Psychiatry, 1997; Goodman & Sours, 1994). During the initial assessment, children need to be monitored, since various skills are not transferable across tasks and settings. For example, children may recognize the current date and time on a calendar and clock yet be unable to recount the day and time when a particular event occurred. In addition, the anxiety that is usually engendered by a formal interview can influence interview data. When interviewing children due to academic problems, an initial inquiry about scholastic performance should be avoided. In these circumstances, it is known from the outset that children are experiencing difficulties in school. What remains unknown, however, are the factors that contribute to their difficulties.

Children are generally anxious about an impending interview and perceive it as analogous to having to report to the principal's office (an experience they understand, if only vicariously). Depending upon their age, children may not fully understand the purpose of an interview. Those who have a better understanding still may worry about the implications of what they say or do not say. Helping children understand the purpose of an interview can be a challenging process. However, this process is critical if the goal is to alleviate anxiety and dispel misconceptions. To help young people to relax, the initial focus of an interview should be on strengths and interests. For example, the professional can state, "I don't just want to know about your problems or difficulties; I also want to know about your strengths and abilities. I want to know what is difficult and what is easy for you. Please tell me about some of the things you like about school, and things that you are good at."

THE ROLE OF SOCIALIZATION

Socialization is a complex process operating on many levels, ranging from parental to familial to cultural. The way that we are taught to behave influences personal experiences and interpretations of the world. It affects all areas of development beginning at birth. Infants have mainly an internal focus, but they turn to others to have their desires and needs met. Toddlers and young children begin to shift toward a more external focus. Stipek et al. (1992) found that after the age of 21 months, children become more socially-oriented. They visually reference parents and adults when attempting to complete tasks, thus indicating that they are seeking social recognition of success or failure. These authors described a gradual process of child socialization through three phases of self-reflection: (a) children younger than 22 months old do not engage in self-reflective evaluation nor social evaluations of performance; (b) by 2 years of age, most children are aware of approving and disapproving evaluations; and (c) by 3 years of age, children begin independently to compare their achievements to internalized standards. Based on this model, it becomes clear how children gradually internalize external standards and perhaps, accompanying beliefs and values of family, community, and society. Bruner (1990) contended that children learn to make sense of the world as they gain the ability to tell stories about it. Furthermore, he viewed narrative, a social action, as the mechanism whereby children learn to integrate what they and others think, feel, and can or cannot do.

Although growth is a gradual and continual process, Damon (1977) suggested that by ages 10 to 12, children achieve a remarkably advanced level of social understanding, including knowledge of authority, positive justice, friendship, and social regulation. As a result, professionals may be tempted to treat them as if they have adult experience and insight. Damon cautioned against adult-anthropomorphizing children's lives. For example, one may be tempted to apply adult conceptions of friendship to two playmates, and judge one who shares a toy as kind or generous and another who shoves as hostile, when neither interpretation may be correct. A child may be sharing or pushing out of curiosity, imitation, or an attempt to socialize.

Professionals need to empathize with children in order to see the world through their young eyes. During an interview with two sisters, a pattern emerged wherein the younger sister would take a piece of the game away and run around the room. In response, her older sister would pursue her, retrieve the piece, then strike her sister who would cry and eventually withdraw. At first glance, one could assume that the younger sister was attempting to create a conflict with her sibling. As the pattern continued however, the older sister removed herself from the game and began to nurture her sibling. Consequently, the interactional pattern between the siblings became more evident.

SOCIAL-DEVELOPMENT FACTORS

Social-developmental factors can influence the interview process. As stated previously, children arrive at interviews without a working model for what an interview is. As a result, they draw on personal experiences to form a template for their interaction with professionals. Stipek et al. (1992) suggested that toddlers and young children have difficulty telling the difference between adult-prescribed behavioral norms and adult-prescribed achievement goals, meaning that these children may interpret a request to "answer these questions as best you can," as an expectation or demand to respond to all questions in a prescribed way. Children may previously have experienced criticism when trying something new (an achievement goal). Consequently, they may be anxious and anticipate criticism from a professional, especially if they are unable to respond to a question or request. In some cases, parents may instruct their children to cooperate, listen, and behave. Each one of these instructions may have a detrimental effect on the subsequent professional-child interaction. In any of these situations, professionals will be met with unexpected responses that require skillful management, including reorienting the children to the interview context (e.g., situation, goals, and process).

Gender-based and age-related socialization can also affect child-focused interviews. For example, although 2-year-old boys and girls initiate conversations about feeling states equally as often, their mothers are twice as likely to initiate feeling state conversations with their daughters as with their sons, a likely contributor to later gender differences in emotional expression and willingness to discuss things of an emotional nature (Dunn, Bretherton, & Munn, 1987). Remaining cognizant of this can help professionals become sensitive to a young boy's inability to express and articulate his feeling states. The assumption that young boys do not want to discuss their feelings may be erroneous. Rather, they may not have had the opportunity to practice speaking and receiving feedback about their feelings. This important information has major implications for how young men respond to personal issues and how they interact with others as they mature.

Age-related socialization also occurs. Until about 8 years of age, children gain their sense of accomplishment from parents and significant others, but by age 9 or 10, positive value judgments emerge from interactions with friends and their peer group (Dupont, 1994). Developmental changes impact on socialization, and can assist or impede the work of professionals. Stone and Lemanek (1990) reported that around 8 years of age, children begin to provide more details about experiences and situations than their younger counterparts; however, social desirability also begins to influence their responses negatively.

Cultural differences are also surmised to exist in children's development (Graham & Weiner, 1991). In some cultures, children quickly learn and begin to apply social display rules, masking their inner thoughts and feelings because it is expected of them. Kitayama, Markus, and Matsumoto (1995) noted that such masking behaviors exist in the North American culture, but not as commonly as in some Asian cultures. Obviously, masking behaviors will make it increasingly difficult to assess inner worlds, especially if children believe that they are not supposed to talk about certain things. Professionals who attempt to collect information of a cultural, gender, or age-influenced nature will be impeded in their efforts and will have to move sensitively and carefully if they are to be successful in eliciting responses.

CONCEPTUAL DEVELOPMENT

Even very young children have some form of inner working model of the world and how its various parts operate. According to Astington (1993), children construct this working model through their life experiences and emerge into the community with pre-obtained understandings and beliefs about the world. Wellman (1990) found that as early as 3 years of age, children typically have both an experiential and a theoretical foundation for beliefs, desires, and dreams, while Astington added that by 4 years of age, they understand that their mind construes and interprets situations and things. Although Carey (1978) stated that children's concepts or theories evolve over time, with new ones replacing the old, Pramling (1983) found that old theories are not always abandoned and may be retained for particular situations or events. If this holds true, then conceptions can be perceived as integrally tied to the meanings attributed to each unique situation (e.g., interpretations). In accordance with this belief, Feldman (1992) suggested that professionals should strive to understand and interpret the meaning accompanying behavior rather than to explain and predict the behavior. If this perspective is used as a guideline, professionals cannot expect their knowledge of developmental literature to be predictive since it applies to the mythical, but nonexistent, average child, while they deal with specific children.

Until recently, research on children's conceptual development has been scant. Jean Piaget was one of the early researchers to study a child's view of the world, work that he carried out in France in the early part of this century. Much of his initial research (e.g., Piaget, 1926, 1929, 1930) was pure exploratory inquiry that attempted to understand children's views of the world, and pre-dated his stage theory. More recently, researchers have explored children's conceptions of a variety of things including: self, mind, reality, and knowledge (Broughton, 1978); friendship, authority, positive justice, and social regulation (Damon, 1977); learning (Pramling, 1983, 1986, 1988, 1990); and mental experiences in contrast to imagery, photographs, smoke, and shadows (Wellman, 1990). These explorations prove that it is indeed possible to obtain useful self-reports of preschoolers' conceptions of experiences.

SELF-AWARENESS IN CHILDREN

To be self-aware, an individual must have a sense of self as distinct from others, a memory of personal actions and experiences, and the ability to recall those events. To be self-reflective and self-evaluative, children must have a relatively stable self-concept (Stipek et al., 1992), a reference point which Lewis and Brooks-Gunn (1979) refer to as a categorical self-concept. By 15 months of age, infants begin to recognize themselves in a mirror, videotape or photograph, an ability present in most by 2 years of age (Lewis, Sullivan, Stanger, & Weiss, 1989). This recognition appears about the same time as toddlers begin to use personal pronouns (Kagan, 1984), evidence of their emerging awareness of a physical self, and their growing ability to self-reflect (Stipek et al., 1992). By 18 months of age, children begin to be able to solve problems by insight, to talk about past events, things that are out of sight, and hypothetical situations. These abilities crystallize in most children by 2 years of age (Astington, 1993). This cognitive growth parallels children's advancing ability to engage in pretend play (Astington; Wellman & Hickling, 1993). Stipek (1995) presented evidence for children's self-reflective capacity emerging possibly by 2 years of age, and most certainly by 3 years of age. Using a methodology that allowed researchers to witness children's success and failure behaviors with an adult present, Stipek et al., (1992) reported that children begin to anticipate adult reactions to their achievements sometime within the second half of the second year, with nearly half of 21-month-olds calling their mother's attention to some achievement during a 10-minute free-play period. In addition, Stipek (1995) noted that between 36 and 42 months of age, children shift to autonomous self-evaluation that does not require adult mediation.

Wellman (1990) suggested that before the age of 3, children conceptualize the mind as a type of container, a repository of information related to their desires, and that around 3 years of age this conceptualization changes significantly. As they reach this transitional age (3 years), Wellman reported, preschool children begin to understand that their mind is capable of perceiving, construing, and interpreting information about the world, after which they see it as capable of hypothesizing, conjecturing, and reasoning. Once this initial breakthrough in understanding is made, it remains relatively stable, although 4-year-olds are much more fluent in explaining inner beliefs than their 3-year-old counterparts. Astington (1993) called this development a representational theory of mind, an understanding that the mind constructs a representation of reality. Johnson and Foley (1984) reported that by 6 years of age, children are able to clearly distinguish between thoughts (ideas, notions, fantasies) and experiences (events, actions). In experimental research conditions however, children sometimes had trouble distinguishing between what they actually said aloud and what they were asked only to think about. Since children have been found to have no trouble distinguishing between thought and action in the real world, this series of studies demonstrates how previous research findings can be shown to be an artifact of experimental conditions and misinterpretation of language rather than a reflection of real differences in children's ability to discriminate between fact and fantasy.

Some open-ended interview data has suggested that during preschool years most children conceptualize and describe themselves in physical terms (Bierman & Schwartz, 1986; Broughton, 1978), with little distinction between inner experience and overt behavior. However, the notion of a bodily-based sense of self may not be an entirely accurate representation of reality, since preschool children have been found to report on social and psychological self-conceptions and causes of behavior, though not as often as they do later in life (Damon & Hart, 1982; Livesley & Bromley, 1973; Stone & Lemanek, 1990). Additionally, preschool children have the ability to manipulate mental representations, although they have difficulty holding more than one concept at a time and have trouble inferring the thoughts and feelings of others (Bierman & Schwartz, 1986). Miller and Aloise (1989) suggested that the internal-external dichotomy utilized by some developmental researchers is simplistic and unhelpful, especially given the overwhelming evidence that preschoolers are able to describe internal states and make social-causal attributions.

Between 6 and 8 years of age, most children shift their peer comparisons from behavioral to psychological constructs (e.g., I am bigger versus I am smarter) (Barenboim, 1981). At about 7 years of age, children are able to discriminate between their actions and feelings in different situations and gain a relational/ situational sense of self (Stone & Lemanek, 1990). For example, children can begin to see themselves as competent in one school subject and not so capable in another (Harter, 1986). Between 7 and 12 years of age, they

gradually demonstrate more flexible conceptions of social roles and relationships, a growth that leads to a more complex, adult-like view of self in relation
to others (Damon, 1983).

Following a thorough review of the literature on self-concept development, Damon and Hart (1982) advanced a working model of self-understand-
ing that (a) progresses from physical to psychological, (b) includes an emerging sense of stable social personality characteristics, (c) includes an increasingly self-reflective and metacognitive awareness of self, and (d) proposes a
gradual integration of diverse aspects of self into an integrated and unified
conception. Using this model as a guideline, it is possible to monitor children's
growth on a continuum of understanding.

In the domain of emotional experience, Stone and Lemanek (1990) suggested that until about 8 years of age, children are not able to provide accurate
reports of their own emotions, recounting the internal-external dichotomy to
support their position. Given the current information regarding children's developing self-awareness and the discussion regarding mental and bodily-based
self-conceptions, this cut-off seems extreme. In contrast to this position,
Bretherton, Fritz, Zahn-Waxler, and Ridgeway (1986) found that by 3 years of
age, children have a general understanding of themselves and others as emotional beings, can label basic feeling states, make simple causal attributions
regarding feelings, and involve themselves in pretend play with emotional
expression. These findings have been supported elsewhere (e.g., Smiley &
Huttenlocher, 1989). Although controlled experimental studies that assess
children's verbal knowledge of emotion seem to underestimate their conceptual understanding, observation-based studies of children's emotional behavior have consistently revealed that even very young children have a substantial working knowledge of emotion (Heckhausen, 1988; Jennings, 1993;
Terwogt & Olthof, 1989).

In addition to understanding single emotions, several authors (e.g., Harter,
1986; Harter & Whitesell, 1989) have identified five stages of development in
children's understanding of dual emotions:

1. At 5 years of age, children deny that two feelings can occur together.

2. By 7 years of age, children believe that two emotions can be experi-
    enced simultaneously as long as they are the same valence (either
    positive or negative) and as long as they are directed at a single
    target.

3. By 8 years of age, children believe that they can feel two same-valence feelings simultaneously as long as the targets of the emotions are different.

4. By the age of 10, children are able to appreciate their experience of opposite valence emotions directed at the same target.

5. By 11 years of age, children are able to understand that they can experience both negative and positive feelings about the same person at the same time.

Future research may determine that these are late estimates of emerging ability, but existing information can guide child-focused interviews.

Although much of what has been reported is representative of typical groups of children, not all children are the same and there will be a wide variance of behaviors at every age level. Children with special needs or circumstances may present with even more extreme differences. Bierman and Schwartz (1986) stated that developmental trends must be weighed against the individual growth of each child being interviewed, since differences exist in both age and speed of growth, with varying levels of achievement in different domains of ability and different circumstances.

Besides the natural range of differences, Wilson (1985) outlined four conditions that can influence accurate self-awareness of mental states, including motivated self-deception, incorrect adoption of a feeling vocabulary, the child's ability to process prior attitudes, and the effects of self-reflection. In addition to these noted conditions, existing circumstances can influence children's ability to reflect and express themselves (e.g., hunger, pain, exhaustion, fear, anxiety, threat, or coercion). Finally, mental and physical diseases or conditions can play a significant role in current or permanent level of functioning (e.g., autism, mental retardation, schizophrenia, depression, anxiety, posttraumatic stress, or substance or medically-induced amnesia, delirium, dementia, or psychosis).

MEMORY, RECALL, AND SELF-REPORT OF CHILDREN

During infancy, it is obvious that children store and recall information. The fact that children repeat what they have learned supports some form of operational memory. Although preschoolers' memory skills may be confirmed through either direct observation or careful study of their behavior, it is not until they are approximately 2 or 3 years old that they possess sufficient language skills to be tested with research paradigms similar to those used with older children and adults (Bjorklund & Muir, 1988). Even then, experiments must be designed cautiously with children's language abilities in mind, otherwise accurate findings are jeopardized. Because studies of memory utilize methodologies with wavering ecological validity and different recall times, variable results can be difficult to integrate. Consumers of such research are encouraged to pay careful attention to the findings, and to favor ecologically valid methods when results differ.

In naturalistic observations of children, Todd and Perlmutter (1980) indicated that 1- and 2-year-olds will recall information following cued prompts, and that, by the age of 3, children typically have the skills to independently recall and narrate events that have happened to them, generally in the form of basic outlines that lack detail. Research consistently reveals that children spontaneously recall less than adults, with the amount of information provided increasing steadily with age, until it matches adult levels at around 12 years of age (Cole & Loftus, 1987). Hamond and Fivush (1991) discovered developmental differences in children's recall of events. Although younger children (4-years-old at the time of the interview and 2½ at the time of the event) recalled as many main events as older children (5 years old at the time of the interview and 4½ at the time of the event), they did not provide as much detail surrounding those events. Apparently, the amount of detail provided by children has more to do with age at the time of the event than the age at the time of recall. Children who were older at the time of the events were able to spontaneously offer more detail than the younger children, who needed prompts to provide additional information.

Findings reveal that, although they may provide less information than those of their older counterparts, children's autobiographical memories, even in those as young as 2½ years, can be quite accurate (Fivush, 1993; Marin, Holmes, Guth, & Kovac, 1979). Preschoolers are as accurate as older children or adults, but are most accurate when reporting main events rather than peripheral details (Goodman & Reed, 1986; Warren & Swartwood, 1992). Overall, young children seem to be better at recalling actions rather than peripheral details, a determination that will affect their performance on experimental tasks that require them to recall minutiae (Cole & Loftus, 1987). Not surprisingly, children are more accurate when reporting familiar and personally meaningful events that they have experienced than when reporting those that they see as unimportant, such as stories and events fabricated for research studies (Bjorklund & Muir, 1988; Steward, Bussey, Goodman, & Saywitz, 1993). In fact, when asked to recall activities they are quite familiar with, children's memory abilities tend to be comparable to or better than adults (Johnson & Foley, 1984;

intense emotions provided more consistent and extensive reports, though their stories deteriorated the more frequently they retold them. In similar research with children, Warren and Swartwood (1992) indicated that emotional response was not found to increase children's recall, although it did result in longer narratives. In a review of literature on the effects of emotion on memory, Reisberg and Heuer (1992) reported that emotion has variable effects on memory, sometimes enhancing and other times undermining it; emotion generally slows the process of forgetting yet creates unusual intrusion errors. Saywitz and Snyder (1993) reflected on the role of emotional factors in recall performance, and suggested that memory for emotionally laden material may be either heightened or impaired. These authors reported that memory for events may be impaired if children are asked to recall them in stressful surroundings such as a courtroom; strategies for emotional self-regulation may influence recall (e.g., avoidance, denial); and finally, preexisting emotional disorders (e.g., posttraumatic stress, depression) may affect concentration, motivation, mood, or self-esteem which in turn influence recall.

DECEPTION: CAN CHILDREN LIE?

Even very young children have a conception of truthfulness and the morality associated with it. By 4 years of age, and perhaps earlier, children know that deliberately misleading someone is wrong, and the majority of 5-year-olds state that it is always wrong to lie (Eckman, 1989). Children as young as 4 years of age can differentiate lies from truthful statements (Haugaard & Crosby, 1989). Although those younger than 3 years of age may unintentionally make a mistake and tell a lie, they have not been found to tell deliberate lies (Eckman, 1989). They are more likely to make errors of omission than of commission (Steward et al., 1993).

Even though Piaget (1959) suggested that children under 7 or 8 years of age do not believe that they can conceal their thoughts from others, current research findings suggest that by 3 or 4 years of age, children know that people can deliberately mislead others. By 3 or 4 years of age, some children will lie deliberately, especially if the negative consequences of being caught lying are minimal (Eckman, 1989) or if the anticipated consequences of telling the truth include punishment (Bussey, 1990). Based on parental and teacher reports, Eckman reported that although the vast majority of children do not lie often, about 5% of children at all ages do lie often. Eckman also reported that strong emotions create involuntary changes in behavior that are not easy to conceal. Although young children have the psychological capacity to lie, it is very difficult for them to hide strong emotions (as seen through changes in facial expression, hand movements, posture, or sound of voice) and convincingly tell an untruth, a task that even experienced adults find difficult. Interestingly, Ceci and Crotteau Huffman (1997) have demonstrated that once false memories and beliefs have been planted in preschoolers' minds and reinforced, experts are unable to identify them as lies (likely because the children believe them to be true and do not exhibit tell-tale signs of discomfort).

ARE CHILDREN SUGGESTIBLE?

Children tend to communicate most accurately when their recall is grounded in real-life experiences and events, especially when they are personally significant or emotionally salient (Steward et al., 1993). Young children will also recount information more accurately, albeit in less detail, during free recall, and they will provide more complete accounts when direct questioning is utilized, although the integrity of what is recalled is affected (King & Yuille, 1987; Schwartz & Schwanenflugel, 1989). These findings underscore the influence of suggestibility when children are asked more direct questions, or at least the encouragement of creative thinking that distorts what is remembered.

Ceci, Toglia, and Ross (1987) indicated that preschool children are more easily influenced by suggestive or misleading information than are older children and adults, although much of the reviewed research was conducted using children's recall of stories rather than their recall of personal experience. In instances of personal experience recall, even younger children are less sensitive to suggestion, as long as the event is personally significant (Fivush, 1993).

Loftus and Davies (1984) reviewed a number of research studies regarding children and adults to determine whether children are more or less suggestible than adults. They reported variable findings (in studies on children of different ages under differing research conditions), and reached the conclusion that children and adults are both susceptible to suggestion, given the right circumstances. These authors further proposed that the children's interest in what they are seeing, the time delay between exposure and request for recall, and their reduced language capacities all have potential for impact on both suggestibility and recall.

Cole and Loftus (1987) determined that children under 7 years of age are more susceptible to misinformation regarding peripheral details than are adults, particularly in stressful situations, though they do not appear to be any more suggestible than adults with regards to the central elements of an event. Some researchers have suggested that children 4 years of age and older are no more suggestible than adults with regards to central aspects of their direct life experiences that are understood and interpreted as personally meaningful (Fivush, 1993; Melton & Thompson, 1987).

Saywitz (1990) even suggested that 4- to 9-year-old children may be less resistant to suggestibility than their older counterparts when they are recollecting less significant life events. Eckman (1989) stated that, "children are most susceptible to misinformation if their original memory of the area of misinformation is weak; the misinformation deals with a peripheral, not central, event; and the interviewer who provides this information is an adult they respect" (p. 174). Goodman, Rudy, Bottoms, and Aman (1990) supported this latter contention.

Children are easily influenced by suggestion, and seek acceptance from adults, especially their parents, yet have different concerns about confidentiality than do adults (Goodman & Sours, 1994). Apparently, children are interested in describing events but do not want to malign their parents or betray their trust. Any of these factors could make children susceptible to coaching or suggestion from their parents, particularly if their parents have interrogated them using leading questions. Lepore and Sesco (1994) found that children 4 to 6 years of age can be influenced to report false information about another person's actions if professionals make incriminating statements (particularly when children have had only a brief encounter with an adult whom they don't know well). If children have been previously interviewed using leading or suggestive questions, information recalled may be accurate or it may have been distorted by the questioning (Jones, 1992).

Unfortunately, after memories have been distorted, they seem to persist (Loftus & Davies, 1984), and such memory distortions are not always self-evident. In a series of research studies conducted on preschoolers, Ceci and Crotteau Huffman (1997) demonstrated the powerful effects of suggestibility and the persistence of false memories, especially when suggestions are introduced repeatedly over time. Ceci, Toglia, and Ross (1987) highlighted the effects of demand characteristics when they compared children's responses to suggestive questions asked by adults versus the same ones asked by other children. They found that adults were more influential than were other children, although results indicated that some children are highly suggestible while others are very resistant to suggestion no matter who does the suggesting.

Children may sometimes follow adult suggestions even though they realize it is wrong. Professionals can influence children through both verbal and nonverbal cues, whether intentional or not. Morgan (1995) cautioned that professionals must choose words carefully or risk having responses distorted and data challenged by others. Adults have been found to be somewhat susceptible to professional suggestion, while research on children provides us with mixed results. As reported earlier, direct questioning affects the integrity of what is recalled and results in less accurate recollection. Wood and Wood (1983) found that in low-control questioning situations (where comments and reflective statements were made along with open-ended questions), preschoolers showed more initiative in raising topics, elaborating, commenting, or asking questions. The frequent use of direct, closed questions, however, led to passive children providing unreliable information. (More is said about questioning in Chapter 4.) Unfortunately, the younger children are, the more difficult it is for them to recall freely, with the result that professionals use more questions and increase the potential for suggestibility.

Although much has been said about how suggestibility can change children's memories, and therefore their self-reports, this is not always the case. In King and Yuille's work (1987), some children admitted to going against what they knew to be true because they felt compelled to do so by the professional. In such a case, although the report has been distorted, the memory has not been transformed and the original memory will persist as opposed to the misinformation.

CREDIBILITY OF SELF-REPORTS

Perry and Wrightsman (1991) suggested that a child's credibility should be assessed via, "consistency of the account, vocabulary appropriate to the child's developmental level, lack of motivation to fabricate the account, appropriate affect (e.g., fear, guilt), spontaneity, consistency with the laws of nature and with corroborative evidence" (p. 246). These authors also indicated that competence to testify is usually decided by the trial judge (though psychologists, psychiatrists, or social workers may be involved), based on children's ability to observe, remember, and be truthful. Research reveals that most children can do these things by the age of 2 or 3 years.

In closing, Lepore and Sesco (1994) noted that experimental research often has limited external validity. Therefore, professionals must be cautious when interpreting and using research findings. However, Saywitz (1990) asserted that as studies of children's recall approach ecological and contextual validity, children's accuracy and ability to resist suggestion improve. When naturalistic research paradigms are used, children tend not to be very suggestible (King & Yuille, 1987). At the same time, professionals are wise to remember that every child is unique, and although they may be familiar with even well-designed research studies, they must always view each child as a distinct case in point. Given the mixed research results, professionals need to approach each child as a unique individual and to do everything possible to ensure that the interview is not contaminated by suggestion or leading questions. In the final analysis, all children should be seen as competent and truthful unless proved otherwise.

A thorough working knowledge of pertinent developmental research is important when working with children. To this end, relevant areas of the published literature, including social growth, self-concept, self-awareness, memory, self-report, and issues of suggestibility and deception have been reviewed. Other related areas that have been addressed include developmental psychopathology and family dynamics. Knowing what the literature reports regarding the mythical but nonexistent average child can provide helpful guidelines for what to expect of children in various age groups; however, the uniqueness of each child must never be overlooked. The skillful application of orientation, rapport-building, and observation will help ensure that children's self-reports are rich and useful. In order to individualize interviews with children effectively, a blend of structured and unstructured communicative interactions is recommended. Although it may seem a daunting and challenging task to individualize interview interactions with children and youth, the benefits of finding a successful balance can be extensive.

CHAPTER 2

PROFESSIONAL VARIABLES

Until recently, professionals have paid little or no attention to how they influence children through their actions, statements, and underlying beliefs. Akin to the astronomical concept of perturbation (whereby a planet's gravitational pull influences the progress of another as they pass by each other) the influence of professionals on the outcome of an interview is direct and noticeable. With a growing appreciation of the reciprocal nature of interviews, interest has developed in understanding the subtleties of interpersonal transactions and the mutuality of the interview process.

McNamee (1989) contended, "What adults learn from talking with young children has as much to do with the adult's competency, sensitivity, and knowledge about the child and his way of thinking and speaking as it does with the child's linguistic competencies" (p. 90). In addition, what professionals learn from youngsters has as much to do with their personal awareness of their own beliefs and experiences as it does with the beliefs and experiences of the children being interviewed.

In the final analysis, the outcome of interviews will be a direct result of the nature of the interview topic, the questions that professionals choose to ask, the interpersonal climate between children and professionals, and the communication process.

THE INTERVIEW TOPIC

When reviewing research proposals, ethics review committees look for potential negative effects that the research topics and processes can have on the study participants. Similarly, investigations that utilize an interview format as a source of descriptive data should be subjected to the same close scrutiny. Even if professionals are not interviewing children as part of a research study, they need to consider carefully any potential negative effects on children. At first glance, it seems that little harm could result from simply asking children questions. However, closer inspection reveals that potential problems do exist and need to be considered in regard to child-focused interviews. For example, while interviewing children, routine questions are asked about physical, emotional, or sexual abuse. Although some children will not have been victimized, having such questions asked could invoke personal anxiety and contribute to a fear of being victimized. They may also have illogical but highly emotional fears about being removed from the care of their parents. The prospect of being apprehended by child protective services is a common concern of children and one that is often intensified in those who have actually been abused. In such cases, the act of inquiry may contribute to children's emotional despair and a reluctance to disclose vital information.

Furthermore, children who disclose abuse will frequently request that their disclosure remain confidential to protect their parents or to avoid reprisal from a perpetrator or others. For example, during an interview with a 6-year-old, one of the authors (PJM) became acutely aware of a child's reluctance to describe the abuse he had endured while in the care of his adolescent male babysitter. The youngster eventually disclosed during the interview that the babysitter threatened to kill his pet rabbit if he were to tell anyone about the abuse. Only after a trusting relationship had been established was the child able to discuss his fear for the welfare of his pet.

In another example, during an interview with an 8-year-old girl who had been struck across the back with a belt by her mother, the other author (MLZ) was admonished by the girl not to tell anyone. "My mom is getting help because she gets mad all the time. So it's okay," the girl reasoned. The response was, "If your mother is getting help, and she is still getting mad enough to strike you with a belt, then the help she is getting isn't working, and the person who is trying to help her needs to know that." She said that if the author told someone, she and her sister would be taken away from their mother. The response was, "I know that you love your mother very much, and you don't want to be separated from her [acknowledgment of her fears]. Child protective services might separate you from your mother, or they might not [demonstration of several possible outcomes]. However, it is dangerous and wrong for your mother to hurt you when she gets mad, and I need to make sure that you are safe from being hurt and that your mother gets the help that she needs [expression of concern and explanation of purpose]."

At that point, the youngster was advised that the law required a report to child welfare; then she was asked if she would like to disclose the abuse to a child welfare worker herself, or if she would like to be present when the telephone call was made. She decided to sit nearby and listen while the author spoke on the telephone. The youngster visibly calmed down, and seemed to gain a sense of control, when she knew that she was able to listen in. In both case examples, initial queries heightened the anxiety and fear of each child, and appropriate responses were necessary to calm and reassure both children. Children need not feel an increased sense of disempowerment or violation when being assisted.

Most professionals are sensitive to the possible problems that can arise from discussing topics such as child abuse, drug use, sexuality, or criminal acts. However, not all professionals are sensitive to the possible negative consequences of apparently less provocative topics of investigation. Effective interviewing requires a sensitivity to children throughout the interview, regardless of the focus. Topics that may appear innocuous can contribute to children's anxiety, discomfort, or distress. Children, for example, will sometimes begin to discuss issues that they fear will portray them as abnormal or bad. In these circumstances, they worry that they will be judged for their thoughts, beliefs, or experiences and are concerned about whether professionals who are conducting the interviews will accept them. If such reactions (e.g., heightened anxiety) are noticed in children, the professional should take ample time to reassure youngsters that they are not being judged or evaluated, that there are no right or wrong responses, and that they will be accepted for who they are as individuals. In some circumstances, children may become upset by something that is totally unpredictable.

For example, while talking with a young boy about cars, a topic that is commonly of interest to young boys, MLZ found him becoming tearful. After closer investigation, MLZ discovered that this boy's aunt had recently died in a car crash. While asking another boy about his home life, MLZ noticed that he began to talk very quietly while describing his bedroom. With some probing, he acknowledged that the room he slept in had once been his uncle's room and that his uncle had committed suicide in the same room. "My uncle hung himself from the neck when he was drunk," he said. He went on to describe his reaction to entering the room and discovering his uncle's body.

Although it is difficult to predict what will upset a child, potential topics that can trigger distressing thoughts or memories (e.g., death, violence, abandonment) require attention. For youngsters who are reluctant to express their feelings, their inner distress may go unnoticed unless they are observed carefully and queried about their feelings. More than likely, they will also require continual reassurance, particularly before and after a significant disclosure. Although some children may not appear upset by questions about contentious subjects, each child needs to be evaluated individually. As potentially sensitive information is gathered, personal reactions, thoughts, and feelings that pertain to the content of the interview and the behaviors of children must be monitored (Corey, Corey, & Callahan, 1993).

Although some children are cautious, others will readily disclose transgressions to professionals. Following disclosures, some children fear reprisal and request that their parents not be informed of their transgressions. During school-based interviews, children may express similar concerns about teachers or principals. Although many children will speak candidly, others are reluctant and fear censure or reprimand. Under these circumstances, children need to be reassured that they will not be reprimanded by professionals or others for choosing to disclose or not to disclose.

Corey, Corey, and Callahan (1998) reviewed salient issues facing professionals conducting child-focused interviews within a school context. These authors emphasized the need to be aware of dynamics within the school setting and specific state laws regarding confidentiality. In the case of the criminal or court system, such assurances may not be possible. When such options are available, children need to be fully informed of their rights and responsibilities under the law from the outset of an interview. They need to be cognizant of potential penalties, as well as available support and protective services. Such information can reduce defensiveness and psychological distress. More detailed information pertaining to confidentiality and related issues is discussed in the chapter on ethical interviewing.

Following interviews during which sensitive information is disclosed, it may be useful to inform parents or guardians about the topics discussed (aside from issues of confidentiality) and the potential emotional ramifications. If parents and guardians are not present following an interview, it is recommended that they be contacted by telephone. Since the effects of an interview cannot always be observed directly following an interview, professional-parent communication can occur regardless of a youngster's apparent disposition. Contacting families shortly after an interview can also ease parental anxiety and demonstrate a genuine concern. Never underestimate the difficulty parents can experience when their children are involved with professional services. Conducting interviews can become common-place for helping professionals and they may overlook the significance that parents (and children) attribute to this process.

Being available to process interviews can be helpful to children who are institutionalized (e.g., in groups homes or hospital wards) and separated from their parents or guardians. These children may lack immediate family support and an opportunity to process their emotions. Feeling isolated while grappling with highly charged emotions, can have unfortunate consequences. While working in a number of group homes, we have often witnessed children return from interviews and begin to act out their internal turmoil through volatile and disruptive behavior. Far too often, their reaction led to physical restraints, police involvement, more restrictive care (e.g., hospitalization, secure treatment in an isolation room), or all of these. Had we anticipated the relevant topics or concerns raised in interviews, we might have been able to continue to offer psychological support in order to process the children's intense emotions.

LEADING AND FOLLOWING

Regardless of the particular interview circumstances, preconceptions, beliefs, and even prejudices can influence the process and outcome. According to Mishler (1986), professionals carry into an interview "a set of assumptions and implicit criteria about the adequacy of a response" (p. 57). Those underlying mindsets affect the questions asked, the manner in which they are asked, and how children are responded to. To lessen the impact of professional skew, it has been suggested interviews should be conducted with open minds, biases set aside, and an attitude of innocence and open curiosity devoid of either assumptions or expectations be assumed (Goodwin, Sahd, & Rada, 1982; Jones, 1992). In some cases, this may require challenging and rethinking established beliefs about children and information collecting philosophies.

Data can be lost when professionals are inattentive or blind to the emerging content. Children may communicate important information that might be overlooked or misinterpreted. For example, a sexually abused child might state, "I don't like it when grandpa plays with my toys." The word "toys" may be a euphemism for sexual body parts, a fact that might be overlooked when the professional hears only the surface message. In remaining attentive to a child's verbal affect (e.g., emotional tone, sense of urgency, and importance) and nonverbal body language (e.g., eye-aversion, stilled body), the underlying meaning conveyed and how it affects the child may be better understood. So as not to miss important content, preconceived ideas regarding how children will respond need to be bracketed.

QUESTION SELECTION

The selection of questions used during interviews requires careful consideration for a number of reasons. First, questions highlight personal interests and can miss significant arenas of exploration. Second, selected questioning reflects preconceptions and misconceptions. Third, the same question may be asked in a number of ways by a variety of professionals, each communicating different messages through verbal and nonverbal cues. Fourth, questions can be interpreted by children in a variety of ways, depending on the language, on delivery, and on the children's previous experience. Professionals should not assume that all children understand questions in the same way, mean the same thing by their answers, or share similar meanings with researchers. To understand children's language and communications, new methods of eliciting information while questioning children must be developed (Wells, 1989).

Appreciating the mutuality of an interview, and realizing that children can be inadvertently influenced to respond in certain ways either through acts of omission or commission, needs to be underscored. Wells (1989) asserted that adults have historically suppressed children's experiences by interpreting their language rather than examining its meaning. She pointed out that traditional methods of interrogation were characterized by threats and entreaties to tell under heavy adult authority, with the result that children would reveal only what was expected. A child's responses can be influenced by leading questions (Lepore and Sesco, 1994). This may be especially true if professionals have preconceptions about what children know or may have experienced. Inadvertently, professionals mold children's reports by including misinformation or misinterpretation in questions. Additionally, children's responses might be reinterpreted, or aspects of their self-reports might be selectively reinforced or ignored. For example, Kahn (1994) warned that psychologically trained professionals gathering affective data unavoidably tinge interviews with psychological interpretation. Kahn stated, "Interviewers' inquiries, as well as their direction and points of follow-up, strongly affect the course and content of the interview" (p. 92). These concerns are present within the interview itself and, following the interview, when the data is reviewed and analyzed.

Important information can be lost if professionals do not know where to begin. Furthermore, initial inquiries need to be open-ended and inviting. If appropriate questions are not asked or children are not invited to speak openly, youngsters may filter out or never share valuable information. According to Lukas (1993), "The purpose of the (initial) question is to begin eliciting the child's understanding of why *she thinks* she has been brought to you and get a sense of her expectations and concerns" (p. 67). Once this is known, misconceptions can be corrected before proceeding. In addition, once questions have been posed, professionals need to be open to the children's responses. Because children do not possess well developed experiential and cognitive tools to describe their lives verbally, they tend to communicate symbolically or metaphorically (Lukas, 1993). Professionals can respond by joining children in exploring the meaning of their experience as they understand it.

Although it can be anticipated that children will understand what has been asked, this will not always be the case. When children do not understand a question, their confusion is generally reflected in a disoriented gaze, pause, or a specific request to rephrase a word or the entire question. When misunderstood, professionals should stop, indicate that they have been misunderstood, and rephrase their question (Saywitz, 1990).

Although wanting to ensure children's comprehension, Hughes and Baker (1990) advised that asking children whether or not they understand is unproductive and inappropriate since young children do not have a well developed ability to monitor their own understanding accurately. When children are unable to answer a question, a common response is, "I don't know." This response should be accepted at face value. Generally, when children say they don't remember or don't know, it means they really don't know, and rephrasing of the question only leads to frustration and breakdown in communication. Repeating or rephrasing questions tends to agitate the children and lead to a more fervent "I don't know," as if to say, "Weren't you listening the first time?" After being asked again, children may think that the professional does not believe them. They may also feel pressured and coerced to respond and may even fabricate an answer to avoid further queries. Moston (1987) asserted that children's first replies should be accepted, as continued probing will result in a deteriorated response. King and Yuille (1987) suggested that children be told explicitly that it is appropriate to say they don't remember.

Due to their inability to evaluate their own understanding, and their desire to please adults, children are likely to answer questions that they don't understand (Dickson, 1981). If they are given a yes-or-no question, children's desire to please may lead them to agree without actually understanding the question. In some cases, children will respond to a part of the question that they may have understood and ignore the rest of the question, with the result that answers can appear totally irrelevant (Saywitz, 1990). Television has used this tendency to great comic advantage (e.g., Alan Funt from "Candid Camera" and Art Linkletter from "Kids Say the Darndest Things"). Language that is familiar and understandable to a child is preferable. In clarifying communication, appropriate language and terms can be used rather than oversimplified or simplistic words that may offend children. More is said about language and the use of questions in Chapter 4.

THE INTERPERSONAL CLIMATE BETWEEN CHILD AND PROFESSIONAL

Interviews entail much more than adults speaking with children. They involve a discourse between two human beings who mutually influence each other. Personal qualities of professionals are obviously crucial to the creation of a comfortable environment for children (White, 1990). Professionals may influence children through their style, dress, or manner. Rich (1968) contended that one's appearance, manner, and behavior set the tone and influence children's impressions and expectations of the interview itself.

Appearance and Attire of the Professional

How professionals dress for child-focused interviews deserves attention. Professionals should dress so as to not intimidate children. For example, formal attire (e.g., shirt, tie, and jacket) can be associated with authority and may inadvertently intimidate children. The white lab coat worn by some physicians can also intimidate youngsters. Dressing in a practical manner that allows for flexibility in terms of seating arrangements and activities is encouraged (e.g., paint or work with clay). PJM once supervised a child-care worker who was dressed in a very fashionable outfit but struggled to move freely in her high-heeled shoes and skirt. In later sessions, she found it much more practical to forego high fashion for comfort while at work.

Manner of the Professional

An acceptance of children can be conveyed through words, tone of voice, and physical demeanor. Assuming a judgmental stance (whether positive or negative), a patronizing or condescending attitude, or using inappropriate behaviors such as baby-talk, should be avoided. In attempting to gain a child's acceptance, inexperienced professionals may resort to unnecessary and fatuous behaviors. When this occurs, professionals risk losing vital credibility with the children they interview. When such behavior is taken to an extreme, children may begin to withdraw and become uncommunicative, or behave in an infant-like manner. In such situations, professionals are faced with the additional task of having to reestablish rapport and restore the children's age-appropriate behavior in order for the interview to continue productively.

Case Vignette

During an interview between a male counselor and a 5-year-old female, the counselor began the interview by spending a long period of time playing with the child in an attempt to make the youngster feel comfortable. The counselor's manner was child-like in both behavior and expression, which served to entertain the little girl. The interaction became quite disjointed when the counselor attempted to change the pace and focus the interview. The child continued to play and interpreted the counselor's behavior in the context of what she had determined to be the unspoken contract for their interaction. The interaction intensified when the counselor noticed the time and insisted that the child calm down in order for the actual interview to proceed. The child appeared unsure of the counselor's intentions and continued to invite the counselor to play. Needless to say, prompting the girl to set aside her toys and sit still to talk only served to anger her. The interview was unsuccessful.

Lukas (1993) contended that the purpose of the interview is not to entertain children but, rather, to gather valuable information. An abrupt interviewing style can hinder the process and increase tension and anxiety, thus jeopardizing the child-professional relationship. This outcome commonly occurs with sudden and unpredictable changes in voice, tone, or behavior. Such shifts can negatively affect the flow and direction of the interview. When professionals spontaneously change the course of a conversation or activity without any forewarning or transition time, children can become confused, disoriented, or agitated and withdraw.

Although professionals may be willing to avoid gross shifts in topic or flow, a case can be made for the selected use of interruptions. For example, professionals may want children to clarify a point. When clarification or elucidation is required, Geiselman, Saywitz, and Bornstein (1993) suggested that professionals wait until youngsters have finished their story rather than interrupting the narrative that is in process. Children do not cope well with even brief clarifications during their discourse. It is far better to make a mental note to probe further, and return to it later rather than interrupt the verbal and cognitive flow. In addition, interruptions may inadvertently occur (e.g., by not disconnecting a telephone or paging system, or by leaving a door ajar). Children, like most adults, do not respond well to interruptions. Besides expressing subtle signs of frustration (e.g., long sighs, resting face between hands, rolling eyes), children tend to lose their train of thought and become unable or unwilling to return to the topic of discussion that was interrupted. Permitting interruptions conveys an implicit message that what children are communicating is unimportant. As suggested by Basch (1982) when empathy towards children is significantly lacking, the result may be "defensive behavior with which the child seeks to protect himself from further frustration, hurt, disappointment, overstimulation and so on" (p. 16).

Behavior of the Professional

Interactions with children can be suffused by a range of behaviors, including subtle and overt actions. Many actions will be habitual and deeply ingrained, yet can have serious effects on the children being interviewed. A professional's way of walking, including the speed, range of arm swing, and accompanying noise such as shuffling feet or clicking heels, communicates a level of confidence, assertion or aggression. When they speak, the natural tone and volume of their voice can communicate similar information and may be interpreted in a range of ways. While talking, professionals use accompanying hand gestures, eye-gaze, facial expressions, and whole-body movements, all of which send information. In addition, various activities (e.g., offering toys, playing games, writing notes, glancing at the clock, adjusting the window blinds, flipping through a book) communicate messages to children. Professionals need to appreciate the influence of their behavior (e.g., proxemics, speed of movement, range of gesture—small or large, and level of noise). For example, children can be greeted in the waiting area with an extended hand to shake or by a gentle touch on the shoulder. Some children may have experienced such interactions and may welcome them as forms of greeting. Other children will not recognize them or will become threatened by them.

The initial greeting is critical in establishing the child-professional relationship, and professionals need to be responsive to their body language in order to interpret how their actions are being received, so that they can adjust their interactions accordingly. For example, when children are observed clinging bodily to their parents in a waiting area, any kind of physical approach must be done cautiously. Quick, expansive, movements or loud interactions will almost certainly be interpreted as threatening. In this circumstance, an extended hand will most surely be ignored by the child, and a touch on the shoulder will not be welcomed.

Although experienced professionals may be familiar with the aforementioned pitfalls, even the best can become nonchalant or overconfident, and therefore neglectful, of the basics underlying all effective practice. In addition, even experienced professionals will sometimes encounter situations and factors over which they will have little or no control. Although many aspects of the child-focused interview can be managed, others cannot. Rich (1968) commented that children may be inadvertently affected through unpredictable environmental or physical factors (e.g., clothing may remind a child of an intimidating figure, the professional's tone of voice may be annoying to a child) and suggested that professionals may also fall prey to similar prejudgments of the child or less conscious influences and may experience potentially unfavorable results. Such circumstances may be unique and unpredictable, however, professionals should become aware of these possibilities and not assume that all appraisals will be neutral or positive. Interviews need to be conducted with an active sensitivity to the child-participants. The successful gathering of preinterview information, as discussed in Chapter 3, can help to alleviate these potential problems.

THE CHILD'S DESIRE TO PLEASE

From the moment of conception, children need adults to meet their physical, emotional, and psychological needs. Consequently, an inherent power differential between children and adults operates on a physical, economic, and political level. In addition, children are encouraged to obey adults, and for the most part they acquiesce with little resistance (though the parents of a strong-willed child might disagree). In fact, young children tend to idolize parents and authority figures, even seeing them as infallible. As a result of this imbalance in power and status, children tend to seek approval from adults, especially adults in positions of authority. In the interview situation, this particular characteristic is considered a double-edged sword. Children will often willingly and enthusiastically enter the interview situation. But some children will respond in ways that they think will please adults. Jones (1992) suggested that children are often keenly attuned to the reactions of adults, which may result in a change of responses, or potentially withdrawing from the conversation. Mishler (1986) further noted:

> Respondents learn from how interviewers respond to their answers—restating or rephrasing the original question, accepting the answer and going on to the next question, probing for further information—what particular meanings are intended by questions and wanted in their answers in a particular interview context. (p. 54)

Children can be highly skilled at reading adult nonverbal cues and may quickly tailor their responses and either curtail or change answers. Behaviors that constrain children from expressing themselves may be either verbal or nonverbal. For example, children may notice something as innocent as a professional's cursory glance at his or her watch and assume that the professional expects a brief response.

Case Vignette

   MLZ observed a 6-year-old girl with severe developmental disabilities and a measured IQ below 50 being questioned on her knowledge of colors: "Is this red or blue?" asked the adult while holding up a blue cube. The girl began to respond "Re..." but noticed the subtle frown and headshake of the professional and immediately changed her response, midvocalization, to "Blue." Although she did not know the difference between the colors, her performance on the activity was better than chance and suggested that she knew the two colors.

This case example shows how children of varying abilities are capable of responding to subtle verbal and nonverbal cues. An intelligent color-blind child may get a correct answer to a color scenario by attending to a professional's vocal signals! The professional knows the answer and inadvertently discloses it through intonation, inflection, or subtle facial and body movements.

Eckman (1989) suggested that children may exaggerate or lie in order to please a parent, especially during conflicts and tensions such as those following family dissolution. These findings have implications for the professional-child relationship. Children need to be informed that there are no correct answers and that there will be no pressure to respond in a certain way or even to respond at all. Professionals have a responsibility to monitor both the children and themselves and ensure that appropriate measures are taken so that children are minimally influenced to answer a certain way. Although professionals are sometimes tempted to compliment (e.g., "That was a great answer.") or encourage (e.g., "I like your response.") a child, such statements are positively reinforcing and suggest that the child has offered a more appropriate response (implying that there is an inappropriate response). Under these circumstances, children will work diligently to discover the most appropriate answer.

A more effective way to support children during the interview is to acknowledge their responses through verbal and nonverbal expressions: head nods, smiles, leaning forward, or verbal comments such as "un-huh," "yes," "I see," or "okay." Once again, self-monitoring is necessary to ensure that responses do not become subtle value judgments. For example, if a child's answer is favored, a response might be "Un-huh," accompanied by vigorous head-nodding, and if an answer is unfavorable, a response might be "Mmmm" with no accompanying head movement. Although the differences may appear minute, they can influence children's responses. Over time, children will learn that some answers are more acceptable than others. Inflection alone can convey approval or disapproval.

Professionals should try to offer encouragement rather than praise for children's specific efforts. They can thank children sincerely and honestly and avoid using language which emphasizes the existing hierarchy. In describing a method used to avert unnecessary power struggles, Morrissette (1989) wrote:

> If one examines the dynamics of power struggles which typically occur between young people and child care staff, this symmetrically escalating transaction makes perfect sense. For the young person to feel in control, he or she will initially reject any evaluative report from the child care staff. Typically, when evaluative reports are shared by the child care staff they are usually delivered with the child care staff assuming an elevated position in the client-worker relationship. This constructed hierarchy (worker telling young person) tends to perpetuate a power struggle around control. (p. 32)

Several statements that can be used to avoid the punctuation of a hierarchy include: "Thank-you for talking with me," or "I appreciate your taking the time to explain what happened." In contrast, statements such as "You're a real hard worker," or "That was easy, wasn't it?" are heavily value-laden, evaluative and patronizing, albeit well-intended.

THE COMMUNICATION PROCESS

An interview is a complex communicative act that involves intentions, expectations, leading and following in a bidirectional interaction. Rich (1968) identified several potential stances that can be assumed by professionals and children during an interview: (a) professionals and children may agree on the purpose of the interview; (b) professionals and children can agree on the intent of the interview, but either party may have reservations or an alternate agenda; (c) professionals and children may disagree on the purpose of the interview and recognize their differences; (d) professionals and children disagree and do not recognize their differences; (e) professionals and children may have a motivational conflict based on their relationship (e.g., the child wants to tell but is afraid of upsetting the professional); (f) either of them may have motivations that are not entirely conscious; (g) professionals and children may engage in a kind of dance of intentions whereby one may try to offer what he or she thinks the other wants, rather than what he or she honestly thinks or believes; and (h) both professionals and children may miscommunicate due to differences in lexical understanding. Consequently, professionals must recognize that such circumstances can exist and then work diligently to minimize them through self-awareness and monitoring of the children.

To help professionals clarify their own stance, Barker (1990) poses salient questions before beginning the interview process:

1. For whom is the interview being conducted?

2. What is the wider context of the interview?

3. What information is to be obtained during the interview?

4. What will be done with the information obtained?

5. What are the limits of confidentiality that will apply to the interview?

6. How much time is available for the interview?

7. Will it be possible to arrange for further interviews?

Although Barker specifically addressed the clinical psychological interview, many of these questions bear on the work of all professionals who conduct a variety of child-focused interviews. After having considered the answers to these questions, the next step involves conveying these intentions to children. This step may involve some negotiating of intentions and expectations. For example, children may need time to play, take breaks, or may want to talk about their recent acquisition of a pet or video-game. Although it may take time, interview goals and processes must be clarified and negotiated in order to avoid unnecessary problems. In addition, the negotiation process can help children and professionals appraise each other.

SMOOTHING OUT THE WRINKLES

Regardless of how carefully interview parameters are established, miscommunications can still ensue. Minor rifts, however, can be relatively insignificant if professionals respond in a sensitive fashion. Again, to ensure that children do not blame themselves for miscommunication, professionals are advised to assume responsibility and apologize. The occasional apology, offered as a sign of respect and concern, should serve to strengthen the child-professional relationship. However, if apologies occur frequently, professionals should suggest a session break or even end the interview in order to take time to reassess their work and consider what may be contributing to the faltering communication. Typically, miscommunications result when: (a) professionals use words that are above the children's developmental understanding; (b) children present with an unrecognized language or communication disorder; (c) children become tired, lose interest, or lose concentration; (d) either children or professionals are defensive, feeling attacked or threatened by something the other has said or done; or (e) cultural or language differences exist between children and professionals. If appropriate steps are not taken to resolve emergent problems, both children and professionals are at risk of becoming frustrated and conflicted, and the interview is at risk of deteriorating beyond repair.

SOME GUIDELINES

Once an interview is underway, children's narratives should be supported. To do so, rapport must be established so children feel comfortable enough to share openly and honestly. Barker (1990) emphasized the importance of rapport and defined it as a state of understanding, harmony, and accord, a sympathetic relationship characterized by warm feelings toward each other. Looff (1976) identified ways to positively influence the flow of the interview with young children and included: (a) anticipating children's responses given any previous information; (b) putting children at ease when they greet the children in the waiting area, a transition time during which professionals can structure, define, and provide clarification for children; (c) talking about and reflecting feelings (especially those feelings pertaining to the interview situation) back to children; (d) using relevant examples or stories; (e) universalization and generalization which help children to see themselves in a social context; and (f) using summary statements to rephrase what children are sharing. In addition he cautioned against overidentifying with children. With older children and adolescents, he suggested speaking on a more egalitarian level, discussing confidentiality issues more explicitly, and sharing personal information (self-disclosure) in order to establish rapport.

Communication is a reciprocal process and to establish or maintain rapport, professionals may sometimes need to answer questions posed by children. Although professionals must consider what they want to reveal in response to questions (especially if the content of the answer may influence the child's opinions thereafter), there is rarely time for careful reflection. Much will have to be decided on the spur of the moment.

CROSS-CULTURAL INTERVIEWS

Communicative intentions and interactional patterns need to be monitored. Such patterns reflect social-cultural experiences. To ensure that children understand the context and are comfortable responding, a broad range of effective communication skills are available and provide children ample time to adjust to the interview situation. Professionals should also reflect on their own social-cultural experience and how it influences their expectations, the way they understand and interpret things, and their attitudes and values.

PROFESSIONAL SELF-REFLECTION

To increase personal awareness, professionals are encouraged to practice self-reflection. Self-reflection can be defined as a systematic process through which professionals can independently monitor and direct their own professional development. Essentially, self-reflection is intended to help identify blind spots, strengths, and needs. Self-reflection entails drawing the present clinical situation into focus while considering the context of past experiences and future potentials (Morrissette, 1996a). The self-reflection process can also be considered a valuable preventive procedure, or a way to lessen the probability of unfortunate incidents occurring during the interview (e.g., ethical violations, professional-client conflict).

When professionals are uncertain or ambivalent about a particular situation, self-reflection offers an opportunity to consider options and alternatives. To set the stage for the self-reflection process, professionals can pretend that they are supervising themselves from behind a one-way mirror. Professionals previously supervised in this manner may recall the advice of mentors who effectively slowed down the interview process, diffused anxious moments, and encouraged a pensive posture. Their ultimate goal was to restore a sense of perspective and optimism.

Reflectivity can be traced back to Dewey (1933) and is designed to help professionals better understand themselves in relation to their clients. During reflection, professionals develop hypotheses about their clients and themselves. These hypotheses emerge when present interactions with the client are combined with prior knowledge and experience. Reflection becomes a means for reliving and recapturing experience in order to understand it, learn from it, and develop new insights and appreciations. Through the reflective process, the less obvious aspects of our experience become more apparent and can be connected to our present and future actions. Reflection may take place at any time and need not be assigned to any specific schedule. Professionals may even decide to take a break during an actual interview in order to process specific feelings or thoughts that surface and begin to threaten the interview process (e.g., anger, sadness). Schon (1983) recognized that reflection-in-action appears to be a contradiction in terms, and addressed the concern that reflection-in-action may interfere with and paralyze the ability to act spontaneously. Although the term *reflect* tends to connote a return to past events, Schon contended that professionals often think about what they are doing while doing it, which brings an immediacy to the act.

The importance of reflectivity in professional development has been associated mainly with such professions as education (e.g., Copeland, Birmingham, De La Cruz, & Lewin, 1993; Diamond, 1991; Munby & Russell, 1989), and with nursing (e.g., Mitchell, 1995), although Schon (1987) researched self-reflection in the development of architects, master-class musicians, and psychotherapists. In essence, reflectivity is considered a valuable methodology to develop clinical wisdom and judgment. Shapiro and Reiff (1993) remarked:

> It is assumed that reflective inquiry by the professional practitioner and cohorts will raise the level of consciousness of the various features of one's practice. This increased awareness, in the author's experience, often results in spotting some inconsistencies or identifying the guiding principles of one's arrangements and uses of personal resources and the constraints which formerly had not been entirely conscious. (p. 1385)

Reflectivity involves bracketing personal assumptions and beliefs while looking inward at internal processes both during and following interactions. Used properly, self-reflection can help professionals become aware of various intrapsychic, interpersonal, and larger systems issues. Neophyte professionals can enhance their skill-evaluation through knowledge gained by self-reflection (Bernard & Goodyear, 1992) and can even effectively replace some traditional supervisory functions (Kurpius, Baker, & Thomas, 1977). As they become more experienced, professionals can continue to expand their repertoire of skills and improve their effectiveness. Williams (1995) proposed using a self-reflective process to develop the self-consultant, with the goal of creating a systematic routine (Lewis, 1991) that novice professionals can continue to utilize after the formal academic supervision period.

During their studies, prospective professionals have many opportunities to discuss clinical issues while receiving support and direction on cases. After graduating, however, the context changes and support for professional development will vary. After leaving the academic setting, beginning professionals are often struck with the stark reality that they no longer have easy access to supervision, and they often find themselves working alone. The skilled application of self-reflection can help to fill this void.

Regardless of skill level, professionals should reflect on issues that impact their work with children. To identify relevant issues, a specific process of self-examination is recommended. The first step is to identify and record personal reactions during interviews and to reflect on those reactions during a later audio/video tape review. During the self-reflection learning process, it is important to notice personal reactions (either physiological or emotional). Rather than dismissing and ignoring subtle personal reactions, reflective professionals consider the implications associated with their experiences. For example, professionals who are annoyed that a child has arrived late for an interview may perceive this response as normal. What they might not consider without taking the time to reflect, is how this initial reaction can affect the engagement stage of the interview process. With more experience, professionals can expand their self-evaluations and compare issues that emerge during interviews with known or unknown personal issues (e.g., violence, abandonment, trust).

A formalized and systematic process of self-reflection involves more than a consideration of the interview process and its overall context. Self-reflection is a complex endeavor that moves beyond general discernment to encompass self-introspection, self-awareness and, self-evaluation. It is a process culminating in greater insight, skill, and functioning on the part of the professional. To achieve these goals, professionals are required to assume an active self-regulating role, and consequently, become responsible for their own clinical decisions and actions.

Self-reflection appears to be best suited to professionals who have achieved a level of development whereby they demonstrate a basic understanding of interpersonal dynamics, reasonable insight into their work and the interview process, self-initiative, and an ability to face their own vulnerability while exploring personal strengths and needs. Successful self-reflection involves objectively reflecting on one's work, identifying and extracting data that is significant, processing the extracted data, and effectively integrating what has been learned through the reflective process. Self-reflection is typically appreciated by professionals who see their development as an ongoing process and recognize the complexity of the situations that they encounter along the way.

Potential Benefits of Self-Reflection

Two advantages of self-reflection include cost-effectiveness and increased quality assurance. Economically, self-reflection is beneficial in that additional personnel are not required to perform traditional supervisory functions. In many situations, changes in the health care system have resulted in the reduction of personnel and in a decrease in the amount of supervision available to professionals. Subsequently, professionals have less clinical support and are having to rely increasingly on their own intuition and skills. Furthermore, with professionals focused more intently on personal process and skills, there is a greater likelihood that treatment will be of a higher quality and, therefore, more productive.

Although self-reflection might prove valuable for professionals who conduct child-focused interviews in a myriad of contexts, it will be especially beneficial for individuals working in relative geographic or professional isolation. For professionals, particularly those working in rural areas, conventional supervision is not readily available and they are left without face-to-face supervision. Without a colleague with whom to discuss ethical, professional, or clinical issues, beginning professionals are left grappling with sensitive issues in isolation.

Preparation for Self-Reflection

To self-reflect effectively, professionals need to step back from their work, become introspective, and consider overt and covert responses that influence their interactions with clients. This process typically involves careful and intentional review of audio and videotapes, detailed clinical notes, documentation of personal experiences usually in the form of a journal and consultation with colleagues. Video-assisted self-monitoring can be useful in identifying and adjusting specific behaviors and in developing confidence. During the planned review process, professionals identify issues (either positive or negative) that merit closer inspection and perhaps consultative feedback. Emphasis is placed on punctuating and mobilizing professional resources through increased self knowledge. To assist in the review process, a series of process steps and questions are outlined below:

1. What outside pressures are influencing my work?

2. Why is it important for me to succeed in this particular interview?

3. How am I feeling toward this child (e.g., distant, protective)? Why?

4. How did I feel during the interview (e.g., disappointed, hopeful, excited, frightened)? Why?

5. What did I like or dislike about my interactions with the youngster whom I was interviewing?

6. What am I experiencing emotionally and/or physically as I think about this child?

7. What specific child behaviors am I reacting to?

8. Is there a central theme triggering my reaction?

9. Does anything remain unsettled for me?

These questions are not intended to be exhaustive, but rather are provided as a starting point. Professionals are invited to build on these questions and to develop their own self-reflective line of questioning. When considering the information that emerges from these questions, professionals should attempt to identify and consider personal issues that affect their interviewing style. Examples include preoccupation with the interview process or skill acquisition and general performance anxiety (Morrissette, 1996a, 1996b).

Teyber (1992) contended that, although it is relatively easy to see the reenactment of a client's conflicts in his or her interpersonal process, it can be exasperatingly difficult to recognize one's own interpersonal process while involved in an intense, affect-laden relationship. Professionals must exercise patience and realize that the ability to recognize and respond at the process level is acquired slowly. It seems only reasonable that professionals will require time to acclimatize to self-monitoring. The duration of this period will depend upon the unique circumstances of professionals. In addition, the development of specific skills will hinge on the theoretical model subscribed to by these individuals.

Pragmatics of Self-Reflection

On the surface, self-reflection seems straightforward enough; however, it can be difficult to do effectively. The specific details of self-monitoring are often vague. A common assumption is that professionals possess the natural ability to self-reflect, that they will evolve toward a self-reflection mode, or that they will develop the ability to self-reflect by chance. To enhance the self-reflection process, careful consideration needs to be rendered to its gradual implementation. The fundamental and immediate questions of who, what, when, where, and how must be considered. To assist in this process, a number of activities have been developed. These are discussed below. The suggestions are preliminary and are not intended to be exhaustive.

Flexible Thinking. Before beginning to self-reflect, professionals must remain mentally flexible. Insights will rarely emerge if one's thinking is restricted. While brainstorming ideas and alternatives, it is important to remain curious about possible discoveries. This practice can promote self-discovery and personal empowerment (see, e.g., Amundson, Stewart, & Valentine, 1993; Cecchin, Lane & Ray, 1992; 1993). However, due to the influence of their academic programs—which may have endorsed a specific theoretical conceptualization—some professionals are faced with the challenge of becoming less orthodox, more creative, and more flexible in their work. This usually entails challenging ingrained beliefs about self in relation to children. A fascinating study conducted by Henson-Matthews and Marshall (1988) suggested that professionals who demonstrated high self-monitoring skills were more flexible and endorsed multiple therapeutic approaches as compared to low self-monitors who gravitated to a single theoretical approach. Interestingly, the two theoretical orientations endorsed by high self-monitors were behavioral and systemic.

Audio/Videotape Reviews. Videotape supervision offers an ideal way to conduct self-reflection. While reviewing audio or videotapes of their work, professionals should pay careful attention to, and make note of aspects of the interview that they find rewarding or disconcerting. In both situations, professionals can attempt to identify personal reactions, as well as to note precisely what was said or done that affected them personally and interpersonally. Self-reflection is rarely an easy task and invites the development of specific questions that can serve as a guiding framework during audio/video review. Several questions that professionals might ask themselves include:

1. Why am I feeling so responsible for the outcome of this interview?

2. How have I become so invested in this particular child?

3. What is generating my concern about the interview?

4. Why did I respond or behave the way that I did?

5. How did I expect myself and the child to respond in the situation (speech-act or behavior)?

Connecting Notes with Corresponding Tape Segments. Even when a session is audio or videotaped, clinical notes collected during or immediately following the interview, can provide us with valuable information to reflect upon in conjunction with the mechanical recording. With substantial information at hand, professionals can begin to articulate their reactions, dilemmas, or confusions and begin to entertain different perspectives. After completing this process individually, professionals can invite colleagues to share their reflections and views, which will extend the benefits of the reflective process beyond the professional's own breakthroughs.

Inviting Client Feedback. There is merit in inviting children to share their impressions of the interview process. This strategy can be both useful to the professional and an empowering experience for children. When using this specific strategy, professionals regularly ask children about how they perceive the interview and whether or not the process is helpful. The potential benefits of such consultation include helping professionals form a respectful and collaborative relationship with their young clients, opening up child-professional communication and rapport, and helping children remain focused on the interview process.

Involving Others. Self-reflection does not have to be a solitary venture; it can include the use of peers, as long as issues of confidentiality are carefully considered. Disclosing and discussing salient material generally requires a certain amount of trust between professionals and those with whom they share their work. Some professionals may experience difficulty shifting from traditional supervision, which is usually conducted in a top-down fashion, to less formal self-supervision.

SELF-REFLECTION: PRELIMINARY GUIDELINES

A substantial degree of individual responsibility underlies the self-reflective process. In an attempt to provide a preliminary guide to self-reflection, several focus areas, intrapersonal and interpersonal, have been developed. These focus areas may be helpful for beginning professionals and for those who are newly embarking on the self-reflection process.

Intrapersonal Aspect of the Interview

Objective #1. Work toward understanding the significance of identifying personal emotions and feelings during an interview (e.g., disappointment, relief, fear, anxiety, anger).

Strategies.

1. Create a relaxing environment that is conducive to self-focus while attending to internal processes.

2. Direct energy toward personal awareness, needs, and growth as opposed to problem-solving.

3. Appreciate the importance of self-care and reiterate that self-reflection is a time for self-development and, ultimately, improved performance.

4. Carefully review meaningful issues or incidents that occurred during the interview.

In order to ensure accurate description, it becomes important that professionals complete their notes as soon as possible following the interview. Although professionals commonly believe that they will be able to recall important relevant information, this is not always the case.

Objective #2. Work toward articulating the possible origin of personal feelings experienced before, during or following the interview.

Strategies.

1. Consider past or current events that may influence one's personal work.

2. Consider how personal issues and life experiences can directly affect professional work.

3. Develop a personal genogram, timeline, and review of personal family history and patterns.

Objective #3. Work toward resolving personal issues through supervision or consultation.

Strategies.

1. Seek appropriate assistance and support.

2. Review additional relevant educational resources (e.g., readings, training audio or videotapes, workshops).

Interpersonal Aspect of the Interview

Objective #1. Review clinical notes and audio or videotapes and identify points where negative or positive feelings may have occurred (e.g., what was said, what was intimated, nonverbal client behaviors).

Strategies.

1. Identify any recurrent interpersonal patterns that prove to be either helpful or problematic.

2. Keep records to help track patterns and make connections.

Objective #2. Consider professional-child relationship issues.

Strategies.

1. Review personal behavior during interactions with children.

2. Review feelings during interactions with children.

3. Review the stages of an interview (e.g., social/engagement stage, interaction stage, session termination).

Self-reflection is a unique process whereby professionals can consider intrapsychic, interpersonal, and larger systems issues that influence their work. This process should prove useful for professionals who are attempting to understand how attitudes, feelings, and values guide and influence their interactions with children. Self-reflection can be a valuable tool in the advancement of professional development. Despite its deceptively simple appearance, self-reflection is a complex process requiring specific skills. Only over time will professionals determine whether or not their self-reflection process is effective. These guidelines are not intended to be a definitive approach to self-reflection. Time and experience are necessary to refine aspects of the self-reflection process (e.g., audio/videotape review components, clinical notes, client feedback) into a working model that improves interactions with children.

Professionals cannot underestimate the impact of their own presence and presentation on the outcome of child-focused interviews. This chapter reviewed the multiple influences of the professional, the interview topic, the questions asked, the interpersonal climate, professional sway over children, and the process of communication. Besides the many ideas included in Chapter 3 on the successful practice of interviewing, specific ideas have been advanced to overcome the identified problems. For successful interviews, professionals must be adequately trained and properly prepared. Research and theory on educational interviews, clinical interviews, legal and criminal interviews, and counseling interviews have made important contributions to an understanding of effective child-focused interviewing. Rich (1968) indicated that it is not enough that professionals minimize blocks to communication, they must maximize facilitative factors.

CHAPTER 3

THE PRACTICE OF
THE INTERVIEW

Before embarking on an interview, the myriad of factors that influence interactions with children need to be recognized. Child-focused interviews pose a number of challenges, including differences in cognitive and linguistic abilities of professionals and children, conditions under which children attend interviews, and various misconceptions that children have regarding the interview process. The importance of creating an atmosphere of safety and comfort cannot be over emphasized. Professionals may be extremely gifted in assessing children and designing treatment plans, but unless the interview context and process accommodates youngsters, it is unlikely that they will return or fully participate in treatment. This chapter highlights and discusses essential elements to effective interviewing practice.

PREPARING FOR THE INTERVIEW

When imagining the interview experience through the eyes of a child, the objective centers on making children comfortable enough to establish trust, enhance communication, and facilitate discourse. The inherent challenge of interviewing children involves striking a balance between the formal and the informal aspects of the process. Interactions need to be formal enough to cover the essential content (e.g., details regarding the presenting problem) yet informal enough to be flexible and responsive to children (e.g., timing and pacing). The overall interview environment, including the personality of professionals and the physical structure of the interview room, is critical to effective interviewing with children. If the interview room is not perceived as welcoming, relaxing, and safe, attempts to work effectively with children may be counterproductive or futile.

The physical environment can convey information to children even before the interview begins (Hazel, 1995; Rich, 1968). The physical structure of the reception area or office, its furnishings, and general appearance are essential to setting an appropriate tone, and they require attention (Barker, 1990; Goodman & Sours, 1994; Halliday, 1986; White, 1990). Accordingly, the interview environment should be quiet, controlled, and equipped with age-appropriate furnishings allowing children to feel comfortable. Appropriate toys (e.g., dollhouse with human figures, play telephones, crayons and paper, small vehicles, plastic animal figures) can be useful in helping children to feel at ease and can be used as effective engagement tools. For example, when first greeting children who are engaged in playing with a toy in the waiting area, professionals can slowly begin to show interest in and begin to inquire about the activity. This process affords professionals and children time to become acquainted with one another. Observing youngsters involved in spontaneous play can also provide useful assessment information. Children may be demonstrating an interest which can be noted and used at a later date.

Whisking children away from a play activity due to a time schedule is discouraged. These activities are not wasted time and warrant consideration for future planning, especially by professionals who are not accustomed to working with children. Professionals can become irritated with youngsters who are perceived as dawdling and disinterested in the interview process. Children work on a different time schedule and require time to turn from one task to another. Expecting children to quickly transition from an activity with which they are enthralled is unrealistic. Forcing this issue typically results in a power struggle.

While working at a child guidance center, PJM provided direct service to children, families, and supervised social work, psychology, and medical school interns. A great source of anxiety for interns was greeting children in the waiting area and trying to guide them into the interview room. These interns discovered that this task was full of surprises including times when children refused to comply because they hadn't finished constructing their Lego® block fort. Over time, the interns became less rigid and more creative, they learned that simply inviting children to bring their partly built fort along into the interview room was effective. They also learned that without knowing it, the assessment had already begun. The trick was to abandon the rigid sequential interview format which they had been taught and continue the process once children were in the interview room. Of course this often involved a willingness to work at a child's level and perhaps sitting on the floor to help in the construction of a Leg® block fort. More will be said about preparing for this type of work later in the chapter.

As with many things in the interview process, there are always exceptions to the rule. With children who are easily distractible for example, excessive stimuli are likely to be problematic or counterproductive and should be avoided. For these children, professionals can consult with parents or guardians to determine the need for additional therapeutic tools. Children with special needs require additional preplanning and therefore, preinterview consultation is necessary. For example, temporarily removing excessive toys from the waiting area may be necessary. Requesting that parents or guardians avoid arriving too early for an interview, and that they bring a personal toy or book may also be helpful.

Once the relationship and its boundaries have been established, a variety of toys can be integrated to enhance the interview process. If special needs are not considered, children may be inadvertently set up for failure. Once again, expecting children to immediately suspend usual behavior in order to convenience professionals is unrealistic.

BREAKING THE ICE

Children generally gravitate toward what is familiar, comforting or fascinating. Therefore, providing appropriate toys and materials can be soothing and facilitative. Toys should be perceived as more than play objects and appreciated as valuable bridging tools between the child's home and the professional's office. In cases where a challenge is anticipated when establishing a relationship with a particular child (e.g., a child who has been mistreated by an adult), inquiries can be made about toys or activities that interest a child. Preinterview information gathering regarding child preferences, activity level, and rest patterns might at first glance appear to be of only minor importance. However, seemingly unimportant data gleaned from an effective intake interview can foster a relationship with children and ease the transition to an interview.

Hazel (1995) described a number of elicitation techniques which are briefly discussed below. These strategies are multipurpose and are helpful in creating a safe context wherein children feel free to express themselves. Hazel underscores the importance of privacy and confidentiality when working with children and asserts that failure in either of these two areas can jeopardize the interview process.

Case Vignettes

The use of case vignettes can be particularly helpful at the beginning of an initial interview. This involves having children read aloud a short story. Upon completion, a discussion is facilitated regarding the content of the story and children's reactions. The advantages of this technique are twofold. First, professionals can begin to learn more about the opinions and views of children and, second, this exercise serves as an effective icebreaker and helps relax youngsters.

Important reference points can emerge during conversations regarding the content of the story, and these can be noted and utilized at strategic points during the interview. For example, if children frequently refer to the issue of loss when discussing their interpretation of a story, personal experiences pertaining to this issue can be explored. Attending to themes that emerge during therapeutic discourse is important for a variety of reasons. Two of the more obvious reasons include demonstrating to children that their story is being carefully listened to and being wise enough to follow a trail that has been provided by the young guide.

A criticism of this technique concerns its limited use with children who cannot read, are reluctant to read aloud, or are unable to speak. Although this is a valid criticism, the technique should not be abandoned. Rather, creative variations can be designed to reach a wider audience. For example, to accommodate children who are unable or reluctant to read, a short story can be read to them. Another variation may include children and professionals watching a video that can be followed by a discussion. With children who are disabled or unable to speak, interpreters or writing can be used. Providing services to disabled children presents challenges that can be overcome. Regardless of the strategy, the goals of engaging children and gaining insight into their lives are achievable.

A number of books specifically designed to engage children in discussions about life circumstances (e.g., divorce, childhood/parental illness) are available and can serve as useful aids. Having children create personal stories can also be an effective strategy. The advantage of this technique is that professionals can eventually become coauthors of stories and instrumental in developing endings that are beneficial to children.

Pictures and Photographs

Hazel (1995) suggested that pictures and photographs can provide children with an opportunity to use their free imagination and create their own version of the captured episode. Rather than having to comment on a case scenario, children can become creative and develop their own story. Again, this technique is limited to a specific audience.

Quotations, Phrases, or Popular Culture

Popular quotations, phrases, or other aspects of popular culture can be used to elicit responses from children. This technique is designed to prompt reactions and conversations. Demonstrating to children that their opinion is important is, in itself, a powerful intervention. To determine limits, children sometimes make provocative statements to elicit reactions from professionals. For example, youngsters may express a provocative opinion to which they are not even remotely committed. A common example involves young people who suggest that high risk behaviors (e.g., gang involvement, illicit drug use) are little to worry about. When hearing this, inexperienced professionals tend to immediately react and attempt to convince young people otherwise. Professionals can respond and remain intrigued about a young person's perspective. Rather than contributing to what can result in a highly charged situation, professionals can enter into a conversation and remain curious about the young person's perspective (e.g., "Tell me more about that."). Having avoided being perceived as agents of social change, professionals are then recognized as interested listeners. As discussed more fully in Chapter 8, immediate action must be taken when issues of potential harm, either to self or others, are verbalized.

Problem Setting

Children can also be invited to propose solutions to contemporary problems. This strategy may be particularly helpful with hard-to-reach children. For the most part, these youngsters are outspoken and can present creative solutions to some rather thorny situations. For example, the issues of oppression and personal rights violations seem to strike a cord with children in residential care facilities. They appreciate the struggles of people living in oppressive conditions and generally engage in conversations relating to these topics.

THE INTERVIEW CONTEXT

Creating a comfortable environment involves attending to ventilation, lighting, temperature and space. Ideally, a room with brightly colored walls and natural light from windows that are visible to children sets an appropriate tone. Alternative forms of lighting can be used to create a comforting atmosphere and increase feelings of assurance. The ability to increase or reduce the amount of light in the interview room may be useful. Some children appear more relaxed and function better under subdued lighting. This form of lighting has a calming effect on children who are generally excitable. If an interview room is too warm or cold, children may demonstrate discomfort and become irritable. Depending on their abilities and disposition, youngsters may be unable to articulate discomfort, and instead act out their displeasure. Ample space within the interview room should also be available to gain close physical proximity to children. Allowing space to maintain eye-level contact (e.g., sitting on the floor) is important as well. At the same time, the space should be large enough to accommodate professionals and various play activities without having an overwhelming effect. Ultimately, adjustments should be dictated by the unique needs of each child. What works for one, may not work for another.

The designs of child-centered facilities can become nonfunctional. For example, chalk boards intended for children may be mounted too high for them to access, chairs may be too large to sit in comfortably, and reading material might be age-inappropriate. Consequently, many furnishings become uninviting or unusable. To provide better accommodations, children can be consulted about how they would design a comfortable setting. More often than not, splendid ideas are shared and *Time* magazines are discarded and replaced with Lego® blocks. To accommodate young visitors, professionals need to remain sensitive to the various age groups who frequent their waiting areas, offices, and interview rooms. Special care needs to be taken to inform parents and guardians about what toys are at the disposal of children in order to prevent accidents from occurring. For example, toys that can be dismantled into small pieces can be dangerous around younger children.

Some youngsters may be mesmerized by a new toy, and that can be a distinct challenge to the professional who wishes to gain their attention and engage them. The skill required in this situation involves creatively integrating toys or activities into the formal interview process. In other words, a toy or activity can be used to begin forming the relationship. For example, children can be asked about drawings they are completing or toys that have captivated their attention. In this way, distractions become excellent entry points into the children's world. On the other hand, moving away prematurely from such meaningful activities may result in missed opportunities and an ineffective interview. In addition, spontaneous play may provide observant professionals with useful information (e.g., attention and concentration, skills and interests).

In some circumstances, it might be helpful for children to bring their own toys or activities to the interview. For example, in one case with a youngster who refused to speak about a traumatic event, it was suggested that the parent bring along the child's favorite board game. In that case, prior to playing the game, the youngster was asked to review and explain the rules. Very soon both individuals were involved in a conversation that eventually moved into a discussion about the young boy's trauma. In this case, a sensitive professional effectively empowered the child and thus, facilitated disclosure of important information.

In some extreme cases when working with frightened or highly anxious children, no matter what is done to create inviting and supportive atmospheres, interviews may be unsuccessful. A solution may involve meeting children in contexts wherein they feel safe (e.g., their homes, daycare facilities, or schools). The idea of conducting interviews in children's natural environments, such as their homes or schools, has received some attention (e.g., Barker, 1990). A child's home may be a good place to establish rapport. However, although the natural surroundings may increase a child's comfort level, distractions may emerge in the form of toys, interruptions, or lack of privacy. In these situations, there is a struggle between wanting to demonstrate interest in a child's environment and wanting to accomplish the task at hand. Feeling obliged to take the infamous house tour, professionals must grapple with the issue of boundaries and time. In school-based interviews, other distractions may be present, including lunch and recess breaks, the hours of the school day, bus schedules or nap times (Morgan, 1995).

Using Props

The strategic use of props can also be helpful in child-focused interviews. Pipe, Gee, and Wilson (1993), for example, found that props that were placed as visible cues facilitated more complete free-recall reports of events, even without professionals making verbal references to the props. Research has suggested that physical props can facilitate recall, particularly with younger children. Such props however, need to be used in conjunction with specific questions that relate to the matter at hand and should not serve to lead children by suggestion.

In regards to the ability to recall information with the assistance of physicals aids, Saywitz and Snyder (1993) suggested that children may be taught to improve their recall through the use of visual cue cards. It appears that visual cue cards that correspond to the questions: who, what, where, when and how, may be helpful in stimulating memory regarding specific facets of events without significantly increasing error rates. Although the cards are not, in themselves, leading with regards to content, they can be beneficial in cueing children about what to remember. This can expand the kind of detail spontaneously volunteered by children.

Engaging the Larger System

Except in rare circumstances, parental or guardian consent needs to be secured prior to commencing an interview. When preparing for interviews with very young children, time should be taken to meet with parents or guardians to discuss specific circumstances and personal idiosyncrasies (Morgan, 1995). This process might entail presession meetings or telephone calls that can assist in preparing for the interview and in establishing rapport with significant others. To augment information obtained from the interview, reports provided by parents and significant others can be invaluable in forming a global and comprehensive picture of children. Because children's behavior varies drastically in different settings, teachers and significant others can be consulted to obtain a broad view.

In preparing children to be alone with professionals, preinterview meetings with the parental subsystem and the youngsters can be arranged. Children are much more likely to be comfortable if they are aware of their parents' location and are given permission to see their parents when the need arises during the interview (Jones, 1992). Obviously, each child is unique, and specific needs and circumstances must be considered on an individual basis. Although older children will probably require less parental support than their younger counterparts, any assumption based on age discrepancy must be exercised with caution. For example, assuming that all 8-year-olds should be mature enough to be alone with professionals can be a risky judgment. In general, children are most comfortable if they enter the interview room with their parent(s). Parents should only leave once they and the professional are reasonably assured that the child is comfortable (Hughes & Baker, 1990). Zilversmit (1990) stated, "In a strange office with an unknown person, children normally hang back and stay close to their parents until they get used to the newness" (p. 217). Both verbal and nonverbal indications from children will typically assure parents and professionals that youngsters are feeling comfortable enough to be left alone.

TIMING OF THE INTERVIEW

The timing of interviews can be critical, especially in situations when there is a conflict with a favorite activity or pastime. If children are asked to miss something that they really enjoy or are anticipating, such as a sporting event or the circus, they may appear uncooperative or hurried (Rich, 1968). In such situations, children may simplify responses to complete the interview in record time so that they can return to things that are meaningful and gratifying. Such children may be incorrectly assessed as anxious, defiant, uncooperative or resistant. In reality however, these children are following their job description and are indicating that a valuable activity is being missed.

In addition, understanding children's general routine and health is essential when planning interviews. Expecting children to suspend interests for something that is potentially less fulfilling is unrealistic. When possible, the timing of interviews should be approved by children. If children feel coerced, a power struggle (which the professional is unlikely to win) may well ensue.

Some power must be conceded by professionals through negotiating the pace and flow of interviews. Should professionals incorrectly assess a child's restless or distractible behavior as noncompliant, an adversarial relationship may evolve. For example, if children perceive professionals as becoming impatient, they might become anxious, defensive or withdraw emotionally. In response, professionals might become annoyed, self-protective, and critical. Professionals who feel they have lost control of an interview may take action to correct the situation and restore their status and sense of competency. The resulting emotional discomfort experienced by professionals and children with whom they are working can culminate in a vicious cycle wherein children are perceived to be oppositional, ungrateful, or resistant and professionals are considered to be grumpy, unhelpful, and ineffective. The result is a negative spiral that damages the interview relationship and benefits no one. Children usually dictate the flow and content of the interview. Although this may be difficult for some professionals to accept, when working with children this becomes obvious.

A surprising number of professionals conduct interviews directly after school and discourage the consumption of beverages or food during the interview. What seems to be overlooked in many of these instances is that children are probably both tired and hungry after being in school. Although professionals and parents may be eager to begin the interview process, children may be more interested in unwinding and having something to eat. Prior to beginning the interview, it is suggested that youngsters be asked how they are feeling to assess their general mood and energy level. Children must be afforded time to prepare for the interview. Simply asking them if they would like to visit the washroom before an interview, for example, can help avoid unnecessary discomfort or interruptions.

RECORDING THE INTERVIEW

Recording interviews can eliminate the need to take notes, reduce distractions, and improve accuracy. This process allows for retrospective analysis and in the case of criminal investigations, a videotape can allow others to collect information without having to reinterview children.

Although recording interviews is commonplace and second nature to professionals, potential problems should be considered. Similar to situations where a new toy is discovered, novel objects such as recording apparatus seem to have a magnetic pull. When working in a child guidance center, PJM soon learned the intrigue that one-way mirrors hold for children. Noticing their reflections in the mirror and the light of the monitor behind the mirror was all the entertainment most youngsters needed to distract them from the interview. Children frequently find recording devices intriguing and are tempted to explore these interesting gadgets in detail.

If an interview is to be recorded, written permission must be obtained from parents or guardians and should be consented to by the child. Fogelman and Hogman (1994) suggested that videotape be used for part of the interview and either audiotape or note taking be used when the content is more sensitive to children. Furthermore, recording equipment should be positioned inconspicuously so as not to distract children or interrupt the procedure (Goodman & Sours, 1994). If proper precautions are not taken, interviews can quickly turn into a lesson on the operation (and perhaps the redesign) of electronic devices.

INTERVIEW MEMBERSHIP

Deciding who should be present during interviews remains debatable. In clinical interviews regarding child sexual abuse, for example, Halliday (1986) suggested that children should be interviewed alone and without their parents. This common position is based on the rationale that children may be reluctant to talk candidly with a parent present, especially when more sensitive topics are discussed or if a parent is implicated as a perpetrator. In contrast to this position, children can feel supported by the presence of their mother or father in cases where parents are not implicated. MLZ found children to be open and comfortable, even reassured, when parents are present during such interviews.

When several professionals need to be involved, for instance in the case of sexual abuse, Pence and Wilson (1994) suggested that interviews be conducted jointly. Although such a process may not be restricted to one session, it could be more comprehensive, limit the duplication of questions, and allow professionals to collect information simultaneously and compare notes afterwards. The potential drawbacks of increasing interview membership beyond a single professional and child includes difficulty in establishing rapport and the reluctancy of children to share sensitive or painful information. Pence and Wilson cautioned that situations that involve two professionals who have not clearly determined who will take the lead in questioning may result in a volley of questions. Professionals from different disciplines or backgrounds may follow personal agendas while disregarding each other or children. In addition, varying interview styles could hamper children's adjustment. Recommendations include (a) parent(s) be present and leave once children are comfortable, (b) as few professionals as possible be present to reduce the intimidation factor, (c) a bug-in-the-ear be used so others could observe and make suggestions, or (d) a two-stage interview with the interview team identifying areas for further questioning following the initial interview.

SETTING THE STAGE

The initial introduction stage can be awkward for professionals. Wells (1989), for example, cautioned professionals against introducing themselves as a friend. Although well-intentioned, this message is misleading and potentially confusing. Situations arise where parents, in an attempt to help the child relax, refer to professionals as uncles or aunts. Parents should be dissuaded from such practice. For many children, the interview process is confusing enough. Adding to this confusion serves no useful purpose. Whatever the purpose of the interview, rapport between professionals and children is vital.

The skill involved in conducting child-focused interviews is underscored by the integration of two conflicting attitudes. Professionals need to maintain an empathic stance while remaining detached to allow for objective and accurate observation (Rich, 1968). This is a delicate and important balancing act. Yarrow (1960) stated, "An interview that probes feelings, attitudes, and deeply personal orientations requires a deeper level of relationship in terms of warmth, sensitivity and responsiveness than one concerned primarily with obtaining factual data" (p. 569).

The clarification of roles and the socialization of children both are crucial to the interview process, and they are discussed later in more detail. To acclimatize children to the interview context, professionals must explain their role while emphasizing their interest in the interview process. Flin and Boon (1989) contended, "A willingness to make the child feel comfortable, and a genuine interest in what they have to say, will help children to talk about their experience" (p. 51).

The main objective of interviews is to enter into a discourse wherein children are invited to reflect upon and explore thoughts and experiences in detail. Pramling (1983) referred to this discourse as a "developing interaction." In this interactive dialogue, requests for clarification may allow a more thorough understanding of what children intend by their statements.

Wells (1989) suggested that professionals begin by clearly explaining who they are, their function, and the role of the child. Assuming that children will understand a professional's role or the purpose of the interview would be presumptuous. Ethical responsibility dictates that the purpose of the interview be explained in a way that children can fully comprehend (Boggs & Eyberg, 1990). To accomplish this, a short introduction is usually sufficient for younger children, whereas with older children several minutes of description may be warranted. Barker (1990) noted that interviews should include fact-giving just as much as fact-finding, stating that "those concerned need to know about the nature of the interview process, its confidentiality, the time frame and other relevant facts" (p. 11). Issues such as confidentiality (especially with school-aged children) and any preconceptions the child may have about the interview need to be resolved. Hughes and Baker (1990) stated that when interviewing children 7 years old or older, confidentiality should be discussed regarding the purpose and context of the interview and children should be told in advance what will be shared and with whom.

The importance of getting off on the right foot with children cannot be overstated. To accomplish this, activities or conversations that are calming reassuring can be employed. The anticipated flow of the interview can also be explained. For instance a professional might say, "I will be asking you some questions at the start and I would like you to explain your answers to me as best you can. If I am unsure about something, I will ask you for some more information to help me better understand." To avoid having children feel as though they answered poorly, emphasis is placed on the professional's ability to listen rather than on the child's ability to report or explain. Similarly, children are invited to seek clarification: "While you are speaking with me, if I say anything that you do not understand, or if I ask a question that confuses you, please let me know and I will try to say things more clearly. If you want to ask any questions you may, and if you get tired and want to take a break then please let me know."

In spite of the most careful precautions, communication blocks can be encountered when eliciting information, either due to youngsters' inability or unwillingness to express themselves. When this occurs, Rich (1968) suggested using neutral phrases such as "Could you help me understand?" or "I don't quite understand." If children remain unable or unwilling to articulate, rather than persist, the professional can reintroduce the topic at a later time. When information is unclear, professionals can apologize to children while asking them to repeat their story. This microintervention is important in terms of relationship building and interpersonal engagement. To empower children further, professionals can invite them to ask clarifying questions. Sufficient time needs to be provided for children to ask questions or seek clarification (Pence & Wilson, 1994). Encouraging children to pretend they are detectives injects a playful element into the interview and enhances the child-professional relationship. Obviously, children are more likely to provide information when they are feeling relaxed and trusting of the professional.

ENGAGEMENT AND PACING

The basic principles of engagement and pacing with children are often overlooked. Moving too quickly from this stage, professionals jump into the formal interview process. When interacting with children it is important to realize that joining is an ongoing process, therefore the interview process needs to be carefully assessed, since completing an agenda in haste may strain and possibly jeopardize the relationship. Professional responses are typically guided by several factors including personal anxiety, time restraints, years of repetition, and boredom. Experienced professionals may mistakenly assume that they know when a child is comfortable. To avoid potential problems associated with moving hastily, professionals are encouraged to establish realistic goals. When attempts are made to accomplish a larger agenda, professionals place themselves under unnecessary pressure and jeopardize the professional-child relationship. Therefore, professionals have to consider the developmental stage of children with whom they are interacting.

Initially approaching children in a low-keyed manner has proven effective (e.g., soft voice, controlled movements, relaxed body, and smiling or neutral facial expression). Simply saying hello or making eye contact may be sufficient. Children commonly appear apprehensive in a new environment. As hosts to these children, professionals must be gracious and respectful of them. Youngsters will typically remain close to their parents until they become more familiar and comfortable with their new surroundings. Children explore first with their eyes and then slowly become more curious and begin to explore with their hands. Relying less on words and more on action (simple play with toys) to engage children seems to ease the transition period.

STAGES OF THE INTERVIEW

To conduct orderly and efficient interviews, several models have been developed (e.g., Boggs & Eyberg, 1990; Hughes & Baker, 1990; Jones, 1992; Barker, 1990; Yuille, Hunter, Joffe & Zaparniuk, 1993) and specific strategies have been recommended (Morgan, 1995). A review of the literature indicates that common components and fundamental ideas exist.

Although the detail provided differs across these models, the overall sequence is similar. Barker (1990), for example, separated interviews into three stages which includes getting to know each other, the exchange of information, and the conclusion of the interview. Such a format provides a simple framework within which to collect information in an orderly fashion. Jones (1992) elaborated on possible stages of the interview and advocated for a semistructured interview format, within a preplanned but flexible framework involving: establishing rapport, initial inquiry, facilitation using toys and materials if necessary, gleaning specific detail, and terminating the interview. The stages within this model are not necessarily lockstep. Another detailed scale, the Step-Wise Interview created by Yuille, Hunter, Joffe, and Zaparniuk (1993), includes nine steps designed to overcome problems when interviewing children—particularly in sexual abuse cases.

Initiating interviews with a conversation or activity that calms and reassures children is recommended. During this time period, misconceptions can be dispelled. When first getting to know children, a focus on interests and hobbies is recommended. Sensitive topics can be pursued once a trusting relationship has been established. In an effort to ease children into the interview process, models that are flexible, sensitive, and respectful are beneficial.

The possibility that an interview may not go as planned, should be anticipated. To respect the needs of children, it may be necessary to terminate the interview prematurely rather than attempt to elicit information under unfavorable conditions. Trying to coax or pressure children to participate will serve no purpose and is usually to no avail. Goodman and Sours (1994) were mindful that people are living organisms and children are developing organisms who will change and adapt to internal and external stimuli over the course of the interview. The time needed for this process must be provided.

Rich (1968) suggested that interviews should take the form of either a funnel or an inverted funnel, dependent upon the nature of the topic. The difference is that one form begins with generalities that establish the frame of reference, while introducing as little bias as possible, and progresses toward more specific, precise, and concrete questions. The other works in the opposite direction—a helpful approach when the topic is one that children may previously have spent time thinking about. The form of an interview is dependent upon its circumstances. In crisis-oriented interviews, for example, professionals are under time constraints and it becomes important that as much information as possible be obtained in minimal time.

LANGUAGE AND MEANING

To facilitate open communication with children, interviews should not resemble interrogation sessions (Barker, 1990). The age and abilities of children need be taken into account, and the language of professionals should be age/ability appropriate. Again, the onus is on professionals to conduct themselves in a manner that is suited to a child's age, personality, and ability. Several skills have proven helpful in establishing and maintaining rapport and they are discussed below.

Interviewer Anticipation

The ability to anticipate comes with experience and can eventually be acquired when working with children on a regular basis. Anticipating and appreciating the apprehension of children prior an interview is instrumental in respecting the experience of youngsters while recognizing their vulnerability. Professionals can   ally predict with relative accuracy what a child's reaction will be to the initial interview and how he or she will respond to being questioned. When uncertain about the interview context, children are generally hesitant to discuss even nonspecific and innocuous issues, let alone to disclose significant information.

A general acknowledgment of a youngster's circumstances, along with supportive behaviors (e.g., "Un-huh," raised eyebrows, head nods), can demonstrate an interest and understanding of children. Descriptive statements about behavior, appearance, or demeanor (e.g., "You look a little nervous," "You laughed when I asked about your sister") can also indicate that a professional is sensitive to a child's mood. When youngsters present as shy or timid, direct comments regarding their responses should be avoided so as not to in-crease their discomfort. Highlighting the reactions of children can increase their self-consciousness, and they may begin to withdraw to avoid additional attention.

Initial Greeting

Professionals have a marvelous opportunity to influence children positively during the initial greeting. While greeting children in the waiting area, the professional can clarify concerns and put children at ease. Reversing roles with children can be playful and an effective way for children to ask questions and gain confidence in the professional. Rather than simply direct youngsters to an interview room or office, the professional should take time to introduce youngsters to the surroundings. Providing a quick tour of the office area can satisfy children's curiosity. When working with one-way mirrors, youngsters can be shown the observation room. As children sit behind the glass, professionals can step outside into the interview room to demonstrate how the one-way mirror works.

Reflective Responses and Questioning

Reflecting feelings back to children, particularly feelings regarding the interview situation, demonstrates genuine interest and a willingness to understand their story. Rather than assume that children's experiences are similar, the individuality of youngsters should be respected. In situations where children seem to be struggling to explain themselves, the use of metaphors and mutual storytelling (Gardner, 1971) has proven invaluable. Metaphors and stories help children normalize their experience and see themselves in a wider context. Reflecting back to children what they have described and doing so in their own words and language serves to augment and support relationships. Children may feel better understood by a professional's attempt to clarify and confirm their narratives.

Various types of questioning techniques are available. Regardless of the questioning technique used, however, best results are usually obtained when children are trusting and information is gathered in a skillful and patient manner. Interviews can begin with simple, open-ended questions that elicit broad, spontaneous descriptions (Saywitz, 1990). After a relationship has been established, more complex and direct questions designed to extrapolate specific information can be pursued.

Again, the age and ability of children will dictate the interview process. With younger children for example, the use of closed-ended questions is typically more appropriate (Barker, 1990) as they find open-ended questions difficult. In an attempt to elicit information, open-ended questions can be asked (e.g., What were you thinking about? How did you feel?) and followed by summary statements. The intent is to direct the discussion toward specific areas of affect or interest while prompting and encouraging children. This questioning style can support children in organizing their thoughts, feelings, and behaviors. The goal is to create conversational space and avoid an intrusive ambiance. Therefore, questioning skills need to be refined for the purpose of seeking narrative responses (Hughes & Baker, 1990). Questions such as, "Can you tell me about your sister?" are avoided and replaced with questions like, "What happens when you and your sister play together?"

Another effective strategy in eliciting information is to ask questions like these:

I'm curious about how you felt when she said ... .

I'm wondering what you were doing when this happened.

I'm interested in knowing what happened after that.

Wood and Wood (1983) discovered that preschool children who were in low-control questioning situations when reflective statements were made alongside open-ended questions demonstrated increased initiative by raising topics, elaborating, commenting, or asking questions. In contrast, in situations where there was frequent use of direct, closed questions, children became passive and provided unreliable information. Additionally, Moston (1987) indicated that in interviews of children, their first responses should be accepted, even if they are "I don't know." Repetition of the question often culminates in deteriorated performance or fabrication of responses. In the latter, children feel pressured and coerced to respond.

Goodman and Sours (1994) provided creative suggestions for enhancing the interview. The techniques of thinking out loud or directing questions to a third person, for example, are useful when working with children who are verbally noncommunicative. These authors also recommended that the speech of professionals should be slow and deliberate. Using the subjunctive mode of the verb "were"—as in "If you were to show someone your classroom, what would he see?"—can also be useful in that children tend to pay more attention to verbs than other elements of speech. Inherent in these approaches, is a flexibility which is necessary to establish rapport with children. What needs to be remembered is that, perhaps for the first time, children have the undivided attention of an adult with whom they are unfamiliar.

To encourage cooperation during interviews, Sattler (1992) suggested: (a) using hypothetical questions such as "Imagine that ..."; (b) describing the already known details of hard-to-discuss situations; (c) commenting on topics children may be avoiding, and then following up with questions based on children's verbal statements or behavioral responses; (d) presenting two acceptable alternatives; and (e) allowing positive responses to be given before requiring less palatable or critical responses.

Professionals need to be wary of children's suggestibility when using any of these strategies. Glasgow (1989) cautioned that when interviews last for extended periods of time, children become distressed and succumb to the perceived demands of professionals. Remaining vigilant to signs of fatigue, distress or the loss of concentration is important particularly with younger children. When initial signs emerge (e.g., fidgeting, resting their head on an arm which is rested on the table, rapidly changing the subject, asking for their parent/guardian), interviews should be brought to a close efficiently. Expecting youngsters to exceed their limits can jeopardize the relationship and accuracy of the information provided.

Summary Statements

After children offer lengthy stories or descriptive replies, it is important to follow up with summary statements. Summary statements are used to condense and rephrase what children have shared in a segment of the interview. Framed in a positive tone, summary statements are used to demonstrate that children are being heard and appreciated. Summarizing what children have said ensures that professionals have correctly heard and understood what children have said. Although it may seem obvious, critical or judgmental statements are avoided. Children will usually be quick to correct professionals when they are incorrect.

Summarizing also serves to encourage children to continue with their narratives, knowing that they are being listened to actively. When summarizing, evaluative, judgmental, or critical statements should be avoided. Although summary statements may occasionally be used to highlight discrepancies in order to sort out conflicting testimony, professionals are advised to proceed cautiously and monitor children for signs of defensiveness. When children feel threatened, Hughes and Baker (1990) suggested, professionals should respect children's defenses and provide them with the emotional and personal space they require rather than pressing on with a confrontation (although this may not be an option for those employed in the judicial system).

Boundary Maintenance

To work effectively, it is essential not to overidentify with children. To maintain appropriate boundaries, it is necessary to reflect on the interview process while remaining cognizant of thoughts, feelings, attitudes, values, and biases. Older children, however, can be spoken to on more of an egalitarian level and confidential issues can be discussed more explicitly.

In summary, to obtain a child's report, Boggs and Eyberg (1990) reminded us, the interview should focus primarily on learning the child's perceptions, cognitions, and feelings. This information can only be obtained from children. These authors recommended progressing from least to most threatening topics, providing time for the child to trust that their descriptions will be valued and respected.

CLOSING THE INTERVIEW

To close interviews, children can be asked if there is anything else they would like to share (e.g., Boggs & Eyberg, 1990). Such invitations, provide children with ample opportunities to elaborate on personal stories. Professionals are often pleasantly surprised with information that is volunteered and which they may have forgotten to inquire about or have down played in its significance. Children can also be asked how they felt about an interview and if they have any questions or concerns. Children can be encouraged to contact professionals should any further thoughts or concerns surface. Securing parental/guardian permission before extending this offer however, is important. In bringing closure to interviews, themes and comments can be summarized and children's willingness to cooperate and discuss important information can be highlighted.

Children should leave interviews with a clear understanding of what is to follow (e.g., follow-up interviews, sharing of research results, etc.). Morgan (1995) suggested that children should be praised for their participation and that notes should be reviewed with children to ensure that documentation is correct. Whenever possible, interviews should end on a positive note. This usually involves a discussion centered on cherished interests or hobbies.

CHAPTER 4

LANGUAGE OF
THE INTERVIEW

Language is at the heart of interviews. Like a thread that weaves its way through the fabric of the interaction, it is vital to the exchange between professionals and children. Over the course of an interview, professionals and children observe, listen, and verbally interact (Looff, 1976). Language is an integral component of this interaction, it is a part of the general orientation, and it is crucial to the establishment of rapport. A knowledge of language, of its development and function, and of the ways in which it can aid or hinder the communicative process and the use of questions can help professionals interview children more effectively.

WHAT IS LANGUAGE?

Language is symbolic communication by which individuals can share inner thoughts and experiences. Language can be a powerful and effective tool when word meanings are commonly understood. Effective communication, however, remains a challenging task even for adults who have had years to master their mother tongue and to practice communicating with others. When children are at the other end of a dialogue, the task can be a daunting one. Since children's cognitive and linguistic abilities differ from adults, effort must be made to avoid inadvertently talking either above or below them (Barker, 1990).

Common examples include failing to accommodate children and using sophisticated language and clinical terms. Asking children if they are depressed for instance may prompt a variety of answers that range from a direct response to no response at all. In order not to appear ignorant children may provide affirmative answers without understanding what depression is. Children who are unresponsive on the other hand may be considered noncompliant but, in actuality, may be unable to respond. Language is learned over time, and knowledge of its subtleties develops from experience. Children lack the experience necessary to associate and attach words to meaning, as well as to consolidate the acquisition of this form of communication.

SECOND LANGUAGES

When second languages are involved, children and professionals may experience additional difficulties. Typically, people perform best when they are interviewed in their first language. However, when children are learning a new language, they may become less functional and fluent in their first language while improving in the second. This typically occurs if the second language is the dominant language outside of the children's home, if use of the minority language is discouraged, or if the minority language model is characterized by colloquial or idiosyncratic and generally weak structure (Lefrancois, 1990). Besides language differences, a professional's cultural background may affect the cross-cultural interview. Even if translators are used or if children speak the language used in an interview, misunderstandings may occur due to a lack of familiarity with the language structures of an interview, varying understanding of words in the translation, and varying dialectical uses of words (Pence & Wilson, 1994).

THE DEVELOPMENT OF LANGUAGE

Communication begins before birth, with external messages transmitted inward, and vice versa. While in the womb, an infant's brain begins to process sound, hearing voices and other noises. Infants hear and feel maternal heartbeats and respond to changes in maternal moods, positions, and activities. As prebirth infants move, their mothers feel movements such as kicks and hiccups.

Following birth, an infant's earliest communication is without language, as the infant cries and makes noises to communicate needs and interests. Many emotions are communicated through facial expression, and infants, who keenly observe faces, imitate expressions and become familiar with nonverbal communication. Some early communication occurs through sound. For example, parents and others use language to communicate to infants and infants respond with sounds but not words. The tone, volume, and intensity of sounds carries a great deal of information that infants begin to screen and understand. Slowly, almost miraculously, infants begin to decipher the confusing melange of sounds that make up the systems of language.

An ability to understand and use language is one of the most significant accomplishments of children, and much of it occurs before the child enters school. Of course, parents and guardians teach children through role-modeling, and adapting their language to a child's level in a fine tuned, bidirectional process (Bruner, 1977). For example, mothers tend to talk to their infants using the present tense, knowing instinctively that a newborn's world is present-oriented (Lefrancois, 1990). This process is refined as children acquire expressive language. To assist children, mothers of toddlers tend to reduce or use simpler, briefer, and repetitive phrases and sentences (as they do with infants) and to expand or scaffold onto what they have said. For example, child says, "Big doggie," and mother responds, "Yes, the dog is big" (Boyd, 1976).

Language development begins with listening (oral receptive), and is followed by speaking (oral expressive), then shifts to reading (visual receptive), and finally onto writing (visual expressive). In all but the rarest cases where children have specific disabilities, children's ability to understand language is better developed than their ability to express themselves, both at the spoken and the written level. For example, a typical 18-month-old will understand about 50 words but only speak about 10; a typical 6-year-old child understands around 14,000 words but uses only about 2,500 (Carey, 1978; Swanson & Watson, 1989). Educated adults are able to read and understand a Shakespearean play, yet few would attempt to imitate the level of vocabulary used. For children, the lag between receptive and expressive abilities is typically between 6 months and a year. Although early acquisition tends to be slow, the language learning curve has a steepened trajectory over time, with children learning about 6 to 10 new words a day between ages 4 and 6.

Broad language development in the first few years has been charted and separated into several stages:

1. *Prespeech*—prior to age 1—typified by babbling and cooing (e.g.,"muh-muh-muh").

2. *Holophrases*—by 1 year—typified by words combined with gestures to signify larger meanings (e.g., "ball," intended to communicate, "Give me the ball").

3. *Two-word sentences*—by 1 year to 18 months—typified by words and modifiers (e.g., "big doggie," "want more," "where mommy?")

4. *Multiple-word sentences*—by 24 to 30 months—typified by subjects with predicates and some basic grammatical structures (e.g., "I helping," "That a pretty doggie," "I want more!").

5. *More complex grammatical structures*—between 30 months and 4 years—typified by more complex understanding and application of nouns, verbs, prepositions, and simple joined clauses (e.g., "That doggie is big," "I want some more," "Give me the ball," "Read it, my book").

6. *Adult-like structures*—after 4 years—making complex structural distinctions (e.g., "I promised to eat it all," "Ask me where the dog is!" see Lefrancois, 1990).

At 1 or 2 years of age, children can communicate their needs and wishes using several words and can take turns in play activities. By 2 to 3, children will begin to ask for repeat readings of simple picture books. By 3 to 4, children enjoy simple conversation and will more readily verbalize past experiences. By 4 to 5, children understand verbal sequences of events (narratives), can retell the contents of a story with few factual errors, and can provide connected accounts of recent events and experiences. By 5 to 6, children can retell previously heard stories in the correct sequence, can retell experiences in an organized manner, and can take appropriate turns in conversations (Feeney, Christensen, & Moravcik, 1983).

Although these and other developmental guidelines are helpful when working with children, children must be appraised individually. In addition, the possibility that children may be presenting with some form of communication disorder must be considered, in which case interviews require significant adjustment. Further ideas on interviewing the language disabled child are discussed in Chapter 5.

THE USE OF LANGUAGE IN THE INTERVIEW

In addition to minimizing and eliminating communication roadblocks, facilitative factors need to be enhanced (Rich, 1968). The foundation for effective child-focused interviews can be viewed as a reciprocal process in which professionals and children influence one another (Beekman, 1983; Rich). This reciprocal process involves initiating a discourse wherein professionals invite children to explore their thoughts, then clarify and probe the children's responses to glean a thorough understanding of what was meant (Pramling, 1983). A developmentally sensitive interview format is preferable to highly structured questions, which can inhibit children's communication (Hughes & Baker, 1990).

Developmentally sensitive interviewing should begin with general probes and minimal direction and include:

1. increased directive questioning as needed;

2. the use of a less formal and structured conversational style;

3. the provision of a retrieval context that resembles the encoding context;

4. the reduction of task demands;

5. the provision of concrete retrieval cues;

6. the reduction of complexity questions;

7. the reduction of complex child responses; and

8. the reduction of threatening questions (Hughes & Baker).

Interviews should not be interrogations, words should be suitable to the child's age and ability, and a professional's manner should be suited to a child's age and personality (Barker, 1990). For an effective interview, Morgan (1995) suggested:

1. short, simple sentences;

2. one- or two-syllable words;

3. moving from general to specific questions;

4. avoiding vague chronological references such as, "last month" or "a few weeks ago";

5. avoiding double-negative statements;

6. avoiding double-positive statements;

7. using names rather than pronouns when referring to specific people;

8. observing children for any nonverbal indicators of confusion or inattention;

9. using literal and concrete words as descriptors; and

10. when using words introduced by the child, clarifying their meanings with children.

To these may be added a number of suggestions by Geiselman, Saywitz, and Bornstein (1993):

1. Use open-ended questions.

2. Ask single and not multiple questions.

3. Use language that is simple and appropriate for children.

4. Avoid the use of negatives in phrasing.

5. Praise children for their effort and not the content of their discourse.

6. Change to easier topics temporarily if a child's response is "I don't know" to three consecutive questions.

7. Do not interrupt children while they are answering a question. Inconsistencies can be clarified later.

Lepore and Sesco (1994) indicated that children's responses can be inadvertently influenced through leading questions, especially if professionals have preconceptions about what children know or may have experienced, or children's reports may be molded by including misinformation or misinterpretation in questions. Additionally, children's responses might be reinterpreted, or aspects of their self-reports might be selectively reinforced or ignored. Glasgow (1989) identified some other common interviewing mistakes:

1. allowing sessions to extend beyond acceptable time limits, thus contributing to child distress;

2. using leading questions, forced choice, and hypothetical questions ("What if ... ," "Suppose that ... ") which are likely to lead to inaccurate responses;

3. introducing sophisticated, technical, or euphemistic words which may be misinterpreted by children;

4. using language that encourages fabrication, including "Let's pretend," or "Let's make up a story."

Children understand these language formulations by 3 or 4 years of age (Feeney, Christensen, & Moravcik, 1983), and such scenarios can contaminate and bring into doubt the factual basis for anything children report thereafter.

SOME HELPFUL EXAMPLES

Most children have an adequate ability to comprehend adult speech structures by 4 years of age and can respond with understandable language formations. Of course, care must be taken so that terms are familiar to children, that they are asked to report on experiences they have been exposed to, and that they are asked to reflect on ideas and concepts within their developmental ken. In addition, language structures should not be too complex and excessive demands should not be placed on children's memory or ability to follow a train of referents. The following are examples of appropriate and inappropriate applications, along with some discussion and possible solutions to problems:

Terminology

Inappropriate: "I'm intrigued to know about what you and your peers do when you socialize."

Appropriate: "I'm curious about what you and your friends like to play."

Children's vocabulary develops gradually over time. When uncertain about the appropriate level of vocabulary, grade-appropriate literature can be reviewed to gauge the terminology that will work best with a specific audience. Children's ability to understand and use oral language is better developed than their ability to read. Therefore, the materials reviewed should be story books as opposed to basal readers, which will have a restricted language. Reviewing material just above and below the level required is recommended so that professionals have an idea of what language will be too complex or simple.

Experiential Foundation

Inappropriate: "Tell me what you know about Norse Gods."

Appropriate: "Tell me about what you like to do at recess time."

Children communicate more accurately when their recall is grounded in real-life experiences and events, especially when they are personally significant or emotionally salient (Steward, Bussey, Goodman, & Saywitz, 1993). If they are asked to discuss things that they have had little or no experience with, minimal information is given in return. Children's inexperience may lead them to misinterpret intentions, usually by taking words at their face value. For example, a child responding to a knock at the door may answer the question "Is your father home?" with a factual "Yes" and then wait quietly. A follow-up question "Does your father have time to talk right now?" may evoke another "Yes" from the child. In this circumstance, the child may politely continue to answer questions, not knowing that he or she is being asked indirectly to go and get his or her father. The meaning or intent of the questions is implied by the situation (and assumed past experience) and in this case is much more obvious to the frustrated adult than the child. An adult may even erroneously judge the child to be difficult or resistant.

Solution.   Be specific when making requests: "Will you please ask your father to come to the door to speak with me?" Or more succinctly, "Please get your father for me." Even apparently straightforward factual questions—those often used to collect demographic information—can go awry. For example, the query "When were you born?" may evoke a variety of responses from children who do not understand the underlying intent of the question:

- "At noon."
- "Between my sister and my brother."
- "Six years ago."
- "On December 1st."
- "A year after my parents were married."
- "Four days late."
- "When I didn't need to be inside my mommy anymore."
- "In the Chinese year of the rabbit."
- "After 23 hours of labor."

All of these responses are quite different, and quite correct, given their respective points of reference and their relative context. Each invites a potential barrage of further inquiries, all intended to elicit the answer the professional was initially searching for.

Solution. Be specific. "What is your birth date?" or "How many years old are you?" are more likely to produce the desired response than is the original wording.

Ideas and Concepts

> *Inappropriate:* "I'd like you to tell me the differences between Republicans and Democrats."

> *Appropriate:* "I'd like you to tell me how you think a car moves."

Besides the obvious underdeveloped cognitive constructions of children—such as that of the political theory—it should not be assumed that children have an understanding of words that require a particular conceptual understanding, such as those having to do with emotion, time, money, quantity, size, or positional relations. For example, before the age of 7, most children do not accurately understand relational words such as "forward," "backward," and "sideways" (Taylor & Purfall, 1987). As a solution to this potential problem, Saywitz (1990) suggested that before using such relational and directional words, children's understanding of them should be assesed by asking the children to place an object in a similar relation to another (e.g., "Place the little block beside the big block."). The following two sample questions demonstrate how a single word (with its embedded conception) can stop children in their tracks.

Question #1. "If you have two dollars in each hand, then how much money do you have?" Children who do not understand the word "each" will therefore skip over it and hear the question as, "If you have two dollars in your hand, then how much money do you have?" A typical response, therefore, would be "$2.00."

In addition, the question structure, which uses the phrase, "If ... then ... ," may be too complex for the child, who may proceed to ignore the first part of the question and focus on the understandable second part of the question. A typical response would then be to tell you exactly how much money they have in their piggy bank. Note that by 3 to 4 years of age, most children will understand this sentence formulation (Feeney, Christensen, & Moravcik, 1983).

Solution.   To explore children's math concepts, use manipulatives and enact the addition problem, or phrase the question differently: "You have $2.00 in this hand and you have $2.00 in that hand. Put them together. How many dollars do you have?"

Question #2.   "When someone asks you to share your toys, do you feel bad or good?" In this case, children who do not understand the apparently innocuous but highly meaningful word "or" will likely be confused and not know how to respond to the query. Further, the question, as it is framed, is rather leading, implying that children should feel either one or the other feeling. Children may have mixed feelings. They may feel neither bad or good, but rather something closer to "okay" or "neutral."

Solution.   Ask an open-ended question such as, "How do you feel when someone asks you to share your toys?" Or split the statements, offering several possible options with no particular pressure to respond one way over another, "Some children like to share their toys. Some children do not like to share their toys. How about you?"

Language Structures

> *Inappropriate:* "Your mother said that you have many fears, and she's given me her ideas about them. I'd like to hear your side of things in order to compare the two."

> *Appropriate:* "Tell me about things that scare you."

In general, sentences should not be overly complex. The longer the question, the more likely children are to lose track of where the question is going, and become confused. The younger the child, the shorter and more direct each statement or query will have to be. Boggs and Eyberg (1990) suggested that interviewers provide preschool children with only one concept in each descriptive statement or sentence, and that they remain sensitive to school-age children's limited vocabulary, using each child's own descriptors as often as possible. Confusion about what is being asked may lead to perseverance of responses (using the same answer repeatedly), something that tends to occur more often with younger than with older children. As a solution, Yarrow (1960) advocated using clear transitions between topics, especially in free interviews (e.g., "You told me about what kinds of thing make you feel sad. Next, I'd like you to tell me about things that make you feel angry." Or "Thank you for telling me about how your teacher helps you in school. Now I'd like to ask some questions about something different.")

SUPPORTING AND ENCOURAGING RESPONSES

To encourage narrative responses to questions, phrases that invite children to recount events or experiences in their own words can be used. Some examples include:

- "Please tell me everything that happened."

- "Tell it like a story."

- "I'd like to know what led up to it, what happened, and how it turned out."

- "Tell me the story of what happened."

- "Can you tell me about what you did—your story?"

Once questions have been asked or invitations have been made for children to elaborate on a subject, professionals continue to play a key role in determining the depth and breadth of children's responses. The chart that follows (beginning on page 80) identifies a number of specific communication skills that professionals can employ to induce and sustain children's continued cooperation. These skills also encourage and support children's responses, direct discussion toward specific areas of interest (or content such as behavior, thoughts, and feelings), support children in the organization of their responses, encourage children to expand on the detail provided in their responses, and ensure understanding of what children are communicating. A number of sources were used in developing this set of supportive listening skills. However, since many of the skills were originally intended to be used in a counselor-client helping relationship, they were not imported wholesale from the original sources. Instead these skills were adapted to suit the needs of child-focused interviews. In some cases, descriptors have been changed in order to distinguish between skills. Original sources have been footnoted, although such referencing is not intended to suggest that our categories, definitions, and examples reflect the original authors' intentions or designs.

SKILL	DESCRIPTION	PURPOSE	EXAMPLES
Interjecting[1]	Brief interjections and actions that do not interrupt the child's narrative	To show interest and support the child's narrative	"Uh-huh," "Yeah," nodding, raised eyebrows, eye contact
Appreciating	Positive statements that acknowledge the child's contribution	To encourage further participation	"That's very helpful for me, thank you." "I appreciate...."
Encouraging[2]	Statements that encourage without praising or statements of praise related to the child's efforts during the interview	To encourage further participation	"You are doing a great job!" "You are working very hard." "See, you can do it!"
Paraphrasing	Restatements of what the child has communicated, which use the same or similar words with an emphasis on the content of the text	To communicate understanding of a brief message	"You said that...." "You told me three things you like about school." "You went to...and said...and did ...."
Summarizing	Statements that condense content covered in a portion of the interview, with an emphasis on the content of the text	To communicate an understanding of a series of messages	"You've talked about...." "Let's talk about what you've told me up until now."
Empathizing[3]	Statements that reflect the feelings conveyed by the child	To communicate an appreciation of feelings or emotions (and encourage further sharing of feelings)	"You were really happy." "You felt...." "That made you angry."
Clarifying[4]	Phrases, statements or queries that clarify communication	To clarify a message when the professional didn't hear properly or is confused or uncertain (e.g. slang, references, vague wording)	"You mean...." "You're saying...." "What did you mean by...?" "I'm not sure what you mean." "Pardon me?" "Could you say that again, please?"

SKILL	DESCRIPTION	PURPOSE	EXAMPLES
Probing[5]	Open-ended probes or questions	To elicit further information or detail	"Tell me more about that." "Explain what you mean." "Give an example." "What happened next?" "I'm wondering about /interested in knowing...."
Commanding	Commands or demands to provide information	To elicit specific information or to introduce a new topic	"Describe how you felt." "Tell me your best friend's name." "Tell me about your experiences doing...." "Give me some more examples."
Making Descriptive Observations[6]	Observations that point out the child's behavior, appearance, demeanor, or significant statements	To have the child reflect on the possible meaning of behavior and statements	"You laughed when I asked about your sister." "You look away each time you mention...." "You said you were happy when ... but you frowned when you said it."
Making Inferences	Guesses about what a child is feeling or thinking	To elicit a verbal statement (confirmation or disconfirmation) regarding some-the professional has observed	"You seemed/looked/ sounded happy when you said ...." "You appear to be a little nervous .... " "It seems like .... "
Commenting on the Process	Statements about the interview procedure	To raise awareness of the interview-communication process, structure, or progress	"We've been talking about what you think and how you feel about .... " "Our talking is different than what you've done in school .... " "We're getting through a lot."

SKILL	DESCRIPTION	PURPOSE	EXAMPLES
Linking	Statements that connect content or thoughts that the child has offered at different times in the interview	To help the child reflect on several things he or she has said	"Earlier, you said that you liked math and now you said that you like art."
Challenging[7]	Statements that gently challenge the child to explain confusing, apparently inconsistent, or incongruent information	To clarify statements, ideas, or opinions that seem to be in conflict or opposition with each other	"Before you said ... and now you are saying...." "I'm confused because...."
Contrasting	Queries to elicit contrasts (opposites) in the child's words or statements	To help define and delimit the boundaries of a child's concept or construct in order to help ensure professional understanding	"Explain the opposite of that." "Is that different from .... " "You said that you felt ... what would be the opposite of that feeling?" "You said that Susan is kind. What is the opposite of that?"
Aligning[8]	Queries to elicit comparisons or alignments in the child's words or statements	To help find the similarities between concepts or constructs presented by the child, in order to clarify and organize them	"Is that like/similar to/the same as ... ?" "Tell me how these are alike." "You said that Mark is nice and Susan is kind; how are they the same?"
Information giving[9]	Information or instructions provided before, during, or following the interview	To provide directions or factual information, or to normalize an experience	"This interview is designed to .... " "We'll take a break in .... " "Many children feel .... "

SKILL	DESCRIPTION	PURPOSE	EXAMPLES
Self-Disclosing	Statements of personal experience	To communicate understanding through personal experience; to help the child feel more comfortable with the professional; to provide an example of what the professional is looking for	"I have talked with many children about ...." "I feel a little nervous when I meet someone new too." "Here's an example of some things that I don't like to do."

1. Kanfer, Eyberg, and Krahn (1983).

2. Dreikurs, Grunwald, and Pepper (1971) stated that encouragement values children, demonstrates faith in children, gains the confidence of children while building self-respect, and recognizes effort. Dinkmeyer and Dreikurs (1963) suggested that children should be encouraged for agreeing to attempt a task, while attempting a task, and when they have failed a task, or all three. Dreikurs and Soltz (1964) cautioned that praise should be avoided because it may lead to discouragement if it is interpreted as reward (the lack of which may be interpreted as scorn). Children may believe that they have failed and that they have no value if they are not praised for everything they do. During interviews, praising results can contribute to a child's belief that there are certain right or wrong answers, a belief that should not be reinforced. In addition, insincere or unsupported praise (e.g., flattery) may frighten children who question whether they can meet expectations (Dreikurs et al., 1971). Such flattery may also be interpreted as manipulation and may disrupt interactions. Therefore, praise should be used only as it relates to effort, in which context it is viewed as encouragement.

3. Egan (1994).

4. Lishman (1994).

5. Egan (1994).

6. Kanfer et al. (1983).

7. Lishman (1994).

8. Cochran (1980).

9. Lishman (1994).

QUESTIONING

Language forms the system of symbolic verbal communication between professionals and children, and professionals often use questions to direct the interview. Questions may follow the standard five Ws (who, what, why, where, when), or may involve use of the words "how" or "which." Questions may be prepared or spontaneous, but the language that is utilized must be considered carefully with children's developmental abilities in mind. Around the age of 3, children learn to respond to questions that begin with the words "who," "what," and "where" and to questions that have concrete referents (people, places, and objects). Later in the third year, they are able to answer "when," "which," and "how" questions, with "why" questions being the most difficult to respond to since they require an understanding of causality (Saywitz, 1990).

In addition to overt questioning, any of these key question words may be turned into what Hepworth and Larsen (1993) called embedded questions. Embedded questions are *statements* that contain a request for information or an invitation to speak on a topic (e.g., "I'm curious about ... ," "I'm wondering ... ," "I'm interested in ... ," "I would like to know ... "). Such phrases are usually less directive than overt questions, although they may still be used in a demanding manner that is closer to a command than a request (e.g., "Tell me about ... ," "Let me know what ... "). Most invitations to speak can be formulated as either overt or embedded questions. For example:

1. *Overt:* "Can you give me some examples of times when you felt that way?"

   Embedded: "Give me some examples of times when you felt that way."

2. *Overt:* "Would you please tell me what you were thinking about when ... ?"

   Embedded: "Tell me what you were thinking about."

3. *Overt:* "How would children get along on the playground without supervisors?"

   Overt: "Could you tell me how children would get along on the playground without supervisors?"

   Embedded: "I'm curious about how children might get along on the playground without supervisors."

MAKING QUESTIONS WORK

Whatever questions are used when interviewing children, professionals should strive to elicit narrative, story-like responses that will be rich in first-hand data. Children need to be encouraged to share their stories and discouraged from providing short responses. To achieve this, open-ended questions are preferred (e.g., "What were you thinking about?" "What happened next?"), questions that cannot be answered with a brief yes or no, or a simple snippet of information (e.g., "Did you like it?" "How many were there?") In addition, there is less risk of contamination when open-ended questions are used then when closed questions (which can more easily be suggestive or leading) are used.

Saywitz (1990) suggested that professionals begin with questions that elicit broad, spontaneous descriptions (usually open-ended questions), then gradually move toward more specific and direct questions. Barker (1990) also supported this approach, although he indicated that young children will require closed-ended questions earlier in the interview than will older children. He indicated that simple questions are preferable to complex ones, as they are less confusing, and he advocated dividing complex queries into two or more separate questions (Barker, 1990).

Open-ended questions can be especially helpful in encouraging older children to speak, but they can often have the opposite effect with younger children who are uncertain how to respond. In these circumstances, efforts is made to refine questioning skills, still keeping questions as open as possible while avoiding generalities. For example, instead of a general question like, "Would you tell me about your sister?" children might be asked, "What happens when you and your sister play together?" (Hughes & Baker, 1990).

Another effective strategy in eliciting information is to ask children embedded questions like these:

- "I am curious about how you felt when she said ... ."

- "I am wondering what you were doing when ... happened."

- "I am interested in knowing what happened after you said that to her."

These questions are not general, but contain specific referents for children to respond to (e.g., "when she said ... ," "when ... happened," "after you said that to her"). The intent of working this way is to direct the discussion toward specific areas of interest while prompting and encouraging youngsters to provide further details. This questioning style supports children in organizing their thoughts, feelings, and behavior.

Questions will often have a framework or introduction that provides the setting or context (Yarrow, 1960):

- "I'm going to ask you some questions about your family."

- "You have said a lot of things about your mother. Now I'd like to know some things about your father."

- "I'm going to read you a short story about a family of rabbits. Then I'm going to ask you some questions."

Just as questions themselves may be either general or specific, so may these frameworks. For example, when researching children's experiences with bullying, a general framework can be used (e.g., "I want you to think about a time when you have been bullied."). Or you can use a more specific, structured framework (e.g., "Think of a time when someone bullied you while you were on the playground."). Whatever framework is chosen, either general or specific questions may follow it. For example, as a follow-up to the bully scenario, a general question can be employed (e.g., "What happened?"). Or a more specific question can be used (e.g., "What were you thinking while you were being bullied?").

Besides the dichotomy of open versus closed questions, Yarrow (1960) also introduced a continuum of questioning directness, ranging from direct (e.g., "Who is your best friend?") to indirect (e.g., "If you had to choose only one friend to come to your birthday celebration, who would you choose?"), where the purpose of the question is disguised; to projective (e.g., "If a new boy came to your classroom, how do you think he would feel?") using a scenario that involves a hypothetical child. Depending on the purposes of the interview, each level of directness in questioning will provide more or less useful information.

REPHRASING QUESTIONS

Problems are likely to occur when professionals do not understand children's responses. Other times, children will not understand professionals. But assumptions should never be made about children's understanding or lack of understanding. As previously noted, a child's first response should be accepted, even if it is "I don't know," since repetition of the question often leads to deterioration of performance or to fabrication of responses (Moston, 1987). In the former, children may feel accused of lying; while in the latter, children feel pressured and coerced to respond, even if it means making up an answer. Rewording questions often serves to frustrate children and rupture the professional-child relationship.

This generalization does not mean that questions should never be rephrased. There are some circumstances when it is quite appropriate, even advisable, to rephrase questions. As long as the rephrasing or reframing does not happen too often, it can help to strengthen communication. If children misunderstand a question and offer a valid response to what they thought was asked, professionals can accept the answer and then offer a question rephrased as a new question. If done this way, professionals need to ensure that their second attempt clarifies what they intended to ask.

Morgan (1995) advised that professionals self-monitor and phrase or rephrase questions in their heads before asking them aloud. For example, after a child has spoken about a conflict at school, he or she might be asked, "How did you react?" To which the child responds, "Since then, we just fought more." In this case, children interpret the word "react" as if the professional had said "act." A quick rephrasing might repeat the initial mistake (e.g., "But how did you respond?") and frustrate the child. An appropriate rephrasing would be along the lines of "After Maria called you a name, what did you do next?"

There is one other circumstance in which professionals may wish to restate or rephrase a question, and that is when the child didn't hear it or is obviously confused. In such situations, children will sometimes say something like "Pardon?" "I didn't hear that." Or "I don't understand what you mean." Unfortunately, children may not say anything to communicate their confusion.

Sometimes they will pause or be silent after being asked a question. This may indicate that they are simply thinking about the question, or it may mean that they are confused by the question. Even if confusion is assumed to be the case, an immediate rewording of the question should be avoided. Nor should professionals ask children if they understand the question. Hughes and Baker (1990) suggested that asking children whether they do or do not understand is unproductive and inappropriate, since children are unable to monitor their own understanding accurately, and their desire to make professionals happy may lead them to affirm their understanding when they really do not understand.

Rather than asking whether or not they understood a question, professionals can clarify children's possible confusion (e.g., "I'm sorry. Did I ask that in a confusing way?"). By doing this, professionals emphasize their own lack of skill and not the child's. Even if children did not understand the first time, they are unlikely to feel as if they are at fault. Next, professionals can rephrase questions, making sure to apologize for not wording the question properly the first time. Apologies ensure that children don't take responsibility for the confusion and feel frustrated and incompetent.

Goodman and Sours (1994) made some additional suggestions for enhancing interviews when working with silent children. These include asking rhetorical questions or comments directed toward or invoking a hypothetical third person (e.g., "Sometimes children are afraid. I'm curious about what things might scare you."). These authors also indicated that professionals should talk slowly and deliberately and use the subjunctive mood (as in, "If you were to show someone your classroom, what would he see?"), since children tend to pay more attention to verbs than other elements of speech.

With silent children Hatch (1990) advocated that professionals should repeat the question, restate it, offer alternative responses, and finally ask "Is it ... ?" to encourage a response; but such interventions are risky and could jeopardize rapport or pressure children.

FORCED RESPONSES

Children are not experienced in equal-sided conversations with adults. Graue and Walsh (1995) stated that children are used to three types of questions from adults:

1. *Coercive,* whereby adults ask children questions intended to tell them what to do or how to feel (e.g., "Wouldn't you like to give your aunt a hug and kiss?")

2. *Pseudo-test,* where adults already know the answer (e.g., "How many pencils do I have?")

3. *Procedural,* intended to elicit specific information (e.g., "Where are your shoes?")

Unfortunately, none of these interactions encourages or inspires authentic conversation. Based on their past interactions, children learn to please or placate adults.

Yarrow (1960) suggested professionals take steps to limit the effects of children seeking to provide responses that will gain adult approval. He advised that professionals word questions to suggest any one of several possible responses such as, "Some children think that ... . Others think that ... . Maybe you have some different ideas about it. We like to know all of the different ideas that 6-year-old boys have about this" (Yarrow, 1960, p. 565).

Additionally, he suggested that questions be slanted in several directions to ensure stability of responses over time (e.g., "Do you decide when you go to bed?" countered later with, "Do your parents decide when you go to bed?") However, Yarrow cautioned that countersuggestion may strain rapport if children recognize that a question is essentially the same one previously asked. In addition, children may latch onto the first response made and stick with it whether it represents their point of view or not.

Parker (1984) took some of Yarrow's suggestions, but his examples reveal how easily such techniques may be misused. For example, Parker suggested that the question "Do you feel bad when you are asked to share your toys?" (p. 20) be extended to include, "Or does that make you feel good?" (p. 20). His proposed phrase requires the ability to understand the word "or" to indicate an alternate choice, a language structure that could be problematic for young children. In addition, Parker's sentence does not use a parallel structure ("Or do you feel good?" would be parallel), which makes for a lengthier and potentially more confusing question.

Generally, complex questions are difficult for children to comprehend. A possible solution would be to word the question: "Some children like to share their toys. Some children don't like to share. What about you?" A far better alternative would be to ask children to think of a time when they were asked to share their toys and to tell about what happened and how they felt. This approach would avoid leading questions. To circumvent the right-answer phenomena, whereby children believe that professionals are looking for a certain type of answer,

Hatch (1990) advised that professionals accept children's responses, even if they are not fully understood. If a response is confusing for professionals and children become visibly frustrated when probed, it is best to leave the item and move forward. Avoid overprobing. Information supplied by children may clarify what they say or intend to communicate at a later date. Otherwise, when children are more relaxed, the situation may be reintroduced in a nonthreatening manner. "Earlier on, I asked you what you thought about … , and I was a little confused about what you said. I guess I wasn't listening very well. Could you please tell me again what your idea was, so that I can understand it?"

Professionals must do everything possible to reduce confusion and frustration in their young clients. Typically, the younger the children, the less disruption they will be able to handle in the interview. Also, children with attentional, behavioral, cognitive, or emotional difficulties will have a more limited ability to manage even minor rifts in communication. Children can best answer questions that are founded upon their first-hand experiences and that consider their information processing capabilities (Hatch, 1990). If questions relate to things that children have not experienced directly, Hatch advised professionals to make explicit the perspective they are seeking (e.g., "Pretend that you were eating a snack and someone took the snack from you. How would you feel? Why do you think the person took your snack?").

Every consideration should be taken to ensure the integrity of children's responses. Children's testimony, however, may have been tainted before their first interview. In some rare circumstances, children may have been told or taught how to respond. Lepore and Sesco (1994) found that children 4 to 6 years of age can be influenced to report false information about another person's actions if professionals make incriminating statements, particularly when children have had only a brief encounter with an adult that they didn't know well. If children have been previously interviewed using leading or suggestive questions, information recalled may be accurate but it may also have been distorted by the questioning (Jones, 1992), and distorted memories seem to persist (Loftus & Davies, 1984).

Further, caution needs to be taken when conducting cross-cultural interviews. Weeks and Moore (1981) reported that while the ethnicity of professionals does not appear to influence responses to questions about nonsensitive topics, it can be a factor if sensitive, race-related questions are asked. Campbell (1981) theorized that this is the result of deference to a professional, and reported such responses in research with both adolescent and adult respondents.

APPROPRIATENESS OF QUESTIONS

Professionals can prepare questions in advance and have them reviewed by psychologists, educators, and parents who are sensitive to and experienced with children. When formulating questions, Yarrow (1960) recommended three basic considerations:

1. Questions should be readily understood by children.

2. The meaning or interpretation of questions should not vary significantly from one child to another.

3. The format of questions should not lead children to any particular response.

If possible, questions may be tested on a sample of children in advance to uncover potential problems. Professionals should try to keep questions as simple and as clear as possible. Long, complex questions only serve to confuse children and make them feel uncomfortable (Hatch, 1990). Selected questions and examples must relate to the child and the circumstances they understand. For example, if researching moral development, questions that have adult content or adult issues should be avoided (e.g., "What would you do if your sister needed medication and the only man who had it was charging too much money?"). A more appropriate scenario would be, "What would you do if you were at school and another child did not have lunch and you did?"

At the same time, it may not always be helpful to ask direct questions. For example, if we ask a child "Have you ever stolen anything?" we are likely to get a quick denial in response. Rather than asking children's opinions about topics that may make them feel self-conscious, Parker (1984) suggested using questions that generalize to the peer group (e.g., "I'd like to know what children your age think about stealing," or "I'm talking with children to understand their ideas about stealing, and I'm wondering what children your age think about it.")

Drawing on knowledge about interviewing adults, Yarrow (1960, p. 580) made additional suggestions for formulating questions to encourage responses to delicate or difficult topics (examples are not drawn directly from Yarrow):

1. Suggest in questions that other children might feel the same way: "All children feel sad sometimes. When do you feel sad?"

2. Present two alternatives, both of which might be considered acceptable: "Some children want to be alone when they are sad; some children want to be with someone else when they are sad. What do you want to do when you are sad?"

3. Choose words that will soften an undesirable response or present the response in a context that might make it more desirable: Instead of asking, "Why do you want to hurt someone else?" ask, "What has to happen to make you angry enough to hurt someone?"

4. Avoid placing children in a position where they have to deny some undesirable behavior and do so by wording questions so as to assume

that they have engaged in this behavior: Instead of asking, "Have you ever hurt someone else?" say, "Tell me about a time when you did something to hurt someone."

5. Provide children with an opportunity to express a positive response before presenting questions that will require a negative or critical evaluation: "What do you like best about living with your family?" Follow this with, "What do you like least about living with your family?"

Finally, questions should be distinct from each other. Although it may seem obvious, professionals must avoid asking double questions or bombarding children with questions. Mischler (1986) found that many physicians would ask questions quickly, one after the other, in a manner that took firm control of the interview and encouraged respondents to shorten their replies. As he said, "responses are not simply answers to questions but also a reflection of the professional's assessment of whether a respondent has said *enough* for the purpose at hand" (p. 55). In general, the goal is to create conversational space with children and not to interrogate or interrupt them. Professionals must monitor their interactions to ensure that they don't become overly directive or intrusive when questioning children.

CHAPTER 5

DEALING WITH
UNIQUE CHILDREN AND
CIRCUMSTANCES

Professionals typically approach interview situations feeling optimistic that the interview will unfold as planned. Although most interviews are successful in revealing information, problems can arise when professionals encounter unexpected challenges. Unique circumstances occur when youngsters express their fear, anxiety, or displeasure by threatening to boycott the interview process through either acting-out (e.g., belligerence, overt attack), or acting-in (e.g., withdrawal, refusal to speak or interact) behaviors. These situations may also include children who face emotional challenges or who are culturally different from professionals.

The purpose of this chapter is provide professionals with a conceptualization and practical suggestions to sidestep power struggles and avoid conflicting relationships. Strategies are designed to help professionals build rapport with children and elicit useful self-reports. Although the following strategies may prove helpful, they do not always guarantee success. Professionals must concede that there will be some children whom they will be unable to help due to personality conflicts, presenting problems or other circumstances. As disappointing as such an outcome may be, it remains a reality when interviewing children.

DEALING WITH CHALLENGING CHILDREN

Children who are perceived as challenging may present as uncooperative and noncompliant. Problems typically arise when these youngsters are forced to attend interviews against their will. Consequently, they believe that the interview will be unproductive and a waste of their time. As a result, they are defensive when they attend interviews and reluctant to engage with professionals. From the outset, it becomes clear that they perceive themselves as powerful and able to control the interview process. Children behaving in such a manner can be disruptive and contribute to an unproductive interview. Unfortunately, uncooperative children frequently behave in ways that distance even skilled professionals, leading to disappointment, frustration, or anger. Professionals are generally well-intentioned but if they fail to accomplish their tasks, they may feel mistreated and personally attacked. To remain sensitive and respectful, and to control emotional reactions in these challenging situations, professionals must be appropriately prepared.

Some children are naturally reluctant and will require time to adjust to the interview situation. To encourage reluctant children to cooperate during interviews, Sattler (1992) suggested (a) using hypothetical questions such as "Imagine that ... ," (b) describing the already known details of a hard-to-discuss situation, (c) commenting on the topics children may be avoiding, then following up with questions based on children's verbal statements or behavioral responses, (d) presenting two acceptable alternatives, and (e) allowing for a positive response before requiring a less palatable or critical one. Unfortunately, such interventions are not always effective. Some children's resistance will be intense and will require creative intervention.

Although difficult interviews cannot always be anticipated, professionals generally receive advance notice from parents or colleagues that a youngster is unlikely to collaborate. When preparing for challenging interviews, appropriate steps can be taken to avoid unnecessary difficulties. Professionals should not expect all children to engage immediately but should anticipate reluctance and make necessary accommodations. Changes can be made by meeting children where they feel safe, connecting with children, reducing interview time, and acknowledging resistance when it emerges.

Meeting Children

Rather than interviewing children at a clinic or office, professionals can meet children in places that are already familiar to them (e.g., homes, day cares, classrooms). When they are accommodated, youngsters are less likely to feel threatened and are more likely to engage with professionals. By making this accommodation, professionals convey to children that they are important. This can be a helpful strategy for building alliances with children who are insecure and easily threatened. When working within school settings, professionals can arrange to meet children in their classrooms before asking them to relocate to a separate space. Sometimes, children need only a few minutes to become acquainted with professionals. Other times, they require a series of classroom-based meetings to help assuage their fears. Another helpful strategy is to establish relationships with adults and friends whom children know and trust. If necessary, these allies can be recruited to help escort children to interviews.

Making Links

Professionals can invite parents or guardians to bring favorite toys (e.g., a stuffed animal) or snacks to increase a child's comfort. These items allow professionals to forge links with children while exhibiting a sensitivity to their needs. For example, professionals could ask about or comment on the objects: "Does your teddy bear have a name?" Or, "That looks like a special blanket." In addition to inviting children to bring along toys or games, professionals can allow time for children to play while beginning to connect with them in a nonthreatening manner. Learning about children's meaningful objects can provide important information concerning their lives.

Reducing Interviews

Initial interviews can be purposefully abbreviated to familiarize youngsters with the interview space and to ensure that the environment is relaxed and nonthreatening to them. In such circumstances, the majority of time can be devoted to rapport building. Children can be informed that their visit will be brief, which can be reinforced when the interview commences (e.g., "We will be together for about 15 minutes today. That's not a lot of time. I just wanted to have a chance to meet you and to let you see this room. I'll take you on a tour, and then you'll be able to spend a few minutes playing, if you like.").

If an interview goes well, it is advised that the established time limit not be extended. Interviews should end positively, with a feeling of anticipation for the meeting. When interviews extend beyond agreed-upon limits, professionals may cross an invisible line from comfort to discomfort and children may decide not to return. Difficult children tend to respond best when clear boundaries are consistently adhered to. They may not initially notice that a proposed time limit has been exceeded, but when they do, they may become upset and distrusting.

At the end of a brief interview, children can be casually informed that a longer meeting will be arranged. To avert defensive reactions, future interactions could be referred to as planning meetings or discussions instead of clinical interviews or counseling sessions. It can also be underscored that future interviews will be collaborative in nature. Framing interviews as meetings or discussions can also have a normalizing effect. Utilizing a collaborative approach empowers young people and emphasizes strengths and capabilities. As such, children can engage in a partnership and eventually work toward making changes in their lives. They are also less likely to experience cognitive or emotional dissonance or feelings of inferiority. Although such a simple reframing procedure may seem rudimentary, there is a tendency to professionalize interviews in order to maintain a sense of hierarchy and control even when circumstances warrant an alternative approach.

UNDERSTANDING PERCEIVED RESISTANCE

Professionals can begin an interview by showing interest in children's reluctance. For example, professionals can say, "Your parents said that you didn't want to come today. I'm wondering how you were able to come even though you wanted to stay away?" If professionals appear intrigued by children's perceived resistance, it is less likely to fester and worsen. Instead, resistance is acknowledged and utilized. When professionals offer reasons why children may be reluctant to attend interviews, they communicate that they anticipate a level of resistance and that they are open to discuss and work through concerns that prompt resistance. In using a subtle approach, professionals can generalize and say, "Some children don't want to come in to see me. Sometimes they are afraid of hospitals. Sometimes they think it is going to be boring and a waste of their time. Sometimes, they think that they are going to be forced to talk about things they don't want to talk about." They may add, "I wonder if you have similar concerns?" Through the appropriate application of joining strategies, resistant behavior can be replaced with insightful talk, productive play, and an eventual willingness to participate in the interview process (Marshall, 1972).

When challenging interviews are anticipated, careful preparation can increase the probability of success. When difficulties occur unexpectedly however, professionals will have to resort to general guidelines. Although there are several reasons why children are reluctant to engage with professionals and why they become obstructive and combative, professionals are encouraged to interpret such behavior as fear-based and not consider it to be a personal attack. Reframing behavior can be useful to sidestep power struggles and avoid conflicting interactions with children.

Case Vignette

One child PJM met for an initial interview went to an extreme to criticize not only the physical features of the interview room but also the way he pronounced many words, insisting his pronunciation was "dumb." His behavior was interpreted as an indicator of his fear of having anyone become emotionally close to him, where they would potentially be in a position to hurt him emotionally. In order to protect himself, he did everything he could to be discredited and rejected by yet another professional. Rather than react defensively to his remarks and enter into a power struggle, PJM complimented the child for his interior designing skills and for paying close attention to how PJM was speaking. Using his observations to advantage, PJM began discussing his Quèbèçois accent and sharing a little about himself and his background. To PJM's surprise, the child mentioned that his grandfather spoke German and also had an accent. Not only did PJM diffuse his attack by not reacting defensively, but he also began to build rapport by listening to the child's ideas and using appropriate self-disclosure. From this brief beginning, the two began to build on their shared stories.

WORKING WITH PROFESSIONAL–CHILD CONFLICT

An issue that has remained underinvestigated is the conflict that can develop between professionals and children. This element deserves attention because it is central to resolving many problems that arise within interviews. Professionals are advised to consider how their own transference reactions and defense mechanisms contribute to conflict and how they manifest in the interview. To support this active self-reflection, a model for recognizing and analyzing conflicting interactions is discussed and a range of interventions, designed to diffuse conflicts and build rapport, are offered.

Understanding Conflict

Conflict occurs when two parties are oppositional. To avoid conflict, professionals need merely to step away from arguments and agree with children. By agreeing, the highly charged situation is immediately diffused. Similarly, professionals can diffuse conflict at any point by refusing to participate in it. Furthermore, they can align themselves with children so that they agree with them, see things from their perspective, and understand their difficulties. It can be argued that intervention concedes power to children, fuels their sense of power, and can lead to a loss of professional control. On the other hand, when children are acknowledged, respected, and listened to, they tend to respond well. For example, imagine attempting to lead a child around a room with a rope. If you begin to pull and the child resists, you are unlikely to complete the journey. However, if you first follow the child's lead, you may be in a better position to negotiate the journey. Similarly in the interview context, when professionals take time to first join and follow children, youngsters are more likely to reciprocate.

The same approach used to diffuse a verbal conflict can be applied when diffusing a physical conflict. In the Japanese martial art of Aikido ("The Way of Peace"), defenders (or receivers) blend with attackers, harmonize with attacks, and neutralize potential harm. Although unlikely to be Aikido masters, professionals can apply the underlying principle of this strategy to their work. Some practical applications of Aikido have been illustrated by Crum in his 1987 book *The Magic of Conflict*. The foundation for successfully intervening in potentially conflictual situations is a nonconfrontational stance. Such a stance, based on mutual respect, promotes the achievement of mutual goals.

How Conflict Develops

Conflict within professional-child relationships generally emerges when expectations remain unmet and when personally meaningful positions are challenged. When this occurs, a sense of incompetence can surface. The concept of complimentary coupling provides a framework to understand how a sense of incompetence contributes to conflict between professionals and children. For example, a professional may become frustrated with slow progress in an interview and begin to act impatiently (e.g., completing sentences, interrupting, or unilaterally changing the focus of the interview).

Children who notice professionals becoming impatient might become anxious and defensive (e.g., suggesting that the professionals don't understand, deciding to withdraw emotionally). In response to the children's defensiveness, professionals might become self-protective and criticize the children (e.g., telling them that they need to focus, advising them to stop sulking). When professionals incorrectly interpret children's restlessness, distractibility, or reduced cooperation as willful noncompliance, an adversarial relationship will likely evolve.

If professionals perceive themselves to have lost control of a session, they may become annoyed and take action to correct the situation and restore their own status and sense of competency. In doing so, they may project their personal shame and discomfort onto the children, in effect holding the youngsters responsible for their personal despair. The resulting emotional discomfort experienced by both children and professionals can easily spiral into a vicious, conflicting cycle. As a result of the increased anxiety and tension, the interview process becomes mutually reactive and adversarial, effectively damaging the interpersonal relationship. Coyne, Wortman, and Lehman (1988) described a cycle that results from professionals becoming overinvested in a successful interview outcome:

> With each exchange, the helper has invested more and more of his or her self-esteem and well-being and interprets the partner's lack of progress in a highly personalized way. Having become involved, the helper has accepted some of the responsibility for a positive outcome and part of the blame if it is not achieved. (p. 317)

To alter a developing negative interaction, problematic patterns need to be interrupted. In this quest, personal agendas are put aside and the mutual nature of the relationship is considered. Assuming full responsibility for a poor outcome disregards the bidirectional nature of the professional-child relationship. Conversely, projecting blame onto children for difficulties in the interview might help professionals disengage from the interview process and divest themselves of responsibility for its outcome. Unfortunately, in the latter situation, professionals remain unaware of their contribution to the perpetuation of the situation.

Professional Behaviors That Contribute to Conflict

Professionals are influenced by personal perceptions and cognitions that trigger both emotional and physiological reactions. Personal reactions are often subtle and may be outside of one's conscious awareness. To minimize the impact of such conscious and unconscious judgments and reactions, professionals should carefully examine their values and beliefs. Values and beliefs are influenced by several variables including: age, marital status, gender, and ethnic, religious, and social-cultural background. Effort should be made to remain cognizant of personal reactions to children, including overt and covert responses to their appearance, speech, and behavior.

Problematic situations seem to develop more often when professionals are rigid and unable to adapt or adjust their interactions with children. Rigidity often intensifies when professionals attempt to master a specific interview style or model. Under such circumstances, professionals are more focused on the theory and the mechanics of the interview than on the subtle interactions that comprise the interview process. Despite the benefits of adhering to a guiding framework, professionals need to remain flexible. An unyielding adherence to a specific interview style or model can produce inflexibility and can make the interview an oppressive rather than liberating experience for children. This sense of oppression may be enhanced for children who come from extremely oppressive environments (e.g., violent homes) or for children who have previously had negative experiences with professionals. When there is a poor fit between children and interview style, both children and professionals will feel uncomfortable. Unfortunately, children's discomfort may be misinterpreted by professionals as ambivalence, uncooperativeness, or resistance. When professionals react to children as if they are being willfully uncooperative, the outcome can be mutual feelings of frustration, disappointment, anger, or all three. To be successful, professionals must respect the individual needs of children. Although some children will persist through difficulties, others will quickly lose momentum and withdraw to avoid feeling out of control, incompetent, or helpless. Some children need structure while others require flexibility.

Professional behaviors that contribute to conflict in the interview process can be manifested both directly and indirectly. Such behaviors may be subtle or obvious and are more likely to occur when professionals become hurt, fearful, anxious, annoyed, frustrated, or angry, or lose interest in continuing the relationship. They can include direct or indirect verbal indicators and direct or indirect nonverbal indicators, as described below:

1. Direct verbal indicators can include insulting, demeaning, or critical remarks made to children, or confrontations that are harsh or aggressive. Such behaviors sometimes emerge when children do not respond in ways that suit professionals, who then interpret children's actions as a lack of investment in the interview process. Professionals become disappointed and frustrated and, in response, children become frightened or equally disappointed.

2. Indirect verbal indicators can include insulting, degrading, or critical remarks about children that are made to other people. This behavior is commonly exemplified by professionals who, in the presence of colleagues, make comments about the children after they have become frustrated during the interview process. A common indirect, verbal indicator is illustrated in written or oral reports that tend to criticize children and depict them as troublesome and noncompliant.

3. Direct, nonverbal indicators can include professional facial and body expressions during interactions with children. For example, profes-

sionals may respond to children's unwillingness to share information with a sarcastic facial expression that suggests doubt in the youngsters' commitment to the interview. Professionals may fold their arms, scowl, look away, or look disgusted.

4. Indirect, nonverbal indicators can include a general lack of empathy and authenticity towards children and is demonstrated by the creation of boundaries that are either too rigid or too relaxed. Such behavior is sometimes demonstrated by professionals who believe that children are unlikely to benefit from the interview process. In such circumstances, professionals may spend more time monitoring the clock or looking away than they do listening to the children's stories. Children who notice these types of behavior, frequently respond by losing interest in the interview and withdrawing from the interaction.

Children possess unique life circumstances and personalities and, as a result, will present new challenges requiring professional adjustment. Professionals will usually recognize the types of behaviors that contribute to personal discomfort. Assumptions and biases that prompt reactions (e.g., profanity, aggressiveness) must be identified and adequately processed. For instance, PJM once had a colleague who described her discomfort with children who were physically clingy. She explained that she had little tolerance for loose boundaries around personal space. She realized that in order to work effectively with children, particularly children who require a great deal of reassurance, she would have to evaluate her own discomfort and develop a better understanding of these youngsters. Rather than work through personal issues however, some professionals simply decide to rerefer such clients. The rereferral process might not always be an option, however. For example, professionals who work in child clinics are unlikely to have the luxury of client selection. Therefore, gaining exposure to a wide variety of clients while identifying and addressing personal issues either through appropriate supervision or personal therapy, is recommended. During this process, there is an opportunity to experience personal and professional growth.

Inroads to Change: Conflict Analysis

To avoid conflict between professionals and children, it is important that professionals remain sensitive to personal issues and significant patterns in their work. Critical incident reporting can be an effective way to document emotional or behavioral experiences during interviews. This process is explained by Pedersen (1995) who wrote:

Each incident describes a specific example of success or failure where the observer describes (1) the events that led up to the incident and their context, (2) what the person did (or did not) do that was effective or ineffective, (3) the apparent consequences of this behavior, and (4) whether any of the consequences were under the person's control to change. (p. 15)

Direct feedback can also be requested from children. Implemented appropriately, this strategy can be useful while simultaneously empowering children. By taking responsibility and being personally accountable, professionals disarm themselves, interrupt the cycle of conflict, and establish a positive tone. For example, if children become annoying or disruptive, the interview can be interrupted and the source of the behavior can be pursued with children. A descriptive observation (e.g., "I noticed that you started to make a lot of noise when I asked you about your friends at school.") or an inference (e.g., "Is this difficult to talk about?") can be made. These two skills often work well together (e.g., "You were sitting in a chair and now you're running around the room. Are you getting bored?").

TRANSFERENCE AND COUNTERTRANSFERENCE

To minimize professional-child problems, possible negative transference and countertransference issues require attention. The term transference refers to the projection of subjective unconscious material onto other people. Although the term countertransference was originally used by psychoanalysts to describe reactive feelings in the helper invoked by the client's behavior, it has more recently been used to describe any form of conflict that emerges during interactions. Aside from the overt, conscious relationship and interaction between professionals and children, four types of transference are identified:

1. client transference which may be projected toward professionals;

2. constructive professional countertransference wherein professionals feel a reaction to a child's projection and respond to it consciously;

3. destructive professional countertransference wherein professionals may have a reaction to a child's projection and react to it without awareness (project back);

4. professional transference wherein professionals may project feelings toward children, independent of anything that children initiate.

The following scenario illustrates the four types of transference:

> A foster-child who has been verbally and emotionally abused by his biological parents and then foster parents, arrives for an interview. The child begins to treat the professional as if he had perpetrated the abuse (client transference).

Child: *This place is stupid. I don't have to tell you anything about me.*

The professional feels threatened by the child's defiant refusal to cooperate, begins to feel challenged, and makes condemning statements toward the child (negative professional countertransference).

Professional: *You're an angry and uncooperative child.*

The professional becomes aware of underlying feelings and possible reasons for them and confronts the child (positive professional countertransference).

Professional: *I believe that many adults have hurt you before, and you expect me to treat you the same way as those other adults. I am a different person from those people, and I don't want to hurt or frighten you.*

The child reminds the professional of a youngster who physically attacked and hurt the professional during an interview, and the professional feels intimidated and reacts as if both children were the same individual (professional transference).

Professional: *Sometimes people can't work together. Maybe I'll just have to find someone else for you to work with.*

The professional's goal is to become aware of the various influences on both client and personal reactions to ensure that they don't detract from the interview. Hansen et al. (1977) addressed the successful outcome that is possible:

> If the counselor is successful in the endeavor the client will more or less spontaneously relinquish his illusions about the counselor and accept him as just another human being although often with a feeling of gratitude for the valuable services performed. (p. 266)

The following procedures are suggested as a working model to engage reluctant children and to minimize the negative effects of transference and countertransference.

Display Immediate Respect

Initial contact is significant and can make a lasting impression. The engagement stage of the interview process, therefore, needs to be emphasized. During this stage, nonthreatening gestures help put children at ease, and children should be treated as visitors. The rituals used when greeting guests in our homes are encouraged. It will be particularly important to create a warm, safe, and inviting atmosphere, particularly with children who may be reluctant to share information or engage in the interview process. When initially engaging children, respect can be conveyed through a warm greeting, offering a refreshment and so on (of course, permission to offer a child any refreshment needs to be granted by parents or guardians). In some situations, parents or guardians can be invited to bring along a refreshment for their children.

Children who appear reluctant often have negative preconceptions about helping professionals. Some children have participated in unfavorable interviews and interactions and begin to generalize based on their past experiences. Others have been encouraged by friends or others to avoid the interview process altogether. In such circumstances, time and patience will be required in order to effectively socialize children to the interview context and alter negative preconceptions. This phase must not be terminated prematurely in consideration of personal levels of anxiety and expectations. Reasonable goals and tasks can be established and overly ambitious goals avoided. Sufficient time must be devoted to small talk and the exploration of common interests. Professionals can be uncomfortable when engaging in small talk with children and, as a result, will often want to get down to business. Unfortunately, skipping this important step sends the message that children are unimportant, and that professionals are disinterested in their comfort and emotional well-being.

Conversations can be initiated with children regarding interests and needs (e.g., "I'm interested in knowing about some of the things that you enjoy doing when you're at home/at school/playing with friends." Or, "Your mother told me that you have a pet hamster. Can you tell me about your hamster?"). When engaging children, it is sometimes helpful to talk about personal interests, being careful not to monopolize the conversation (e.g., "I enjoy playing card games too!" Or, "I don't have any pets right now, but I had a pet hamster when I was younger; I called her M.C. Hamster."). During this phase, children are assessing professionals and sensing whether or not they are approachable, accepting, and able to assist them. Children must be given ample time to become familiar with the surroundings and style of professionals.

Interpersonal and therapeutic boundaries also are important. Too often, professionals become overly enthusiastic during the initial meeting and over-whelm children with unwelcome familiarity. Such an approach is often associ-ated with professionals' need for acceptance by children and their caregivers. The prospect of forming an alliance with children is highly appealing for well-intentioned professionals (particularly those who work in private practice and rely on their reputation to find new clients). Unquestionably, personal attributes such as energy, enthusiasm, and optimism are welcome, even necessary, when working with children. However, the timing and intensity of the manifestation of these qualities is paramount to a successful interview. While attempting to engage and explore with children, careful consideration must be given to per-sonal experiences of rejection, disappointment, and self-acceptance.

Professionals must remain cognizant of their own role and expectations. Attempts to get close to children too quickly by delving into sensitive per-sonal life issues can paradoxically create distance. Unfortunately, rather than focusing on interpersonal pacing and rapport-building, professionals often expound on the potential benefits of professional involvement in an attempt to market their services.

Conflictual Transactions and Child Trauma

A conflictive relationship can impact negatively on children and may even create emotional injury. Some children who attend interviews have previ-ously been attacked physically or emotionally by significant figures in author-ity. Reexperiencing conflict during interviews only serves to remind these children of previous danger and adds to their feelings of anguish and distrust. Children who experience animosity during interviews may withdraw from the interview process, refuse to return, or may feel responsible for the negative outcome of the interview. These youngsters can become disoriented, fearful, and ashamed. An increased level of sensitivity needs to be devoted to fright-ened children since they are at risk of becoming overly compliant, subsuming their own needs in an attempt to avoid further harm.

Use Role-Reversal

During role-reversal, professionals purposely reverse roles and suggest that children carefully assess them. Use of this strategy conveys respect and empowers children while helping to alleviate their initial anxiety and apprehension. Also, this strategy underscores the fact that children have some options in their lives. Professionals should encourage children to ask as many questions as necessary before deciding whether or not to proceed. Typically, children do not abuse this power by asking an excessive number of questions. However, if they carry on for too long, professionals can respond by saying, "I realize that you have some more that you'd like to ask. I'd like some time to ask you questions, and after that you can have a chance to ask some more."

If children ask personal questions that professionals are uncomfortable in answering, professionals need to directly communicate their discomfort in responding to the question (e.g., "That's a personal question that I would rather not answer." Or, "I'm not comfortable answering that question."). By establishing personal limits, children can learn how to create interpersonal boundaries through modeling.

Role-reversal is useful with youngsters who have been emotionally, physically, or sexually abused. Such children have experienced a terrible violation of interpersonal boundaries. To avoid a perceived form of boundary violation, the engagement process has to be regulated and children need to be elevated during the interview process. To support this process, professionals can appropriately self-disclose and invite children to share a personal narrative. To begin, it is important to follow a youngster's lead in discussing areas of interest and avoid judgmental statements that emphasize the power differential between adults and children. For example, a statement such as, "I would like to help you," immediately places children in an inferior position relative to professionals, while simultaneously undermining the children's strengths and resources. Statements that suggest power differences can be counterproductive.

In addition to role-reversal, Marshall (1972) presented an interesting strategy with resistant youth wherein he asked young clients to assume a teaching role. For example, children could be asked to assume a teacher role regarding their lives (e.g., "I don't know much about you, so I need you to teach me about you, including what you like and dislike, what you are good at and what you find difficult, and so on.") Children can also demonstrate how to play a game or how to operate a toy. This approach involves taking a one-down position, sidesteps potential power struggles, and encourages children to be leaders.

Caution Premature Trust

When working with abused children, they can be cautioned against trusting prematurely (e.g., not in the first interview!). By doing so, respect is indirectly demonstrated by acknowledging interpersonal boundaries and recognizing client vulnerability. This strategy can be especially effective as children begin to spontaneously disclose personal information. Such benevolent restraining (Morrissette, 1989) assists in pacing children's self-disclosure and building trust. Children can be thought of as individuals who have been exploited and who have experienced violations of personal boundaries. To avoid distancing these children, special attention is given to interpersonal space, being careful to move neither too quickly nor too slowly.

Give Therapeutic Compliments

To further illuminate personal strengths, children can be recognized and complimented. Children can be complimented for personal achievements (e.g., "Congratulations for improving your grades at school. Your mother said you are an "A" student this year."); for skills or abilities ("You are extremely good at communicating your thoughts and feelings. Many children find that hard to do."); for personality or interpersonal attributes ("You have a great attitude toward other people."); for physical attributes ("Thank you for your cheery face. You have a great smile!"); for possessions ("I really like your drawings."); or for their willingness to attend the interview. In discussing therapeutic compliments, Wall, Amendt, Kleckner, and Bryant (1989) wrote:

> Therapeutic compliments are one means of enhancing maneuverability. While most people are accustomed to ignoring advice, they usually are inclined to listen to a compliment. Hence, therapeutic messages couched in complimentary language have a significant chance of impacting the client. (p. 160)

For example, professionals could say, "You have talked about some frightening things that have happened to you. You have shown a lot of courage to talk about your fears with me. Thank you for being so brave." In this example, the ability to remain candid is recognized and complimented. To further acknowledge children's willingness to trust, professionals can describe some unfortunate scenarios that children may have encountered during other interviews (e.g., not being listened to, not being respected). By doing so, professionals demonstrate their sensitivity and support children's resilience, courage, and openness.

Triangulate Nonverbal Information

When dealing with unique children, as much information as possible needs to be collected. This includes information about their mood, behavior, and interactions, much of which will be gleaned through careful attention to nonverbal communication. Yarrow (1960) identified five areas to consider when collecting and evaluating nonverbal information:

1. *Physical—posture:*

   - freedom/constraint; gestures, facial expression (e.g., somber/gay, speed of movement, vigor of movement, energy output, motor coordination)

   - area of free movement (e.g., whether the child is expansive or restricted in his or her use of space)

2. *Physiological—vasomotor instability:*

   - blushing, perspiring, muscular tension

3. *Formal characteristics of language:*

   - loquacity, fluency, tempo, speed of verbal output

4. *Interactional behavior—ways of relating to professionals:*

   - attempts to control the situation, resistance, compliance, dominance, passivity, dependency, withdrawal

5. *Personality style:*

   - spontaneous, inhibited, compulsive, loosely organized, focused, scattered. (p. 593)

Nonverbal information must be supported to ensure that hypotheses about what is motivating it are accurate. Professionals should look for multiple sources of information to form a cohesive constellation of behaviors. For example, if a professional postulates that a child is anxious, he or she must look for supportive behavioral evidence such as tense body with hunched shoulders and bowed head, reddened cheeks, limited physical movement, long pauses between questions and responses, soft voice, and withdrawn and inhibited manner. If these observations match parental reports of the child being a constant worrier, then the professional can have relative confidence in his or her hypothesis.

FUTURE DIRECTIONS IN TRAINING AND RESEARCH

In order to address the issue of professional-child conflict, academic and postgraduate training programs must begin to acknowledge the interpersonal demands and stresses professionals experience. Although the need to recognize and better understand the unique difficulties experienced by professionals has been noted (e.g., Schaufeli, Maslach, & Marek, 1993) there remains a dearth of research in this area, and the emotional needs of professionals continue to be underexamined. New research should attempt to identify precursors to various conflictive interactions. If professionals understand who is most vulnerable to engaging in conflictive relationships with children, they should be in a better position to develop preemptive courses and training workshops.

To begin with, professionals must be able to frame adult-child conflict as common, inevitable, and resolvable. Professionals and children are human and fallible, and there will be times when conflict surfaces during interviews. Professionals should understand the underlying dynamics and the transitory nature of conflict and recognize what they can do to reduce their anxiety and animosity towards some children. We believe that professionals are more likely to acknowledge and candidly discuss their frustrations and insecurities if they know that they can participate in the mending of the relationship. Additionally, the normalization of conflict can help professionals to anticipate such periods and minimize their own feelings of failure.

ACTING OUT: AGGRESSIVE CHILDREN

Children may act out during an interview for a number of reasons (e.g., the need for attention, revenge, control, a testing of limits). Children may be angry, anxious, fearful, poorly disciplined, or may have a mental disorder (e.g., psychosis, Attention Deficit Hyperactivity Disorder, Pervasive Developmental Disorder, Posttraumatic Stress Disorder), a communication disorder, a developmental delay, or a disability (e.g., learning, sensory, motor). Unfortunate behavior may result from cultural differences or a language barrier if children are unable to understand the language used in the interview. Professionals may not always be able to identify the reasons for children's behavior, however, they can intervene to support children, minimize disruptions, and ensure a successful interview.

Much has been written about children's misbehavior and appropriate intervention, particularly in terms of classroom management (e.g., Coloroso, 1987; Dreikurs, 1968; Dreikurs, Grunwald, & Pepper, 1971; Glasser, 1969, 1986, 1990), parenting (e.g., Coloroso, 1994; Dreikurs, 1972; Dreikurs & Soltz, 1964; Phelan, 1994), and residential settings (e.g., Redl, 1966; Redl & Wineman, 1951, 1952; Treischman, Whittaker, & Brendtro, 1969). Although these sources provide a range of ideas, many of them are designed for group settings, residential settings, and long-term placements or interactions rather than for individual interviews. To augment the literature, the following strategies are suggested.

Suspending Judgment

Professionals are usually given advance warning about children's challenging behaviors, either from caregivers or from schools. Once they know that children may experience behavioral difficulties, they can prepare themselves and the environment for these youngsters. While listening to information and opinions from others, they must avoid prejudging children. A professional's apprehension and anger may be fueled by children's negative reputations. However, when these children attend interviews, they are often sad, frightened or angry and need support and understanding, not condemnation. These children should be met with open minds; otherwise they are certain to invoke defensive reactions. Children who frequently find themselves in trouble often feel misunderstood, unsuccessful, incapable, and unlovable. To change these perceptions, children require professional understanding. These children rarely act out intentionally and alternative explanations generally exist. The task is to determine whether or not children can control the observed behavior(s).

Responding Versus Reacting

Often, children who act out have been hurt, and they respond by assuming an offensive stance and attacking before they are attacked. These children are skilled at contributing to a professional's sense of apprehension and discomfort. Some professionals are fearful that they may lose control of the interview process. Difficult though it may be, the challenge is to sidestep power struggles and avoid feeling threatened and behaving defensively. Arguments, power struggles, and oppositional behavior need to be avoided. Similarly, professionals should not bribe, plead, order, coax, or cajole children. If present, parents or significant others should also be encouraged to avoid these behaviors.

Intervening in Troublesome Situations

Regardless of the circumstances prompting unfortunate behavior, several interventions can be used including: bleeding off surface emotions, building rapport, encouraging children to share their stories, and setting gentle but firm limits. Each intervention is discussed in more detail below.

Bleed Off Surface Emotions. To help children, their emotional disposition (e.g., angry, anxious, sad, fearful) first needs to be addressed. Empathizing with children or identifying feelings can temporarily dissipate emotions. Once emotions have been dissipated, children will be in a better position to respond to inquiries. Professionals are specifically advised to empathize with any emotion that emerges (e.g., "You're anxious right now because we've never met before," "You're really angry that I won't let you ... ," "You're mad because you can't play with ... ," or "You've had bad experiences with 'shrinks' before and you don't want to talk with anyone else who might betray you. I don't blame you for not wanting to speak with me.").

Build Rapport. Rapport-building skills outlined in other chapters will be helpful when making connections with children. However, it can be beneficial to connect with children around something they value. Professionals should search for ways to align with the children (e.g., ball cap with a team logo, T-shirt with a rock band.). Professionals could say something like: "I noticed your T-shirt. Do you like Blur?" but should avoid being overly familiar with the children or their lifestyle. Children will likely see through such attempts at alignment and will respond poorly. Connecting with children should occur casually, as an expression of interest, and a sincere desire to understand their perspectives. Professionals should avoid elevating themselves in an attempt to connect with children. The goal is to take the focus away from professionals and to redirect it onto children.

Let Children Tell Their Stories. From the outset, professionals should acknowledge the power that children have and avoid engaging in a competition to get children to speak. The reality is that the children have the power in deciding whether to participate verbally in the interview. Professionals could underscore this power overtly and remind children that to participate verbally is their choice. Professionals who believe that it is their responsibility to make children verbally participate may feel threatened or defeated by silence. Consequently, they interpret children's action as an attack on or a challenge to their authority. These professionals are likely to respond in ways that will further dampen communication.

To engage children effectively and encourage their disclosure, professionals first need to listen to their stories. Even if they doubt the authenticity or accuracy of the reports being made (e.g., "All my teachers hate me. They never call on me when I raise my hand in class." Or, "A robber broke into our house, and I chased him away with a baseball bat. I wasn't even scared."), professionals should consider the underlying emotional message children are communicating (e.g., "I've been wronged." Or, "I feel vulnerable and I want to be brave.").

Set Realistic but Firm Limits. Children who act out behaviorally often feel their lives are out of control. As a result, firm limits need to be established to help them feel contained and secure. These children will likely require specific expectations and guidelines to be delineated (e.g., what to touch and what not to, how interviews will be structured, timing of breaks and activities) without making limits so restrictive that children feel unduly controlled. Clear expectations, including rewards and consequences, need to be set. Any restraints or restrictions should be meaningful and benevolent. For example, a professional could say, "I don't want to control how you chose to act in other parts of your life, but I can't allow smoking or swearing in this office."

By doing this, children become aware of expectations, while being reminded that that they have power and control in other areas of their lives (e.g., "I'm going to have to ask you to turn off your music and take off your headphones. We'll take a break later, and you can listen to your music then." Or, "I'll be asking you some questions. If you don't want to answer a question I ask, we can save it for later."). Providing children with options promotes a sense of personal control (e.g., "We'll have some time to play and some time to work. What would you like to do first?," "We can play with … , or we can draw. Which one would you prefer?"). Professionals can work toward negotiating the use of time with youngsters.

Before inviting children to play, time limits need to be clearly established (unless play will be a main vehicle for the interaction or discourse). Activities that will exceed time limits should be avoided. To help children transition back to the interview, cues can be given a few minutes before it is time to finish playing. Once the play time is over, professionals can casually but clearly reinforce the limits that have been established (e.g., "It's time to set the toys aside." Or, "Play time is over."). If children continue to play with toys, professionals should empathize with children but reinforce any expectations (e.g., "You really want to touch that. Once we're finished you can spend some time playing with it; however, it's time to return to our interview.").

Consequences need to be created for noncompliant behavior (e.g., "If you do … , then … will happen."). However, consequences must be realistic and followed up. Professionals can negotiate with children but should retain control and not let children make inappropriate demands. If all else fails, professionals may have to end the session (e.g., "It looks like this is not going to work. I had hoped to work with you, but I will have to rely on what your parents and teachers have said."). Interviews should only be prematurely terminated as a last resort and without sarcasm, threats, or anger.

Dealing With Specific Identifiable Problems

Specific challenges can arise when working with youngsters who present with unique behaviors. Behaviors that are commonly observed in the child-focused interview and accompanying strategies follow.

The Show-Off. Bright youngsters may want to prove their intellect and may even challenge professionals (e.g., "What benefit is there for me to come here? What if I don't want to talk?" Or, "I'm in a gifted program at school. I don't find your questions very challenging." Or, "What kind of degree do you have? Are you a quack?"). In such circumstances, challenges can be sidestepped by redirecting the focus back on youngsters (e.g., "You are the expert today. I know nothing about you, and I can only learn the things that you decide to share with me."). Even the most defensive of children may feel safer when they are placed in the position of being an expert on themselves. Ginsburg (1997) advised that professionals should not reward vain behavior and should not show interest in the children's knowledge or "correct answers" but should rather encourage them to communicate their thinking process.

The Unfocused Child. Some children will continually chatter, change topics, or behave in distracting ways. Their chatter may prove distracting to both professionals and themselves. These children may not be accustomed to being listened to or may be avoiding fearful topics. They also may be hyperactive, manic, under the influence of drugs, or culturally different. Unless professionals work toward slowing down the interactional process, little or nothing of value will emerge from such interviews. These children will often appear in control of the interview and professionals will be lucky to have any of their questions answered. The pace of the interview can be slowed down by interrupting and speaking slowly and clearly. Children can be encouraged to focus and repeat themselves if necessary. Professionals should also point out topic changes (e.g., "You were talking about ... , and then you changed the topic. Can you finish what you started to say?") or draw inferences from the children's behavior (e.g., "Is this difficult to talk about?" Or, "I realize that this might be difficult to discuss. Would you rather not talk about it?").

The Flippant, Glib, Humorous, or Superficial Response. Some children will respond in a shallow or humorous manner to avoid answering sincerely or honestly. Professionals may respond by acknowledging the first response (e.g., laughing, if it was intended to provoke laughter, or saying "okay" or "thank you"); however, they should not accept the answer as is. Instead, they are encouraged to seek information or explanation (e.g., "That's the quick response, but what do you really think?" Or, "Now I'd like to know the real answer."). Alternately, professionals can confront gently (e.g., "I think that you wanted to make me laugh and that you knew that wasn't a serious answer. I need you to be serious in your responses because what you say is extremely important to me.")

If professionals decide to confront children directly, they need to be certain that children are actually intending to be silly or shallow. If professionals confront youngsters who think that they made a serious attempt at responding, the confrontation will be construed as an insensitive attack and the children will likely close off communication.

The Resistant Child.   Resistance is primarily a protective response, and children will have a range of overt reasons for their resistance (e.g., fear of losing play time, anger over missing a favorite television show, feeling "picked on" by adults, or fear of losing their parents), as well as covert reasons (e.g., threatening topics or content). Children will avoid anxiety-provoking thoughts and real or imagined repercussions for revealing the requested information (Boggs & Eyberg, 1990). For professionals to intervene appropriately, children's fears and discomforts must be respected. Professionals can empathize with children and remind them that some topics are difficult and frightening to talk about.

Children may not always be directly responsible for poor cooperation and may have been coached (either directly or indirectly) to remain uncooperative. In rare circumstances, children resist because they have been directed to do so. Boggs and Eyberg (1990) suggest that if professionals suspect children have been coached or threatened to remain silent, they should be appropriately confronted (e.g., "Sometimes children are warned to not tell some things. Has this ever happened to you?"). Some parents become resentful if other adults establish rapport with their children and send a barrage of verbal and nonverbal messages to their children that other adults shouldn't be trusted. Parents will often do this by speaking for their children (e.g., "She doesn't want to speak with a man. She's very shy and doesn't talk to other adults, but she will talk to me."). In such circumstances, professionals can emphasize the special relationship that parents have with their children. In doing so, professionals are no longer perceived as adversaries and can work toward enlisting parental assistance in helping children feel comfortable.

Hyperactivity, Impulsivity, and Inattention.   Children may be impulsive, inattentive, or overactive for a number of reasons, including age, emotional state, disability or disorder. No matter what the contributing factor, professionals can implement a range of interventions that should support these children and help to ensure successful interviews.

- Work should be planned in short periods, with frequent breaks (e.g., play within the room, have a snack or a drink, engage in some physical activity, take a walk outside of the room). The number of available toys should be limited (e.g., small tub of blocks, a few cars).

- Professionals can maintain eye contact with children before asking any questions, and can encourage children to make eye contact when responding.

- Since many children who have been diagnosed with Attention Deficit Disorders have also been found to have concurrent language disorders (Purvis & Tannock, 1997; Tannock & Schachar, 1996), it is wise to keep questions short and simple.

- The use of props or visual aids can improve comprehension by reducing the need for understanding oral information.

- To help these children cope, interviews should have a clear organizational structure (e.g., "I have five questions to ask you, and then we'll take a break." Or, "That was the third question. I have two more and then we'll take our break.").

- Finally, professionals can support the child's organization of his or her responses (e.g., "Tell me what you did first, then second," or "You've mentioned five different ideas, so let's go through each one separately.").

Sometimes children are overactive, running around, touching, and looking at materials upon entering the interview room. These children can be outgoing and engaging, showing confidence through their actions. Unfortunately, they may also want to control the interview process. Children may be disruptive, unsettled, difficult to manage, undersocialized, loud, or unruly, and may become surly or uncooperative if given direction or limits. These children usually respond to reduced levels of stimulation (visual and auditory); therefore, clutter or objects that may be harmful, fragile, or distracting should be removed.

In some rare cases with children who walk around the interview space belligerently, it may be helpful to avoid a power struggle by overtly giving them permission to walk around the space (e.g., "Feel free to walk around and look at any of the things that are in here."). Often, these children will settle down and become cooperative.

Distractible behavior is sometimes designed to gain attention. In these circumstances, it will be important to ignore inappropriate behavior (e.g., minor noises) and to provide recognition and attention for any and all appropriate behaviors. Some children will strive to get attention for a variety of behavior, and will settle for criticism and negative attention.

Inappropriate Language. Youngsters may resort to profane language during interviews. Again, professionals should try to be as nonreactive as possible, and consider possible explanations for the child's choice of language. MLZ once worked with a 7-year-old boy who was upset one day and said, "The damn pigs busted my brother yesterday." When MLZ told him that he appreciated the boy's anger, but that his choice of words was unacceptable, he said quite seriously, "What word? Damn or pig?" This boy was surrounded by people who reinforced such language, particularly when expressing anger.

If inappropriate language is used to provoke a reaction, professionals can confront children with their supposition (e.g., "I have a feeling that you are trying to provoke me, to find out how I will respond to your swearing."). Professionals who have little or no tolerance for profanity can also respond by saying, "I am not willing to work with you if you continue to swear."

Professionals should set limits if they believe children are simply testing their tolerance. It may be appropriate for some professionals to allow the use of profanity if children are telling a story and repeating what people have said or when expressing strong emotions in a therapeutically beneficial way.

Risk-Taking Behavior. Professionals must ask children about high risk behaviors that could potentially impact their functioning during interviews. For example, the use of drugs or alcohol could affect children's memory, concentration, thinking skills, motor skills, or mood. In addition to inquiring about recreational drug use, there should also be a screening for prescription drug use or over-the-counter medications. Children can be asked if they have ever thought of hurting themselves or committing suicide. Children who are actively suicidal may never tell anyone unless they are asked directly.

ACTING IN: THE WITHDRAWN CHILD

Quiet children can be among the most challenging to deal with. When children act out, they at least provide professionals with a foil to respond to. Withdrawn children on the other hand, can make even the most patient and experienced of professionals throw up their arms in despair and declare their young clients to be untreatable, unworkable, or even hopeless. Unfortunately, professionals do not know what is going on in the minds of these silent children, so they do not always know the best way to respond. Withdrawn children generally enter the interview room and stand or sit in silence. A child's silence may represent a variety of things including:

- fear, anger, resentment, or depression;

- respect and a need for permission before doing or saying anything;

- a strong desire to please professionals;

- an introverted personality;

- physiological or biological impairments (e.g., visual or auditory), a communication disorder (expressive or receptive), or an infection (e.g., ear or throat).

Part of the challenge is to uncover the reason underlying children's silence. Professionals need to proceed on the assumption that children have the best intentions and are simply being respectful. No matter how quiet or impenetrable children appear at the start of interviews, they can usually be engaged in one way or another. A range of helpful interventions for working with quiet and withdrawn children follows.

Provide Space (Physical, Psychological, Emotional, and Social)

By shutting professionals out, children communicate that they feel unsafe or threatened. Professionals need to maintain enough distance to slowly gain children's confidence and trust. Professionals must take time to get to know these children. Planning for extra time or additional sessions to achieve this goal is advised. In many cases, silent children feel that they have not been listened to by adults, and they don't see the point of trying to communicate. Consequently, they may require ample time to adjust. Extra energy will be required in attending to what children are verbally and nonverbally communicating. Many of the supportive listening skills described in Chapter 4 will be helpful in achieving this goal.

Take the Focus Off the Child

By focusing attention on parents or significant others, professionals effectively reduce children's performance anxiety. When parents talk about their children, professionals may occasionally glance at youngsters, being sure to smile warmly. Typically, children will glance at professionals discreetly when they think adults are not looking. If a professional can manage to catch a child's eyes in a brief and positive manner, that professional can communicate an interest in the child and indicate notice of the child's interest as well. Such small connections can set the foundation for further rapport and communication. Professionals working with withdrawn children can look for anxious parents and work toward reducing their anxieties. Once parents become more relaxed, children generally relax as well.

Make Toys Available

Children should be oriented to the interview room even if they stay by their parents or appear disinterested. To connect with children, professionals can note what they play with, then either observe children quietly or make comments about their toys or their play (e.g., "You seem to like that." Or, "Have you ever seen ... before?"). If the children don't move, professionals should watch to see what they look at, and then comment on it (e.g., "I noticed that you looked at that teddy bear.").

Commenting may provide ample prompting for children to go and look, but they may require more overt permission before they will go to a toy. For example, professionals may have to say, "Would you like to see that bear?" In some circumstances the toy might have to be brought to them. If children initially appear disinterested, professionals can set a number of toys close to them and say something inviting like "These are for you," or "You can play with anything in this room."

Follow Children

Children should be encouraged to play in order to track their interests and patterns. Frequently, children will slowly approach professionals and begin to play near them. Once this occurs, casual, but brief, eye contact can be initiated. Sometimes, children will roll a ball, car, or windup toy toward professionals. Once again, this may be taken as a cue to join children in play. When they do this, professionals should receive the toy, pause for a moment while holding it, and then roll it gently back toward the children. Playing a few games may help children to relax in a nonthreatening environment.

To engage reluctant children, professionals can imitate the children's play (e.g., if they are building with blocks, set up a few beside them; if they are pushing a car around, push another car near theirs; if they are drawing a picture, draw one next to them). This technique of imitation is especially helpful with children who have pervasive developmental or communication disorders, and it is ideal as the preface to turn-taking or cooperative play. When children do not initiate play, professionals may attempt to engage them by being casual and inviting. Professionals could gently roll balls to them or send windup toys in their direction.

Encourage and Support Children

Professionals can encourage and support children in a myriad of ways. For example, empathy and encouragement can be used to communicate understanding and appreciation. When children are reportedly afraid to attend an interview, this fear can be reflected back to them through supportive statements (e.g., "Your mother said you were frightened about coming today. Even though you were frightened, you came with your mother. That was brave of you!"). Children's interests can also be supported. For example, if children enjoy playing with dolls, professionals can provide dolls to play with (e.g., "Your father said that you enjoy playing with dolls, so I brought in some dolls and a doll house for you to use."). If children begin to share information, professionals can express their appreciation (e.g., "Thank you for telling me your teddy bear's name. I wanted to know his name, but I was a little shy to ask him myself.").

Sit with Silence

Dealing with periods of silence in an interview can be a daunting task. Nevertheless, it is important to remain at ease without trying to fill the pause with unnecessary words or actions. Showing personal discomfort or pursuing children to answer a specific question will only serve to disrupt the interview process. Similarly, jumping to another question will inadvertently encourage children to avoid responding to the initial question, and by association, any other question. Instead of talking, sitting quietly with children and allowing them to think and respond may be what is needed. Sometimes, waiting is all that is necessary for children to begin to talk. Rather than assuming that children are being difficult, it can be assumed that they are taking time to think about a response.

Children can also be given permission to remain quiet by the professional saying, "Take your time." Following this, children can be asked, "Are you thinking about what to say?" At this point, children may respond by saying "Yes" or nodding. In this case, they can be asked if they need some more time to think about their answer.

If they say "No" or shake their heads, another approach can be attempted. For example, children can be asked if they heard the question, if the question confused them, or if the question made them feel uncomfortable (e.g., "Is this hard to talk about?" Or, "Do you feel uncomfortable talking about this?"). If they respond with a "yes" to any of these questions, then professionals can follow up as necessary (e.g., repeat the question, rephrase the question, or empathize with their discomfort).

Children who are less talkative generally speak softly. Asking them to speak louder has not proven to be helpful. Rather, professionals can acknowledge volume level by saying, "You have an extremely quiet voice, so it was difficult for me to hear." Simply acknowledging the quietness of a child's voice often helps to increase volume. Should the decision be made to skip over a question or topic, children should be informed (e.g., "Let's come back to that question later, okay?" Or, "I will ask that one again a little later."). In this way, the child realizes that no question is insignificant and none will be cast aside.

Start Children Talking

Children are often wary of talking, fearing questions that they are hesitant or unable to answer. Beginning conversations with low-risk topics may be helpful. It doesn't matter what children speak about, as long as they participate in the process. Ideally, professionals want children to talk about themselves, but they are less likely to feel threatened if they can first speak about other subjects. Once children have begun to share, the topic can be shifted toward personal experiences, thoughts, and feelings.

Communicate Through Parents

Some shy children speak through their parents, who act as conduits for communication (Ginsburg, 1997). In this case, professionals can pose questions to parents and allow the child to whisper in a parent's ear. The parent conveys the response to the professional. Eventually, children's voices begin to increase in volume until they are finally openly responding. If parents make an error when serving as interpreters, children sometimes get angry and say "No," loudly and clearly. Such circumstances provide professionals an opportunity to open up communication. For example, professionals could say, "Your mother didn't say it the way you wanted her to." Or, "Your father didn't understand what you meant to say." Thus, they convey that the child's thoughts are valued. Ginsburg noted that gentle patience, persistence, and approval usually suffice to put a shy child at ease and encourage some degree of communication.

In some cases, parents can unknowingly hinder the interview process (e.g., they may inadvertently pressure their children to respond by using approbation or direct commands). When this occurs, professionals can respectfully support parents and ensure them that it is natural for children to be silent at times. This approach allows parents to relax and feel less embarrassed by children's responses. MLZ has also found it helpful to use self-disclosure to recount a time when he was small and felt shy. He describes in some detail how frightened he felt. The person he was to meet seemed to be extremely big and imposing. He felt as if he was looking into a bright light, which hurt his eyes and made him turn away. In MLZ's experience, this personal story helps parents to understand what their children might be feeling. While he is telling the story, he often finds that the children begin to look at him with wonder and curiosity, because they can relate to what he is describing. They recognize that he understands what they are experiencing and most will relax and begin to interact with him shortly thereafter.

Eliciting Support

To elicit support, children's uniqueness and the importance of their perspective can be underscored. To accomplish this, interest can be demonstrated in youngsters and their points of view, thoughts, and experiences. This may be done following a lengthy parental narrative or may be introduced immediately following a statement made by a parent. Professionals can summarize or repeat what their parents have said and ask children if they agree (e.g., "Your mother said that you ... . Is that accurate?" Or, "Your mother thinks you are ... . What do you think?" Or, "Do you agree with what your mother said?").

When parents discuss children's feelings, professionals can empathize with children by restating those feelings either indirectly through the parents (e.g., "He was feeling sad." Or, "She was extremely angry.") or directly to the children (e.g., "You must have been feeling sad." And, "You were extremely angry.").

Asking Parents to Leave

Unless children are extremely anxious about separating from their parents, or have been seriously abused or traumatized, they are generally able to separate from their parents for brief periods of time. Children and parents however, have to be prepared for this stage of the interview. Professionals can let children know where their parents will be should they need them. Curiously, many supposedly anxious or shy children become quite outgoing once their parents leave the interview room. These children may be behaving in a shy manner because they believe that their parents expect it of them. The same response however can indicate abuse, an oppressive parenting style, or circumstances where children do not want their parents to hear their thoughts.

Using Indirect Methods

Indirect methods of communication can help facilitate the interview process. For example, professionals can communicate with children through stuffed animals or puppets. Through puppets for example, professionals can introduce themselves and begin to ask questions. Sometimes children will pick up a puppet and respond as if the puppets are talking to each other. Professionals can also pretend that the puppet is whispering in their ear and can respond as if the puppet had asked a question ("Why don't you ask him?" says the professional to the puppet. "You're too shy to ask him? Well, I think that he's shy, too. Maybe you could offer him a toy.").

Another indirect method involves verbal or nonverbal commentary on children's behavior. MLZ once had to interview a 12-year-old boy who had stopped speaking after he was accused by another child of stealing some small toys. "You're sitting quietly," MLZ said. "Your arms are folded on the table and your head is resting on your arms. You look upset."

The boy looked up and said "I'm not talking to you." This boy had obviously made a decision to say nothing, particularly to MLZ. Unfortunately for him, by voicing his decision, he had already begun to speak, and that was all the encouragement MLZ needed! MLZ said to him, "You don't want you to talk to me. You don't want to say anything. Maybe you're afraid that if you say anything you'll get into trouble. Maybe you believe that nothing you could say will make a difference. It might not; however, it might make a big difference. I won't know unless I know what's going on inside your head."

That was the beginning of a long exchange culminating in his admission of guilt, his expression of sadness about his family's poverty, his expression of guilt regarding his behavior, and his fear of reprimand.

In another situation, MLZ tried to connect with a 10-year-old boy who had also stopped talking. He sat with his hands covering his mouth. Each attempt to verbally engage him failed. He listened to what was said, but said nothing. MLZ then took out a piece of paper and a pencil and began to sketch him. He noticed and glanced up as MLZ drew. Once the drawing was finished, MLZ wrote, "This is how you look" and pushed the drawing toward him. He looked at the picture. MLZ then pulled the paper back and wrote on it, "ON THE OUTSIDE." Turning the paper over, MLZ wrote "ON THE INSIDE." Then he drew a rectangular box with two sentences inside: One said, "I like myself," and the other said, "I don't like myself." Each sentence had a small box beside it.

MLZ handed the boy a crayon. He filled in the box beside "I don't like myself," so MLZ acknowledged his response with a nod, retrieved the paper, and started a second box. Box by box, question by question, a slow and silent conversation began.

After the boy had responded to several questions, MLZ wrote, "Thank You," in large print and circled it. The child acknowledged the expression of support. MLZ then wrote, "What do you want to do now?"

He wrote "Don't know." so MLZ gave him three options: (1) stay a little while; (2) stay a long while; and (3) go home. The boy chose the second option, and then wrote, "What do you want to do?"

MLZ responded, "I would like to be able to read your mind." At this point, he started to talk, and MLZ learned about his abuse and neglect.

In these cases, indirect communication helped to build bridges between professional and child, which then served as the foundation for further, more direct communication.

Dealing with Silence in the Middle of an Interview

If children have been cooperative and suddenly stop speaking, they generally have a good reason for their actions. By using supportive techniques, professionals may have encouraged reluctant children to talk. However, if children suddenly recall their initial vow to not speak, they may withdraw. Sudden withdrawal can be a result of a number of reasons including professionals using unknown words or words with which children are unfamiliar, or it can be the result of hunger, fatigue, anxiety, or insecurity.

When this occurs, a descriptive observation or an inference can be drawn to gain a better understanding of children's silence (e.g., "Some things are hard to talk about." Or, "You became quiet all of a sudden." Or, "Did I say something that upset you?").

If necessary, professionals can negotiate with children and offer some time and psychological space (e.g., "Let's take a break to play, and then we'll come back and talk some more in a few minutes." Or, "That's okay, you don't have to talk about it right now."). With some children, professionals may have to sit on the floor and integrate questions and inquiries with the toys or games. Most importantly, professionals need to remain flexible and respect the needs of children.

SPECIFIC DISABILITIES

To work with disabled children (e.g., visual or hearing impairments, mental handicaps, language disorders, physical disabilities, epilepsy), professionals will need to be creative since standard procedures may not be effective. For example, nonverbal demonstrations such as models, toys, drawings, or photographs can be used. In some situations, it may be appropriate to use translators (preferably individuals who have been properly prepared). To engage children and respond to their needs, parents can be consulted in terms of what they have found helpful with their children. Professionals may also want to observe siblings playing and interacting with these children for the same reasons. Siblings typically know each other well and can offer creative ideas.

For children who have language disabilities, professionals will have to use nonverbal modes to communicate, including props, pictures, writing, communication boards, sign language, and frequent supportive nonverbal communication acts such as smiles, nods, and eye contact. In addition, alternate ways of responding (e.g., drawing, writing, pointing, showing, demonstrating, enacting) can be considered.

ODDS AND ENDS

Effective interviewing recognizes and respects children's diversity. All children are unique, and no two children will present with the same behaviors. As a result, solutions will have to vary with the needs of each child. Besides the many differences already addressed here, children may vary by culture, language, or gender.

When children do not speak the language of the professional, interpreters will need to be utilized. In such circumstances, it will be important to ensure that these professionals are cultural interpreters and can explain what is being communicated from professional to child and vice versa. The communicative intentions of professionals are susceptible to changes by interpreters. The problems of miscommunication are even greater when children are involved. Professionals must clearly state what it is they want to ask and what they are trying to elicit. Open-ended questions and comments should be emphasized and interpreters can be invited to look for different conceptions of words and experiences. In addition, interpreters need to be able to clarify if professionals have said or done anything that may be culturally inappropriate. In some circumstances, children's cultural background may disallow any free communication with professionals. Such children may prefer to be interviewed in a group of peers. Ginsburg (1997) advised that professionals function best if they are from the child's cultural group, or are at least familiar with the cultural group.

When children arrive for an interview either tired or sick, the interview should be postponed and youngsters should be invited to return at another time. There is no sense in a sick or fatigued child trying to participate in an interview. When unsure of children's health, professionals should simply ask youngsters, parents, or guardians. Professionals who suspect presenting symptoms are physiological symptoms of anxiety, can consider a history of avoidant coping behavior with anxiety and distress. In some cultures (e.g., Chinese), many symptoms of depression and anxiety are viewed as physical health problems, and psychological explanations may not be welcomed.

WHEN TO END AN INTERVIEW

Glasgow (1989) cautioned that when interviews last too long, children can become distressed and succumb to the perceived professional demands. Professionals must remain vigilant to signs of fatigue, distress, or loss of concentration, particularly when working with younger children. When initial signs emerge (e.g., fidgeting, resting their head on an arm which is rested on the table, rapidly changing the subject, asking for their parent/guardian) professionals should try to bring the interview to a close quickly and efficiently. Expecting youngsters to exceed their limits can jeopardize the relationship and the accuracy of any information provided.

Finding a common ground upon which to begin the interview process with reluctant children can be challenging at the best of times. Their understandable skepticism and distrust can contribute to an environment that engenders similar qualities in professionals, potentially leading to an ineffective interview. The procedures outlined and discussed in this chapter provide professionals with a basis upon which to initiate and maximize their interactions with children. Attention has been rendered to the resolution of conflict between professionals and children, since it has virtually been ignored in the professional literature. Although children will present with unique challenges, the guidelines offered in this chapter should help professionals to deal with difficult and different children, including those who may act out and those who may act in.

CHAPTER 6

THE RESEARCH INTERVIEW

Few researchers have made a consistent effort to include the thoughts, feelings, experiences, and specific statements of children in their empirical investigations. Notable exceptions include early childhood educator Vivian Gussin Paley, child psychiatrist Robert Coles, and researcher Edith Pramling. Books and articles by Paley explore the lives of preschool children in America (e.g., Paley, 1984, 1988, 1990, 1992). Coles (1986, 1990), a man whose recordings and transcriptions of interviews have been placed in the Smithsonian as a national American treasure, has written extensively on the lives of children worldwide.

Such contributions are invaluable, yet the specific methodologies used by these authors must be inferred from their writings since neither has delineated the process of interviewing (with the exception of some methodological notes found throughout Coles' work, including several sections titled "Method" in his *Children of Crisis* series). Without precise accounts of what they have done, it is difficult to determine exactly how they established relationships and interacted with children or what they said and did to elicit descriptive statements and reflective self-reports. Pramling (e.g., 1983, 1986) is a Swedish researcher whose research innovations have resulted in some outstanding and insightful findings. She is the only one of the three authors to outline, in detail, her methods and techniques for facilitating, capturing, and analyzing oral reports from children.

Pramling (1983) pointed out that although various types of interviews have been used in research with adults, such methods are rarely used when collecting data from children. She acknowledged that interviewing children can be problematic, but argued that interviews provide the most direct way to evaluate children's inner perceptions of reality. Her beliefs are supported by others who suggest that the interview is a useful technique for uncovering children's subjective accounts of their experiences (Hatch, 1990; Parker, 1984; Yarrow, 1960). As Hughes and Baker (1990) stated:

> If one wants to understand a child's beliefs, perceptions, reasoning ability, attitudes, and affective experiences that have relevance to the child's current [circumstances], it is logical to ask the child to report on these self-processes . . . . The child interviewer must learn interview strategies that enable children to communicate competently and to share with others their rich and complex subjective experiences. (p. 1)

In general, researchers are simply expected to know how best to collect data. In preparing this chapter, a thorough review of the literature in the fields of psychology and education was conducted. That review turned up only three articles dealing specifically with the details of research interviewing with children (Beekman 1983; Hatch, 1990; Parker,1984) and only two related book chapters were subsequently uncovered (Pramling, 1983; Yarrow, 1960). In their book about qualitative research in early childhood settings, Browning and Hatch (1995) expressed concern that few methodological or ethical guidelines are available to support investigators, but their edited text added little to the scant literature on the practice of interviewing children.

Information on the research interview with adult participants is also scant, though more readily available (e.g., Becker, 1986; Berg, 1989; Fontana & Frey, 1994; Kvale, 1983; Mishler, 1986; Weber, 1986); however, information that pertains to adult-focused interviews cannot be applied wholesale to children. Just as cross-cultural research reveals differences in thinking across peoples, developmental psychology has demonstrated that many adult assumptions regarding thinking cannot be generalized to children.

SETTING THE STAGE FOR DATA COLLECTION

Research is an organized and coordinated attempt to understand ourselves and the world around us. Marton (1981) distinguished first- from second-order approaches to human science research. He labeled as first-order the traditional scientific paradigm characterized by attempts to isolate and describe various aspects of the world (to classify individuals, to compare groups, to explain, predict, or to evaluate people). By contrast, he referred to second-order approaches as research that aims to describe, analyze, and understand people's experiences of and ideas about various aspects of the world. Whether quantitative or qualitative methodologies are employed, researchers tend to spend much time discussing the results of data collection and relevant inferences drawn from that data, with little attention paid to the actual means of collecting the data. The method by which data is collected may seriously limit, skew, or taint the data itself, along with any subsequent interpretations of the results, yet such possibilities are rarely addressed in any depth.

Second-order, or qualitative, research is descriptive research, in that it relies on rich descriptions of the research subject. As Hatch (1990) noted, "Qualitative researchers depend on their ability to capture participant perspectives in their data in order to report those perspectives in their descriptions" (p. 252).

In most cases, qualitative methodologies have relied on the research interview as a means of collecting raw data, although approaches such as ethnography and participant observation have allowed researchers to participate in the lives of research participants and use observational data and personal experiences, diaries, critical field notes, biographies, and other such secondary sources. These exceptions notwithstanding, much of the data emerges from verbal description. Participants become the data source and the researchers (along with their notebook, tape recorder, or video recorder) become the research instrument. Descriptions may have either observational or linguistic origins, but whatever the source, experiences are eventually transformed into language. Researchers condense and distill diverse data into some type of meaningful written summary, and that ultimately brings into question the reliability of the results, given the source of the data and its subsequent interpretation.

Although qualitative research data clearly requires close scrutiny because of its high reliance on verbal reports, even first-order research often involves the collection of either oral data or linguistic responses to questionnaires and tests. Traditionally, quantitative research has attempted to reduce the subject under scrutiny to a series of statistics or facts that may be manipulated and analyzed mathematically in order to make comparisons and to draw inferences. To investigate the physical world, quantitative approaches have been highly successful in reaching clear conclusions (more notably in the field of physical sciences such as engineering, chemistry, and physics). However, in the field of human science inquiry, no matter how easily the subject matter can be reduced to numbers and statistical concepts, the numerical results must eventually be interpreted and meanings assigned to them. All of the factors that so obviously influence the more purely qualitative research, including topics covered in previous chapters (such as self-awareness, self-reflection, self-report, language, and other related interviewer and child variables) also apply to quantitative forms of data collection and interpretation.

Questionnaire and test-based research is not without its shortcomings. Apparently objective questionnaires may be misinterpreted by children so that their responses reflect what they think they are being asked rather than what the researcher intends to ask. Children may make straightforward technical errors, responding inappropriately because they have misunderstood the response guidelines. Furthermore, children may also be confused by the use of multiple questionnaires that have varied response criteria ranging from the time period evaluated (e.g., in the last week, last month, a lifetime); to the type of terminology used (e.g., always–usually–occasionally–never; agree–disagree; most like you–least like you; choose the one that describes you best); to the type of response required (e.g., written, yes–no, number-based Likert scales as different as 1 to 10 and -2 through +2).

Some questionnaires require check marks to be made, others require numbered circles to be filled in on a separate computer form, still others require written replies, while some incorporate a mix of these formats. Children may be confused by the changing expectations and parameters within and across instruments and may lose track of what is expected of them at any given time. To ameliorate this problem, some researchers administer questionnaires orally, adjusting the wording to suit the children's age and development or the demands of an oral presentation. Although this approach has the potential to rectify one set of problems, it potentially creates a new set if the researcher casually overlooks the influence of the oral presentation on the children (including poor or inappropriate orientation to the task, use of leading statements, tone of voice, body language and nonverbal communication) and the effect on the instruments themselves (and the use of associated normative tables) when the format of administration or wording of items is changed.

Even when researchers do not personally administer questionnaires, and instead ask participants to complete forms in private, responses may be tainted by factors other than misunderstanding directions and misusing formats. Children participating in research may be apprehensive about who will see the results or about what the researcher will think if he or she knows their inner thoughts and feelings or finds out about their past behavior. Children may feel even stronger pressure to fill out forms the "right way" rather than how they honestly think or feel. Group administration of questionnaires opens the door for children to feel pressured by others around them, including their speed of responding, or their concern that others may peek at their answers. All of these factors underscore the need for researchers to become aware of potential influences on the clean collection of data and then to carefully monitor and limit potential sources of contamination.

The Child's Inner World

Adults can help children interpret various aspects of their experiences and provide them with a language to describe their world. Children's uniqueness manifests itself in both the way that they interact with the world and the way that they interpret and store their experiences. The goal of research with children is to gain access to their inner world, including: ideas, beliefs and opinions; feelings and attitudes; memories and experiences; perceptions, conceptions, and aspirations. Such subjective information is unique and valuable, and although inferences based on our observations of children may be helpful, they can never replace the firsthand reports of children. Hughes and Baker (1990) emphasized the dynamic nature of individuality, stating:

> Individuals actively construe meaning from their experiences. Rather than being passive recipients of environmental influences, they selectively perceive and respond to certain aspects of their experiences, interpret experiences in light of what they know about themselves and the world, distort experiences according to their beliefs, formulate expectations about their ability to perform responses, anticipate outcomes associated with different responses, attach values to these outcomes, select goals, and generate plans to achieve goals. (p. 4)

The sheer complexity of individuals makes the task of uncovering and elucidating their inner landscapes a challenging one. However, careful preparation and sensitive exploration on the part of researchers can uncover important information.

Although each child will offer a singular perspective and experience, developmental research has demonstrated that careful examination of children's behaviors, responses, and descriptions (even their misunderstandings) can help us to identify group patterns and to understand the more general experience of childhood. Briggs (1992) suggested that a thorough awareness of one child's vicissitudes can offer insights that will subsequently help to direct inquiries with other children, including identifying questions that would otherwise not have been asked. As noted by Wellman (1990), "Capturing childhood thought ... helps us to understand how we have become ourselves, and it helps us to understand, guide, and interact with our children" (p. 330). Clearly, conscientious interviewing, if utilized reflectively, can lead to valuable insights that can, in turn, lead recursively to more sensitive and effective interviewing.

Researcher/Interviewer Variables

Researchers must keep their attributions to, and conceptions and constructions of childhood from interfering with their investigations (including the expectations they have of children, the range of options that they offer to them, and the way that they receive, respond to, and interpret their responses). Certainly, children's experiences of events may differ from their ability to recall and describe those events. Children may lack the subtly nuanced language and vocabulary of adults to convey inner conceptualizations. They may not have the kind of sophisticated organization and coherence of their ideas that adults gain after years of practice. However, if professionals are not careful, they may disregard or dismiss children's valid attempts to communicate their experiences. Subsequently, professionals may underestimate the significance of children's insights by mistakenly assuming that their thinking is narrow. Matthews (1983) noted that even very young children can have keen insights and make profound statements. He cautioned that, when children's remarks are filtered through narrow developmental assumptions, the ability to take seriously the thinking that may underlie those remarks is limited.

Methodology must provide an authentic window into the world of children. Wells (1989) contended that if unwarranted methods are not changed, there is a serious risk of compromising results. As part of the repression of childhood experience, adults interpret children's language instead of exploring its meaning. Validation of indicators and language require a depth of investigation and shift of perspective, which must necessarily move away from traditional ways of retrieving information from children. Methods of interrogation, threat or entreaty, with requests to tell, reinforced by accommodation to powerful adult needs, mean that children may reveal only what is expected (p. 46).

The main problem occurs when children are perceived as having a primitive mentality and consequently, are spoken and listened to as if they have limited understanding. This process has been referred to as "dumbing down" by Graue and Walsh (1995). Anyone who has heard the artificially high-pitched voice of an insensitive preschool teacher has witnessed this type of intrusive thinking in action. Listen to any effective parent, educator or children's entertainer, and you will be unlikely to find such disrespectful patterns of interaction. Beyond mere style of presentation, professionals must consider what they say and how they communicate it.

Wells (1989) recommended changing patterns of communicating with children "from advising, interpreting and controlling, to listening, hearing, and validating children's experience" (p. 45). This means retaining children's language and forms of expression as unique aspects of culture. Instead of perceiving children as immature, their perspectives must be valued and the interpretation of their communications through implicit models of adult conventionality should be avoided (Beekman, 1983).

To achieve this level of openness, professionals need to discard misleading notions of who children are, as well as ineffective communication practices. This may not be as simple as it appears. The communicative process is complex and inextricably bound up in the social, emotional, cognitive, cultural, and linguistic contexts of children, professionals, and the interactive space created between both parties. Becoming aware of the potential problems and pitfalls of interviewing children will enable professionals to better control for such variables.

Whatever the particular research circumstances, investigators and interviewers (they are not necessarily the same people) bring preconceptions, beliefs, and even prejudices that will impact on the process and outcome of the research. From the outset, researchers must attempt to identify the underlying beliefs that they have about children, how they learn and grow, what they are capable of doing, what they are able to communicate, how they set goals and make decisions, and as many other aspects of children's functioning as are relevant to the particular area of study and method of collecting information. If these implicit assumptions are not made explicit, they are likely to have a detrimental influence on interactions with children, as well as the quality, representativeness, and utility of the data collected.

Once these assumptions and beliefs have been delineated, researchers must next determine those beliefs that may hinder the research process, and then attempt to set those preconceptions aside and to suspend judgment, a process that phenomenological researchers call "bracketing" (Hammond, Howarth, & Keat, 1991). The purpose of bracketing is not to achieve a state of absolute disinterest, but to realize how personal interests in a topic can color one's research activity (Colaizzi, 1978). In short, researchers state their beliefs about the phenomenon under study and explicitly and temporarily set them aside so as not to obstruct their view of the data. At the very least, researchers, while designing research questions, articulating specific queries, running pilot studies, and interpreting results, should be as fully aware as possible of their hidden beliefs in order to limit the detrimental influence of those beliefs.

In addition to questioning their own preconceptions, professionals must also evaluate previous research with an inquiring and skeptical mind. To aid in the process of separating oneself from one's beliefs, it may be helpful to consider how different cultures view children. For example, the Hindu tradition sees children as having a predetermined character at birth. As a result, adults do not take a role in directing or changing children's character, but instead accept children and work to help them fulfill their destiny.

Once some initial parameters have been set for the research study, researchers should begin to collect some sample data during a pilot study. Pilot studies can be particularly helpful to novice researchers who require an opportunity to transfer theory into practice and to determine the effectiveness of questionnaires, interactions, and general methodology. The goal at this stage should be to refine the research question(s) and the methodology for collecting the data. This midstage data may be purely observational or may involve direct interactions with children. For example, researchers may observe and listen to children from a distance to better understand how they represent the research topic to each other, within their natural environment and interactions.

In another case, researchers may decide to join what Beekman (1983) called a child's social/personal/private landscape. According to Beekman:

> It is almost impossible to discover what the *house* means to a child unless you engage in a dialogue with the child in the house. And the dialogue has to be an ongoing one in which the child can talk freely with you at his or her own level. (p. 42)

Whatever the methods used at this point, the goal is to illuminate children's views of the research topic and to hone the research instruments.

As the final data collection phase of the research study is approached, the ways in which professionals may inadvertently influence child participants to respond during the interview itself (through acts of either omission or commission) need to be considered. Mishler (1986) pointed out that interpretation and the interpretive process finds its way into every interaction within the interview process, and that attempts to control for it through standardization of interview schedules, interviewer training, coding, and complex statistical analyses can never fully account for interviewer effects and coder bias.

Mishler cautioned that the texture of what participants are attempting to communicate is superseded by the context of the interview situation itself. For example, Kahn (1994) warned that a psychologically trained interviewer gath-

ering affective data will unavoidably tinge the interview itself with psychological interpretation, stating, "Interviewers' inquiries, as well as their direction and points of follow-up, strongly affect the course and content of the
interview" (p. 92). She suggested that the professional's interactions with participants may even alter their perspective on their own history.

The key to the successful amelioration of professional influence is an
active self-awareness on the part of the professional to monitor personal responses (both internal and external) during the interview. In addition, professionals should be as open and receptive to children's offerings as is humanly
possible, suspending judgment during the interview, working persistently to
appreciate the children's personal experiences and to understand their perspectives on those experiences. Briggs (1992) acknowledged the difficulty in achieving this end, and offered some guidelines to help ensure the integrity of the
data collected:

> Of course, my image of the world that a child is building will never
> match exactly the child's own image. One reason for this discrepancy
> is that I can never have access to all of the material out there in the
> world that the child has to build with; I can never see, hear, smell, and
> feel all that happens to the child. Second, and more fundamentally, I
> am not that child; I do not have the child's accumulated store of
> thoughts and feelings with which to meet the events, react to them,
> create them, and build on them. Moreover, not only do I not have the
> child's thoughts and feelings, I have a great many of my own, which
> interfere with my perceiving accurately those of the child. Neverthe-
> less, by analyzing what I can see of the messages, the plots, simple
> and complex, cross-cutting and contradictory, that these dramas con-
> tain, and by cross-checking what seems to me to be the messages with
> the clues that the child gives to me in the way she reads or fails to read
> the messages, I can, I think, glimpse something of the shapes, always
> changing, always incomplete, of the world the child is building. And,
> more important, I think I can see and understand a good deal of the
> building process. (p. 45)

Finally, Kahn (1994) cautioned that interviews may have beneficial therapeutic effects, but warned that this should not and cannot be the goal of the
research interview; therapists clarify the person's experience in order to alleviate distress, while the researcher does so in order to meet the research goals. At
the same time, she stated that since interviews have the potential for both
disruptive and beneficial effects, researchers should distinguish between clinical and research goals in order to monitor techniques, protect interactions from
contamination, and improve the final evaluation of results.

PRACTICAL CONSIDERATIONS

The actual process of collecting data during the research interview closely parallels that of any other interview with children. Many factors that have been already been addressed in relation to the general interview also apply to the research interview (see previous chapters including the practice of interviewing). However, some additional consideration must be given to the research interview, including benefits and hazards, issues of informed consent, and the use and reporting of research results.

Benefits and Hazards

The researcher's first consideration must be for the well-being of children involved. Ideally, the collection of research data will be at best positive and rewarding for the child participants, at worst innocuous and benign. Professionals cannot afford to be casual or cavalier about potential risks of interviewing children for research. Realistically, however, research has much potential to disrupt children's life. Besides taking time away from their necessary developmental and life activities (or school assignments), research may single out children socially amongst peers. Consequently, they may feel threatened, fearing that something is wrong with them in order to have been chosen for a research study. Children may feel coerced or bullied into joining the study and then into sharing experiences, thoughts, and feelings that are personal. Prior to the interview, children may be fearful of the research situation, unsure of what to expect, and uncertain of what is expected of them.

Once engaged in the study, a potentially stressful and anxiety-provoking situation, children may have strong feelings or disturbing thoughts stirred up by questions asked during the interview. Professionals may inadvertently contribute to children's feelings of helplessness, inadequacy, and even hopelessness. Imagine this scenario: a child enters the research situation with the notion that it is an examination, that there are right and wrong answers, and that the professional is going to report to the child's parents and teachers about how well (or poorly) the child has fared. In this situation, the cards are already stacked against the professional; if he or she is not extremely skillful, the interview could be significantly detrimental to the child and the results useless to the researcher. Once the interview is concluded, children may continue to be affected by the experience and may harbor negative feelings and thoughts.

Besides direct effects on children, investigators should attempt to identify all possible detrimental effects on their ecology, including the impact of a professional's presence, the topic being researched, and the manner of research.

Consideration should be given to direct and indirect effects on peer interaction, family functioning, school (academic and social) dynamics, and greater community interactions. Children may be pressured by others to explain what happened, what they were asked, and how they responded. In addition to negative effects on the individual, others who interact with children afterwards may also be affected. If research is being conducted in a classroom of children, think of how an early disclosure may contaminate the reactions and responses of subsequent participants from the same classroom or school.

Consider how children who are waiting to meet with a researcher, and who observe another child return crying from the interview, may begin to experience anticipatory anxiety and fear. Ecological effects may also be far reaching and enduring.

For example, Robert Coles produced a documentary film for the Public Broadcasting System that has been broadcast nationally and internationally, with copies of the tape distributed far and wide. In the film, children were identified by name and appear with their families, several of them in a negative light. Although Coles did his best to ameliorate and soften this interpretation, many viewers will draw their own conclusions. The social and academic benefits of the film are unquestionable, as Coles urged viewers to consider the societal and family factors that contribute to children's jeopardy or resilience.

However, one must wonder what the immediate and long-term effects of this film will be on the children involved in the film's production. Consider the case of one child who was placed in a group home for disruptive and destructive behavior. Several years later, he may make attempts to change his life for the better, yet the teachers he meets may have seen him on film, describing his inability to control his anger, and may judge him prematurely. Perhaps a potential future partner or employer will have seen the documentary and decide not to take a chance on the fellow whose troubles became public trials. As Parker (1984) stated,

> The ecological effect of securing children's participation and, once secured, interviewing them about their relationships, morals, guilts, feelings about authority, prejudices, awareness, desires, and so forth, are generally not known. When we intrude, we do so with only a limited sense of the long-term consequences. (p. 27)

Hazards and potential problems are easy to identify. What may not be so easy to specify however, are the possible benefits to children participating in the research interview. Professionals anticipate that research will be of benefit to children and society at large. Otherwise why conduct the research? However, they must think carefully through the benefits for children participating in the research. Certainly, a participant's sense of duty or idealism can be called upon, but it behooves us to identify specific advantages for children who are recruited.

What is obvious to therapists or researchers who conduct child-focused interviews is that most youngsters enjoy the attention. In contemporary society, children rarely have the opportunity to engage in a one-on-one experience with an adult. In addition to the pleasure of individual time and attention, children are likely to feel valued, respected, heard, and validated if professionals are sincerely interested in what they have to say and are willing to engage them in an open, receptive interaction. An effective research interview should help children understand themselves better after having expressed personal perceptions, experiences, ideas, and opinions. Such an interaction should provide material to enhance esteem and even engender pride.

Although therapeutic results are not typically a goal of the research interview, they may be a beneficial side effect. During the making of Coles' documentary, for example, child participants (and their families) had the benefit of exposure to an eminent and highly skilled child psychiatrist. Providing therapy to the children may not have been a goal of Coles' research into resilience and moral development, but because of the nature of the data collection, which involved careful listening to and drawing out of emotional themes in a supportive environment, these children may have come away with much positive benefit. In addition, since the nature of the research included the production of a film, these children may have gained esteem in the eyes of their peers and significant others for being chosen to participate in such a production.

Finally, by engaging in research, children may feel positive for having assisted the researcher, society in general, or both. For example, an 8-year-old boy who participated in research with MLZ communicated how surprised he was that someone would be interested in what he had to say, and how thrilled he was to be able to help out. He announced proudly to friends that he had helped out someone from the university!

Informed Consent

Although parental/guardian permission is required in order to conduct most child-focused interviews, it is absolutely imperative for the research interview. Parents/ guardians must be the first line of permission obtained, and it is the professional's responsibility and duty to inform them as fully as possible about the goals of the research, the necessity for the research, the manner in which the research will be conducted, and any possible negative or positive effects on their child(ren). If the parents/guardians agree to allow their children to participate, they should be advised to inform their children about the research project and to answer questions that the youth may have. They should also be cautioned not to cajole, bribe, or intimidate children into participating.

Participation must be free and unencumbered. Ideally, professionals will meet with children in advance of the data collection, to provide them with the same information that their parents/guardians received. That information should be tailored to their cognitive-developmental level. Children should be advised that should they decide to not participate, there will be no negative effects on them from either the researcher or adults with authority over them. Although there is no reason to believe that parents or other adults will retaliate against any children who decide to not participate, the potential exists. To guard against this outcome, all relevant adults need to be contacted and informed of a child's decision to withdraw, while purposively telling them that it is important that their child not feel any negative repercussions as a result of his or her decision. Children may initially agree to participate and then find that they do not enjoy the process.

Although collecting data via interview methodology should be nonintrusive, the process may be stressful for young participants. Children may find it difficult to talk about their own experiences with a professional with whom they are unfamiliar. Therefore, children need to be advised from the outset that they may choose to withdraw from the research at any time, without fear of reprisals or negative consequences. Such statements must be believed by professionals so that they can be spoken sincerely and convincingly.

Professionals must be prepared to lose participants and to let them go freely, no matter what amount of financial, material, or personal resources have already been invested in the participant. Aside from the negative emotional impact on children of being forced to participate in research against their will, professionals must consider the detrimental effect on data collected if children are reluctant or unwilling participants in research. The validity of the data will be seriously compromised.

Use of Data

Participant identity can be protected in a number of ways. Once permission forms have been signed, children can be assigned code numbers identifying their grades and genders. Video or audiotape recordings may then start with the announcement of the code numbers, followed by the actual interviews. Children should not be requested to identify themselves by name on the tape. If interviews are to be transcribed, then the transcripts should also carry only the assigned code numbers. In addition, a decision must be made about the recording of specific names or identifying information that may emerge during the course of the interviews. Number codes or aliases may be used instead of the actual names of children and locations.

All documentation (e.g., permission forms, tapes, notes, computer files, and transcripts) should be secured in a safe location. Ideally, permission forms and code sheets should be secured in a separate location from the raw data and transcripts. If personal references or identifying information should remain intact in transcripts, then that information should be altered in the final written presentation, as long as the altering does not significantly affect the integrity of the findings or the interpretation of results by misleading the consumer (e.g., altering gender, age, or other significant features of the individual relevant to the study would be problematic). In circumstances in which children's words will be quoted, identifying information that exists within the quote must be altered (e.g., names of people, institutions, or buildings) in order to protect participant identity.

The hypothetical outcomes of Coles' documentary film highlight some of the problems that may arise when confidentiality issues affecting participants are not carefully considered. In addition to protection of participants, confidentiality of identity is a key factor contributing to the collection of sensitive data. Many important discoveries have been made because participants felt comfortable enough to share sensitive information, knowing that their identity would remain confidential, even anonymous. When face-to-face individual interviews are conducted, identity cannot remain anonymous to professionals, and in such cases it will be important to ensure confidentiality of identity within the research report.

When working with children, confidentiality issues extend beyond the participants. Parents, schools, and institutional staff may want access to research information, even to raw data. Funding agencies that supported the research may also request access to such information, and it will be the professional's responsibility to ensure the confidentiality of the raw data and participant identity. In cases in which confidentiality cannot be assured (take, for example, the research documentary film), then children and guardians need to be fully informed of both the benefits and the possible hazards of partaking in the project given the limitations on assurance of confidentiality of identity and data.

DURING THE INTERVIEW

The purpose of interviewing children is to elicit rich, unimpeded descriptions of interior landscapes. Such descriptions will be related either directly or indirectly to past life experiences. Briggs (1986) cautioned that if a goal is to elicit oral histories or descriptions of past experiences, children's present life circumstances will color what they remember and report, as well as the way they interpret those events and experiences.

Although this is important to consider, it is not necessarily problematic and should not automatically be viewed as a contamination of data. Unless there is an interest in historical accuracy, children's current views on past events remain valuable to professionals. In longitudinal research, children's changing memories, ideas, and opinions may offer important insights into the functioning of their young minds.

Similarly, Ackroyd, and Hughes (1992) reminded us that people will not always do as they say, but that skilled interviewers can "encourage the respondent to speak authentically; to get respondents to say what they truly think, feel or believe about certain things, report accurately on what they have said or done, relationships entered into, and so on" (p. 117). Consequently, professionals do as much as possible to support the authenticity of reports.

The interview situation itself can color and influence the recollections and opinions offered by children, and it is this form of data contamination that professionals should strive to reduce. An important contribution that professionals can offer to reduce circumstantial contamination is to work toward helping children feel comfortable so that they are able to share their experiences and ideas candidly. During the interview, professionals must be aware of what children say and how they say it. In addition, they must be sensitive to what the children do not say. Just because they are expressing themselves verbally does not necessarily mean that what they say is worthwhile. Conversely, just because they are nonverbal does not necessarily mean that they have nothing worth saying. The role of the professional is that of a facilitator, an interested, accepting, and nonjudgmental listener who helps children to communicate their thoughts related to the research questions.

Rapport and Orientation

At the heart of the researcher-child relationship is rapport and a mutual understanding. Yarrow (1960) underlined the importance of rapport and the general interpersonal relationship between the professionals and child participants, particularly the meaning of the interview relationship to children. Rapport with children needs to be established before introducing questions whether they be paper-and-pencil or verbal. Yarrow suggested that professionals spend time getting to know children before beginning the interview by playing a short game or introducing an item to catch the children's interest and attention. With latency-age children, he suggested using a game that depends on chance (in order to avoid encouraging competition between the adult and child), or taking advantage of children's innate interest in self-mastery by providing them with construction toys to use during the interview.

Children can also be invited to bring in something that they made or earned (Parker, 1984), which would allow them to begin the session by talking about something they are familiar with or proud of. Such a beginning should open the door to candid opinions and descriptions as the interview progresses. Establishing rapport before beginning an interview is very important. However, once gained, rapport must continue to be nurtured throughout the interview. To aid in this process, children need regular assurance that the interview is progressing well (Amato & Ochiltree, 1987).

It is important that children be properly oriented to the research situation, expectations, and circumstances. Children need to be provided with an explanation regarding the professional's role as a "permissive person who encourages the child to express his thoughts or feelings with impunity" (Yarrow, 1960, p. 572), so that they understand the relationship is probably different than any other adult-child role they have previously encountered. The next task is to ensure that children have a clear understanding of the questions being asked or tasks required of them (Damon, 1977).

Finally, children need to be told that they may ask questions to clarify any confusion that they have over wording, expectations, or any relevant aspect of the interview scenario, and they must feel unencumbered in doing so. If such steps are not taken, inaccuracies may result and erroneous interpretations may be derived based on the data.

Recording the Interview

Yarrow (1960) suggested that researchers need to record both verbal responses and accompanying nonverbal behaviors in a manner that does not interfere with the interpersonal relationship. Effective interpersonal communication and responsive interviewing requires careful attention to participants. To achieve this, Pramling (1983) stated that good eye contact and communication be maintained (which is difficult to do if professionals are transcribing children's responses). Note taking may be an effective way of collecting responses, but it may be difficult for professionals to accurately record what children express, especially if they misunderstand or misrepresent what is being said at the time.

Video recording can allow for accurate recording of responses, although the quality and proximity of the recorder will affect the representativeness of data collected. Image and voice recorders are relatively unobtrusive and do not generally distract or inhibit children (Amato & Ochiltree, 1987). This will not, however, be the case for every child. For example, Yonemura (1974) described a preschooler who became upset when he heard his own voice from a tape recorder. He responded by shaking his fist at the machine, gesturing and making faces as he heard the boy in the machine repeat his words, which he considered to be a theft.

If recorders are used, it is the professional's responsibility to ensure that children know they are being recorded and that they agree to the process. Whatever equipment or method is used, it should be tested out to ensure that it achieves the anticipated results without interfering with the interview environment or the data.

SPECIFIC STRATEGIES

The research interview will, of necessity, be an interactive affair and each interview will be a unique interaction. As a result, much of what transpires may be difficult to plan carefully in advance or to teach to others. However, there are many helpful guidelines that can offer some direction to conduct an interview. Yarrow (1960) proposed that the interview must be adapted to the developmental stage of children. Although his stages and suggested adaptations may be challenged, his broad thesis is an important one.

By maintaining a critical eye, the professional can draw many valuable guidelines from developmental research. Normative information should be helpful and not restrictive in guiding the interview process since children will tend to display abilities that fluctuate around typical developmental patterns and trends. Care must be taken to ensure that developmental theories and normative tables do not dictate how professionals treat children as groups instead of individuals, thereby engendering the same problem they attempt to solve. Since children are generally interviewed on an individual basis, they must be responded to as unique individuals and interactions must be adapted with this in mind.

Yarrow (1960) reported that before 4 years of age, a child's verbal response may be difficult to elicit and understand and proposed that professionals use techniques that place less emphasis on verbal responding. He encouraged the use of techniques such as picture-choice (in which problems are provided verbally and children must point at the picture that matches with their perspective), or doll-play (in which children use dolls to enact their responses to questions). After age 4, he suggested that most children have the skills to respond verbally, and that only about 10% of 5-year-olds will refuse to speak (as compared to about half of 2-year-olds).

In middle-childhood, he advised that, in order to limit defensiveness and inhibition, professionals should present a nonjudgmental, accepting, empathic attitude, and a genuine interest in children, with increasing warmth, sensitivity, and responsiveness as the interview probes deeply personal feelings and attitudes. In adolescence, he advised interacting with youth as equals (without being overly friendly) in order to earn their cooperation.

Structure

Interviews may be more or less structured in advance. The standardized approach has questions completely formulated before the interview while the free approach generally consists of an outline of suggested topics that may be introduced in any sequence during the interview. Unfortunately, a formal approach to interviewing children may only emphasize the existing power structure (Hatch, 1990) and may inhibit the children's responses. Although professionals may use standardized questions to ensure the integrity of the protocol across interviews and to reduce professional effects, a precisely scripted delivery of words and intonation can still be interpreted in differing ways by participants. In addition, preselected questions can hamper a professional's ability to adapt queries to elicit responses from children.

Yarrow (1960) discussed the difference between directive and nondirective approaches to interviewing. The first approach suggests that professionals lead the way and maintain a clear focus for the interview, using questions that are specific and are more likely to be closed (inviting a yes or no response). The second approach suggests that children may control the direction and topics of the interview with professionals using a more open-ended set of questions or invitations to speak on a topic.

Professionals may benefit from a combination of these approaches. For example, when collecting factual data (age, grade, family structure) prepared questions will be more certain to elicit the necessary response than would an indirect, unformulated invitation. When eliciting ideas and feelings, an open approach would move away from the question-response pattern that children typically encounter at school, and toward a dialogue that affords children the opportunity to offer content that is significant to them (Yarrow, 1960). Obviously, the nature of the research topic will invite a more or less formal approach to eliciting data, shifting the role and the behavior of professionals.

Pramling (1983) was mindful that, although a fixed goal in questioning and interviewing children must exist, children should not be forced to respond in a preconceived manner. She suggested that the dialogue begin with a broad, general question before moving toward more specific queries. In addition, she recommended that a prepared set of questions be used as a beginning for a dialogue, with spontaneous follow-up questions used to elucidate and elaborate on initial responses (Pramling, 1986).

Generally, questions should move in a funnel from general to specific, although Yarrow (1960) noted that a reverse sequence might be desirable with young children who tend to have more difficulty responding to general questions. The sequence of questions is important, with the initial questions setting the tone for the interview and clarifying role expectations for children. Therefore, initial questions should be easy to answer, with any potentially embarrassing or threatening content introduced later on (Yarrow). In addition, very young children may need to have questions varied in order to maintain their interest, and to reduce fatigue and boredom (Yarrow, 1960).

To conduct effective research, a balance between careful preparation for the interview and flexibility is required. Interviews must be standardized to allow for reliable comparison among children, yet be flexible enough to allow for individual differences between children. Professionals should remain flexible and sensitive to children and use questions carefully (Pramling, 1983). Yarrow (1960) emphasized the importance of sensitivity to issues of defensiveness, level of motivation, age, atypicality (e.g., mental impairment, emotional disturbance, brain damage), or cultural background. Sensitivity to children also includes knowing when to ask specific questions, and when to switch foci in order to maintain children's interest (Pramling).

Context and Content

Research with children has typically focused on their verbal responses to hypothetical scenarios, stories, or questions, and rarely on their life experiences. Many of these techniques may not have good ecological validity because they are decontextualized. Briggs (1986) indicated that decontextualized questions do not always elicit useful data. Traditional research methodologies tend to divert children from their natural inclinations and neglect the spontaneous interests and reactions of children (Damon, 1977).

Generally, the closer to life contexts in which people operate, the more likely that descriptive and useful verbal reports will be obtained. Pramling (1983) suggested that, because children have difficulty reflecting on abstract ideas, professionals should emphasize concrete experiences. She contended that children will do best when providing descriptions and narrative responses rather than attempting to explain something. She also suggested that children are typically more willing to speak if the interview takes the form of a dialogue where professionals do not ask questions, but rather allow children to describe the world in their own words.

Professionals should make interviews conversational and allow children to teach them about their perspectives (Graue & Walsh, 1995). Children should be encouraged to reflect and explore their thoughts as deeply as possible. To accomplish this, professionals should not be satisfied with initial responses, but should allow children to elaborate until they have nothing more to add (Pramling, 1986). The context of the interview can never be eliminated and may in fact, form the foundation for real and meaningful communication. Hatch (1990) went so far as to propose that professionals interview children in the natural surroundings of their classrooms or playgrounds, inviting children to reflect on experiences immediately following their occurrence rather than retrospectively.

Group Interviews

Graue and Walsh (1995) indicated that interviewing in pairs or small groups tended to encourage freedom of expression. However, Amato and Ochiltree (1987) found in their research with Australian children that group interviews made it impossible to ensure confidentiality and were distracting for some children. When children are gathered into groups for interviews, professionals need to remain cognizant of the contamination that will take place as children's opinions and ideas on the research topic are directly influenced by the ideas offered by others, especially as children move toward latency age.

Piaget's Method

The clinical method of interviewing, as designed by Piaget, allowed professionals to investigate the world of children on their terms. In this method, professionals would observe children and record their natural communications. These spontaneous conversations then formed the basis for developing questions. Next, professionals would introduce the topic conversationally, even casually, and allow children's thoughts to unfold. Piaget (1929) stated that it took his assistants "at least a year of daily practice" (pp. 8–9) before they became adept at interviewing. Even with his efforts, Piaget's research has been challenged from linguistic and methodological perspectives, suggesting that the language used was not uniformly understood by children in the way intended by the adults, especially once he shifted his initial findings into a more traditional controlled scientific methodology.

Damon (1977) reminded us that Piaget's clinical method is not a complete methodology in itself. It relies on verbal manifestations of inner knowledge and on hypothetical situations and knowledge, bringing into question the ecological validity of children's reports. Damon (1977) advised professionals to utilize supportive observations and to combine experimental techniques with interviews in order to gain a comprehensive view of the world of children, with a broader range of expressions and contexts.

Utilization of Props

Parker (1984) suggested age-appropriate props be used to help clarify the research topic and focus children's attention and responses, a suggestion supported by Yarrow (1960), who endorsed the use of dolls or drawings to enhance children's responses. Hatch (1990) further suggested that photographs or videotapes of children engaged in activities could be effectively employed to help children recall a situation and offer their thoughts about specific activities or events. Professionals can also play the part of a confused participant who needs the assistance of child-insiders, evoking clearer descriptions, and explanations from children who will then do their best to help the ignorant adult understand.

Duration of the Interview

Yarrow (1960) pointed out that the length of the interview could significantly impact outcome. Excessively long interviews may lead to children offering brief, shallow replies in an attempt to quickly complete the interview. If children begin to look fatigued or hungry, or begin to lose their concentration, a break should be suggested or a second interview scheduled. Older children may be able to forge ahead for a while in such circumstances, but the younger the child, the more likely the professional will have to take a break or schedule a second session. In addition, Yarrow (1960) stated, "Even though the interview is not therapeutically oriented, it may be necessary to help a child achieve some closure on an anxiety-evoking topic that has been opened up in the interview" (p. 582).

Terminating the Interview

As the interview begins to close, Parker (1984) suggested designing a plan in order to return children to a point of equilibrium by anticipating and correcting possible side-effects of the interview. He offered no specific examples of how this end could be achieved. It is recommended that professionals take time at the end of the interview to review what children have shared, to ask them how they are feeling, and to help soothe children if they have been upset or unsettled. This can be accomplished through play or through casual conversation about interests or hobbies. In addition, parents, guardians, and others should be informed that the professional is available to deal with any further questions or concerns. In some cases, professionals may want to schedule a follow-up session to share with children information that they gathered from the interview. Such a meeting could be used to corroborate and confirm the accuracy and validity of data that has been gathered. Furthermore, during this process, it can be determined if there have been any ill-effects associated with the research interview.

DATA ANALYSIS

The manner in which data is collected will limit the way it is analyzed (Yarrow, 1960). If all that was requested was a yes or no response, or an endorsement on a Likert scale then that is all the researcher will be able to evaluate. If long stories are collected in the form of first-person narratives, then the data will afford more detailed analysis, but its density may not lend itself well to checklist-style coding. Clear decisions about how the data will be analyzed must be determined before it is collected.

Before data is analyzed, it must be put in a format that allows it to be analyzed. In some cases, this may require careful transcriptions of every word spoken by the interviewers and children. In other cases, researchers may begin by selecting only statements that are relevant to the research participant. With some, the flow of the text will be important, while with others, content may stand in isolation. Svensson and Theman (1983) emphasized the difference between the oral and the written version of the interview and highlighted the importance of maintaining a clear understanding of what was originally communicated by the research participant.

A significant source of trouble can come from errors in the actual transcription (especially when statements are condensed and colloquialisms clarified). Words may be misheard and lead to confusing or inaccurate written statements (e.g., "the other," versus "another"). Pauses or stammers may be lost and affect the underlying emotional tone (e.g., indecision, discomfort), as could words given emphasis or weight by the speaker. Small interjections could be passed over, yet have important meaning (e.g., "hmm" could communicate negation, assertion, interest, or indecision, or it could just be a casual remark). Pronouns used as referents could mislead the researcher and result in potential misattributions. Svensson and Theman (1983) made a good case for vigilant scrutiny of any transcriptions. An adroit researcher will rely on his or her initial understanding to make deft clarifications of obscure passages.

The process of data analysis requires some sifting and sorting and will differ according to the specific methodology utilized, since some research methods have specific guidelines for data analysis. When there are only one or two research participants, as is common in phenomenological or case-study research, then data analysis tends to move from child to child, and findings may or may not be amalgamated across individuals. For larger groups of participants, data may first be analyzed child-by-child and then compared across individuals.

Data also can be analyzed question-by-question across subjects, coded and entered for statistical analysis. In some cases (e.g., critical incident methodology), data is separated out from subjects, and then all statements are pooled and compared before beginning to sort them into groups or categories. Some researchers will develop categories based on the responses available, while others will begin with a predetermined set of categories (and their respective criteria) into which the data will be slotted. This chapter does not detail the various methods and protocols available, however, it does address some elements that will be important for researchers to consider.

In most cases, researchers are searching not simply for the specific responses provided by the children, but rather for the meanings advanced by them, which are embedded within their statements. If responses are being compared within subjects, then it is the researcher's duty to ensure that distinct responses and ideas are seen as independent entities. The researcher must be careful not to misattribute ideas to children. In addition, the researcher must be careful not to miss distinct ideas or categories offered by the children but hidden within their statements. Especially with young children, statements may be rich with intention and meaning, but lack verbal specificity, so that they at first appear to be shallow or meaningless.

When responses are compared across participants, researchers need to be careful not to make similar errors in attributing certain unintended meanings to children's statements, or to overlook meanings that may not be so apparent. Most errors will occur if the researcher allows his or her own thinking to contaminate the children's responses, or if the researcher is haphazard, rushed, or impulsive in making decisions and attributions. Many guidelines for data analysis suggest that researchers develop hierarchies for categories and themes, with a name or title for the grouping, a prototypical example for the grouping, and specific examples from the individuals.

If children's statements are condensed or rephrased, then the original phrasing should be available for comparison at a later time to ensure that their ideas have not been misrepresented. For example, children might offer their response to a question, following which the professional queries the response to clarify his or her understanding. Children then offer a restatement that may initially appear to be a clarification of the first response. However, Svensson and Theman (1983) reported that in their experience, a detailed investigation of statement often reveals that these piggybacked descriptions often offer distinct conceptions. They found that "respondents, being anxious to clarify themselves when being questioned, deliberately strain themselves to find an additional description when they detect some invalidity or insufficiency with the ones already expressed" (p. 17).

One caution that Winograd (1980) advanced is that researchers should be careful not to make erroneous assumptions regarding the presence or absence of internal representations based solely on the demonstration of a predetermined set of behaviors. He supported the exploration of underlying arguments and logic to understand exhibited behavior. Although researchers may observe certain behaviors, external assumptions may in fact be inappropriate given the differences between individuals.

This certainly begs for the use of research that involves the participant as both data provider and data interpreter; researchers need to be careful not to impose their own representations or assumptions on what someone has said. Similarly, adult eyes and views can color and distort what is seen so that children's conceptions and frames of reference are misinterpreted and their ideas are misrepresented within an adult framework (Yarrow, 1960).

Qualitative data may be analyzed in a quantitative manner to clarify relationships between categories and record prevalence of certain ideas or themes. The second level of analysis pays attention to aspects of commonality and uniqueness. This level of analysis can help to provide information on prevalence and depth of categories. Unless results identify unequivocal developmental cut-offs or turning points, the emphasis of quantitative analysis of qualitative data typically remains on general developmental trends or similarities and differences between groups.

CROSS-CULTURAL FACTORS

Briggs (1984) argued that researchers doing field work in cross-cultural settings must examine the metacommunicative properties of the society being observed and not assume understanding. This examination should include questions about the participants' world view, internal models of authority and power, beliefs about knowledge and learning as well as obvious language differences. If childhood can be considered to have a social-cultural context unique from adulthood, then researchers working with children must necessarily ask themselves similar questions about the ways in which children communicate, including their expectations for the interview itself. The communication norms of the interview situation cannot be imposed on a speech community that views communication differently. Unchecked, the structure of the interview will lead the discussion toward content that is simply a reflection of what the interviewer and interviewee have agreed upon rather than what may exist on its own (Briggs, 1986). Metacommunication events are rich but may be missed completely by researchers who do not gain competence in the culture and, even though a new set of interactional norms may be negotiated, preexisting ones will not be entirely superseded.

When second languages are involved, the problems of conducting productive and representative interviews will be compounded. Weeks and Moore (1981) reported that while the ethnicity of the interviewer does not appear to influence responses to questions about nonsensitive topics, it can be a factor if sensitive, race-related questions are asked. Campbell (1981) reported such a response in both adolescent and adult respondents and theorized that it is the result of deference to the professional. In cross-cultural work, the world of children will never be fully appreciated. However, informants may be able to explain and describe their experiences in a way that becomes helpful for researchers, and ultimately for the consumers of that research.

Effective research interviewing will not come naturally to all professionals. Although professionals cannot control for all of the potential variables, they can be more aware of and limit the effects of developmental concerns and limitations. Professionals can organize interviews to ensure that data is collected in an effective manner.

CHAPTER 7

ETHICAL INTERVIEWING

Professionals working with children encounter many of the same ethical problems as those who work with adults. In addition, they encounter ethical concerns that are unique to children. As a result, there is a need to remain attuned to, and informed about relevant ethical concerns as well as methods of resolution. Although this chapter does not provide answers to questions about ethical dilemmas, it does provide a broad overview of ethical concerns that may arise when interviewing children, including issues of informed consent, confidentiality, assessment, family work, custody evaluation, child abuse, psychopharmacology, and research. Implications are drawn for the education and training of competent professionals.

A BRIEF HISTORY

Ethics once came under the purview of professional philosophers and religious leaders. Monarchs and political leaders would often consult with these early ethical professionals, who were considered to be wise men (or women in some circumstances and societies). Religious interpretations of holy scriptures and edicts generated rules by which many people were advised to conduct their lives. When these guidelines were violated, each religion had different ways of dealing with offenders. Some religions counseled violators to confess their sins and offer some form of penance or to make amends and offer restitution if other people were affected by their transgression. Other religions held counsels, akin to courts, to evaluate the presenting circumstances and determine a judgment. Such sentences could include expulsion or ostracism from the group, or physical punishment in the form of the loss of a body part, and even death.

In many societies, church and state had overlapping jurisdiction, and the rules of the land were often determined by religious decree, if not directly, then at least following ecclesiastical consultation. Legal decisions were often based on religious rules or were reached after having considered religious principles. Although our current legal systems may have evolved over time, the influence of religion remains obvious when witnesses are asked to place their hand over a holy book while swearing to tell the truth and in much of the pomp and ceremony surrounding judicial proceedings.

Professional organizations have also developed ethical principles for the benefit of consumers and their members. Initially, such ethical principles (e.g., respect for individuals, responsibility to society) were considered sufficient to guide the actions of professionals. Through government involvement however, the practice of professionals became further regulated by legislated guidelines. As lawsuits were launched, subsequent decisions began to form a growing body of jurisprudence that helped to guide legal decisions and revisions. Professional organizations began to develop principles of practice that were more or less specific depending on the body involved.

More recently, professional bodies have begun to introduce policies and regulations to help manage their members. Such changes have resulted from professional organizations being unable to enforce nonspecific guidelines and principles in the face of individual practitioners who hire lawyers to argue for special dispensation on technicalities of wording or interpretation. If regulations and policies are too specific, professionals may not have the freedom to act independently. However, professionals may leave themselves open to litigation if they do not adhere to the agreed upon guidelines of ethical practice. Clearly, this issue is complex because there are situations where one professional can act in an unorthodox manner and be perceived as highly effective whereas the actions of another professional who engages in the exact behaviors of the first will be viewed as inappropriate.

For example, a professional could share a joke that is intended to enhance the therapeutic relationship, but the same joke shared by another professional could be a source of concern. Some factors generally relate to the personality of the professional and specifically to a sense of timing, ability to take risks, decision-making skills, and so forth. Some organizations have attempted to work around this issue by developing what are referred to as practice parameters for clinical practice (e.g., American Academy of Child and Adolescent Psychiatry).

In many jurisdictions, the actions of professionals are guided by a confusing and overwhelming array of statutes and regulations from government and professional bodies at municipal, state, and national levels. Aside from regulations that are designed to manage professionals directly, there may be a vast range of additional statutes and acts that influence the actions of professionals who work with children (e.g., schools, family and social services, child protection agencies, medical organizations and hospitals, young offenders specialists, and others with access to sensitive information). The scope of the relevant regulations can be daunting, and professionals may be involved in legal investigations, civil, and/or criminal court proceedings.

ETHICAL GUIDELINES

Until recently, information on the ethics of working with children was rare and available only through sporadic articles in professional journals covering areas such as child psychotherapy (Glenn, 1980), school psychology (Clement, Zartler, & Mulick, 1983), and pediatric treatment and research (Lewis, 1981; McCartney & Beauchamp, 1981). However, a growing interest in the healthy development and care of children has culminated in an increase in the number of books and comprehensive investigations related to this subject matter. Koocher and Keith-Spiegel (1990), for example, addressed a wide range of topics including psychotherapy, assessment, confidentiality, clinical competence in working with families, children in the court system, and research with children. Huey and Remley (1988) provided a thorough review of ethical and legal issues for school counselors, including chapters on ethical standards; legal concerns; privacy, confidentiality, and privileged communication; child abuse; group work; assessment, computers in assessment, and computers in records storage; gender, race and cultural difference; and research. Baylis and McBurney (1993) identified a wide range of ethical concerns in pediatric work including invasive interventions, child abuse, children's competence to decide, confidentiality, parental compliance, parental disagreement, patient selection processes, resource allocation, proxy decision-making, truthfulness, and a balance between the rights of children, families, and society.

In addition, a number of book chapters and review articles have targeted such areas as clinical child psychology (Levine, Anderson, Ferretti, & Steinberg, 1993), pediatric health psychology (Rae, Worchel, & Brunnquell, 1995), and inpatient child psychiatry (Brewer & Faitak, 1989), while special sections in journals have addressed ethical concerns (e.g., *Journal of the American Academy of Child and Adolescent Psychiatry*, 1992; *Canadian Psychology*, 1993). Other articles have tackled important areas, including applied professional ethics in pediatrics (Ost, 1991), social work (Mishne, 1992), and parents as consumers (Johnson, Cournoyer, & Bond, 1995).

Although there is a growing interest in and coverage of ethics in the professional literature, ethical decision-making remains far from facile. Even with codes of conduct, professionals differ in their values, beliefs, interpretation of codes, and actual behavior in their professional work. For example, Lindsay (1991) found variations in values and behaviors of psychologists. His solution was to delineate a clear ethical code of conduct and procedures of enforcement to guide professionals and engender public confidence. Although the development of specific policies and rules seem to offer a simple solution, the complexity of the issues suggest that the resolution of ethical dilemmas will be neither quick nor easy.

One of the most difficult challenges for professionals who work with children is the difference between the beliefs and desires of parents and their children. In addition to the parent-child dichotomy, client-professional differences also exist. Barnett (1987) raised the question of the balance that must be struck between professional opinion and the child's right of autonomy or freedom of choice. Some professionals see the problem in simpler terms. For example, Carroll, Schneider, and Wesley (1985) suggested that a professional view the the person who came with the referral as the client, and work toward meeting that person's needs. Such thinking may be appropriate if all participants are compliant but will engender a confrontative attitude if clients disagree.

In some cases, dilemmas may be resolved by a professional's theoretical orientation. For example, Carroll et al. indicated that a behavior therapist might consider a parent as the client, a psychotherapist would consider a child as the client, and a family therapist would consider the family unit as the client. Again, such thinking may be effective if clients are in agreement however, it will not solve differences in opinion between clients and professionals. Realistically, the input from children, parents and professionals on both legal and ethical fronts must be considered.

Professionals have a role to play in advocacy both on an individual and a societal level. Such advocacy may be as simple as recommending a specific intervention or may involve protracted political campaigning for legislative change. Melton (1987) asserted that regardless of personal beliefs, the best interests of children takes precedent. When appropriate, he lobbied for the direct involvement of the children.

INFORMED CONSENT

Common law, under the Constitution of the United States of America as well as the Canadian Charter of Rights and Freedoms, recognizes the rights of competent minors to consent on their own behalf, with a determination of competence based on cognitive capacity rather than age (Hesson, Bakal, & Dobson, 1993). Other pieces of legislation—both provincial and federal—usually offer specific conflicting ages for the right to consent (e.g., young offenders' act, age of majority, right to consent for health care). As a result, professionals are caught between conflicting expectations and circumstances. For example, a school counselor may be approached by a child to receive counseling, yet the parents may disagree. In the reverse situation, the parents may demand that the child be seen by the school counselor, yet the child may not consent and may refuse to participate.

Crowhurst and Dobson (1993) indicated that although laws have not precisely determined what informed consent is in all contexts, working definitions do exist. For example, Roth, Meisel, and Lidz (1977) suggested that consent involves the ability to understand the nature and consequence of participation, including risks, benefits, and alternatives. Rae, Worchel, and Brunnquel (1995) advised that informed consent must be voluntary and without coercion, must include access to information, and capacity, which involves competence in evaluating options and making decisions. Hesson et al. (1993) contended that since there is no uniform law on consent, it is the service provider's responsibility to determine children's capacity to consent as a mature minor, using existing developmental literature, the law, and their own ethical standards to reach their conclusions.

Crowhurst and Dobson (1993) advanced a multistage procedure to ensure valid consent. These steps include:

1. assessing competence;

2. evaluating legal status of consent;

3. ensuring voluntariness;

4. making the consent specific with regard to treatment procedures, time frames, and so on;

5. providing detailed information of the nature of proposed treatment, potential risks and benefits, alternatives, and method of withdrawing consent; and

6. examining the method of consent, preferably using written consent that details items from the five identified areas.

Langer (1985) described a simpler set of guidelines for obtaining children's consent to participate in research or treatment, beginning first with agreement from the parents and then moving to consent by children, with 12-year-olds clearly considered competent to consent and 7-year-olds competent to offer assent. The younger children are, the more likely it is that their parents' decisions will be given priority.

Professionals may not always be able to include children in the decision-making process, especially with young or incapacitated children. In such cases, professionals have a duty to provide parents with as much pertinent, current, and balanced information to aid them in making their decision, as well as adequate time to come to a determination (should time be available). Information should include a delineation of potential options, known or potential risks and benefits, associated costs and commitments, and, finally, a professional opinion based on knowledge and experience. Where possible, parents should be encouraged to consult others and obtain relevant resources such as books, articles, and pamphlets. In addition, they may benefit from speaking with other parents who have undertaken similar decisions, though referrals should be made to a variety of people and organizations, not just those in agreement with the professional.

Parents are usually deemed to be acting in the best interests of their children, but such suppositions may not be supported in every circumstance. What are professionals to think of parents who refuse treatment for a sick child under the auspices of religious beliefs? How do they determine "best interests" when a parent desires a kidney transplant from his own child, an obvious conflict of interest? In order to be able to consult with parents, professionals need to consider how parents make decisions on behalf of their children.

When speaking about children's participation in pediatric health research, Armstrong (1993) suggested that parents will involve children variably in decision-making, given factors such as their knowledge of children, their awareness of general child development, their past decision-making patterns with their children, and their ability to communicate with their children. Using analogue case scenarios, Gustafson, McNamara, and Jensen (1994) studied parents' informed consent to psychotherapeutic treatment for their children.

They found that mothers tended to make decisions to seek therapy based on the severity of their child's problem and their own personal attitude toward treatment, only weighing risks and benefits differentially when their child's problems were most severe.

Alderson (1993) provided a thorough and balanced overview of the concerns present in children's consent to surgery, including human rights, legal rights, informed consent, competence to consent, and duty of care. In the case of children deemed too young, either by law or cognitive capacity, to consent to or deny intervention, Hesson et al. (1993) suggested that children should still be involved in the decision about the form of intervention and by whom it will be delivered, especially in the case of commitment to an inpatient care facility (hospital, group home, detoxification facility). In the much more delicate case of organ donation, children are often included in the decision-making process by the donation center, although the younger they are the less likely their input is to be considered seriously (Bell, 1986). Since most organ transplants are within families, obvious conflicts of interest exist and have been addressed in a variety of ways through review boards, examination of the donor, and consultation with specialists such as social workers and psychologists (Bell). The decision-making around informed consent must include careful consideration of aspects of balanced information, capacity to decide, responsible care, and legal duty.

CONFIDENTIALITY

Watkins (1989) considered confidentiality to be the foundation of a therapeutic relationship. Although some may disagree with her oversimplification, confidentiality is certainly a prime element in the work of professionals. In accordance with its significance, confidentiality is written into most professional codes of ethics and usually applies to children as the primary clients, though with those under 12 years of age it tends to be more difficult to argue for the confidentiality of information (based on court precedents in various jurisdictions).

Limits on confidentiality differ according to province or state, with several notable exceptions. Known or suspected child abuse must be reported in all parts of the country, as should client expressions of intent to harm another person. Although not required by law, standards for duty of care usually require professionals to report intent or likelihood to engage in self-harm. In some provinces and states, visual, cognitive, or psychological conditions that could interfere with driving or employment must be reported; in other cases communicable diseases must be reported. The former may be relevant for older adolescents, while the latter could certainly apply to both children and adolescents. Finally, professionals may be required to provide testimony in a court of law or to release records to the court, a condition that could preclude confidentiality of any information at all.

Although professionals are not always required by law to maintain records, most regulating bodies require this practice. In circumstances where clients ask that records not be kept, professionals may be required to have the client sign a form detailing the request. When working with children, such a request would have to come from the legally responsible adult. In addition to the direct information they obtain from clients, professionals may have records that others want access to. For example, a professional may see a child and record the child's statements about a parent. A parent may then request that the professional reveal what the child has disclosed or request access to any records. Depending upon the circumstances, professionals may be obligated to provide the requested records (e.g., when employed by a public institution governed by a freedom of information act). However, most access to information acts also contain sections that pertain to protection of privacy. Such protection is not a guarantee, though, and under some circumstances professionals may have to make a case for the nonrelease of information.

In Canada, although there are no current legal precedents, under the Freedom of Information and Protection of Privacy Act, it could be argued that a therapist employed by an institution is not obliged to provide any information if children do not wish to have it communicated. Alternatively, the same legislation could be used to demand that information be released, especially if it relates to potential detrimental actions of professionals, or comments, judgments, and labels applied by professionals. A case was made for this in the circumstance of mentally handicapped children and their families (Dyson, 1986).

If children are wards of the state or if a particular government body has funded the treatment or assessment, legislation may require the release of information. Even though the law may be quite clear on the matter, ethical principles would suggest that professionals consider the well-being of clients prior to releasing any information, with children viewed as the primary clients and the parents as secondary, depending upon the age of the child (e.g., Canadian Psychological Association, 1991). Aside from such regulations, professionals may often maintain a file separate from the legal record. For example, test forms and research protocols will often be kept separate and, like the lab results that physicians use to reach their conclusions and to make their decisions, such records may be secured from the most persistent parents.

Access to assessment results is another area of concern. While the American Psychological Association specifically prohibits psychologists from releasing raw test scores, courts will often order that test results, protocols, and manuals, be released (Tranel, 1994). In order to resolve this dilemma, Tranel recommended that professionals request that they accompany their test records, and/or that appropriately trained professionals be retained by the opposing lawyer or the court in order to interpret results (in this case, results would be released to another psychologist and not the lawyer or court). In Canada, test items are protected under legislation, but raw scores and reports are not. Professional and regulatory bodies, therefore, stipulate that cautionary statements should be made in regard to interpretation of scores and potential problems of misinterpretation and that these statements should accompany the released documents (Foreman, 1996). In addition, professionals should request that all test data have limited circulation and be returned to the psychologist following court proceedings.

ASSESSMENT

Matarazzo (1990) stated that assessment is much more than testing and should involve the collection of data from multiple sources including standardized and nonstandardized measures, interviews and observations; however, tests often provide the cornerstone for assessment in the helping professions. The use of tests in the assessment of children presents a number of ethical problems. Standardized tests require proper validation, analysis of internal and external reliability, correct administration and scoring, and finally cautious and balanced interpretation. Nonstandardized tests require even more care in administration and use, with nonvalidated measures such as projective tests applied and interpreted with extreme caution.

The American Psychological Association (APA) provided broad and thorough guidelines for the use of psychological and educational tests (APA, 1985), as does the Canadian Psychological Association (CPA, 1987). Koocher (1993) proposed a number of guiding principles for professionals who assess children, including:

1. adhere to copyright rules,

2. make reports and conclusions accurate and easy to understand,

3. avoid making decisions that are not warranted by the test's norms or intended uses,

4. use only tests you are trained to administer and interpret,

5. ensure the consent of parents before assessing children,

6. remove obsolete raw test data from files,

7. release tests and raw data only to other professionals trained in the interpretation of those tests and results, and

8. never withhold test results and reports because of lack of payment.

In addition to the general guidelines cited above, specialized cases are made for ethical concerns in computer-based testing (APA, 1986), intelligence testing (Alberta Education, 1986; Bagnato & Neisworth, 1994; Neisworth & Bagnato, 1992), educational testing (APA, 1988; Joint Advisory Committee, 1993), testing of nonverbal children (Leary & Boscardin, 1992), assessment of preschool children (Bracken, 1987, 1994), sociometric testing (Bell-Dolan & Wessler, 1994), forensic evaluation (Morrison, 1986), and identification of deviance (Kauffman, 1984).

WORKING WITH FAMILIES

According to Zilversmit (1990) the literature pertaining to young children in family treatment is sparse. In her review of the literature, she reports two opposing perspectives. On one hand, some professionals believe that including children in family treatment can be beneficial to the entire family. On the other hand, some professionals believe that young children can potentially disrupt treatment and that they obstruct communication and the flow of the interview.

The involvement of children in family treatment depends greatly on the preference of the professional and more specifically, the professional's comfort level with children in the interview room. Zilbach (1986) wrote:

> An obvious and important, yet often overlooked reason for excluding children, particularly younger children, in family therapy, is that they are children. They will not behave or speak like adults—they play and act as children do. Children may not be willing or able to sit still in their chairs and talk for an entire, or even minor portion of, the prescribed family treatment time. They move about and otherwise express themselves physically and motorically, in nonverbal ways which may not be comfortable to adults, parents, and *talking* [italics original] therapists. (p. 11)

Although interviewing children, with parental consent, can be an ethical challenge, interviewing children within a family system can be more complex. To simplify matters, Morrison, Layton, and Newman (1982) suggested that in the case of family therapy, the family unit must be recognized as the client. However, even if the family is viewed as the client, the well-being of its individual members must still be considered. Specific issues such as informed consent, confidentiality boundaries, and fair and equal treatment by professionals must be considered. In addition to these potential dilemmas, O'Shea and Jessee (1982) identified other areas of concern, including therapists' use of power, the related use of paradoxical prescription, the risks of distress to individuals during the change process, risk of deterioration as a result of therapy, and therapist-family-societal differences in values.

Corey, Corey, and Callahan (1993) also raised the spectre of power and influence and caution professionals to be aware of the ways in which they exert their power while working with children as members of families. Watkins (1989) raised some further risks for family therapists, including requests to testify against another family member when the therapist has worked with both, and requests to release information to others outside of the family without the full permission of all family members. Though professionals may feel bound by confidentiality, they may also be required by a court of law to release or share information under threat of contempt-of-court charges. O'Shea and Jessee (1982) stated that conflicts between ethical issues, societal values, codes of professional conduct, and legal issues may be minimized by paying attention to informed consent, therapeutic contracts, and prespecification of policies and procedures. Although such suggestions are helpful, they cannot totally expiate the conflicts inherent in different approaches to values and decision-making. At the same time, legal obligations will often preclude any ethical codes (Bernstein, 1982). When in disagreement with current legal practice, professionals must either work to advocate for change in laws, rules, and regulations, or risk the legal consequences of breaching the law.

Professionals who interview children as part of a family unit must approach children without preconceptions based upon reports from parents and others. Although prior reports should not be ignored, they should be set aside, particularly during the initial interview. Professionals should also inform children of their position. For example, once alone with the child, professionals can say, "I have spoken with your parents already and they have told me their side of things and the reasons why they came here with you. However, I am here to help you and your family, and I am not on anyone's side. I am interested in hearing your side of things. I want to know what you are thinking and feeling. I would like you to tell me your ideas so that I can understand your side."

If there are serious discrepancies between parental and child reports, it may be helpful at some point to discuss with children the evidence of differing reports. However, if such a step is taken during an initial contact, it will likely be detrimental to the establishment of rapport. In some cases, parents may bring children to professionals in order to have them extract personal information, or to have children changed or fixed. Both circumstances can place professionals in an untenable situation, especially if the parental dyad is determined to be a key contributor to family problems.

When working with families, Corey et al. (1993) advised professionals to make explicit agreements about limits to confidentiality from the outset. Taking such steps early will help to minimize potential problems, such as professionals having to side with either parents or children. Decisions must be made about what will be kept confidential and what will be communicated to others. Examples of problematic information could include a previous extra-marital relationship by one of the parents or an adolescent's use of contraceptives.

To allow for flexibility of response, Corey et al. (1993) suggested that professionals should avoid making promises about confidentiality. Professionals may deem some information important for successful work with the family and other information personal and irrelevant. However, some consider leaving confidentiality to professional discretion to be unacceptable (e.g., Zingaro, 1983). While Hendrix (1991) noted that strict confidentiality is neither desired nor required, he advised that professionals who want to disclose information shared by a young person should seek voluntary, informed consent, and help youngsters to see the advantages of sharing significant personal information.

An invitation to discuss confidentiality could be, "I would like to talk about confidentiality so that we can all agree on how we will deal with it. Sometimes we will meet as a group. Other times, I will meet with you individually or I'll meet with two of you at once (for example, your parents). Generally, what we talk about when we are alone is confidential. That means that I will not talk about it in the group without your permission. However, sometimes you may talk about something that I think is important for others to know about. If you disagree, then I will try to help you understand why I think it is important and helpful for others to know. I can't promise that I won't bring it up, but I will talk with you before I do. Is that agreeable for you? Does anyone have any questions or concerns?"

Following the initial discussion on confidentiality, professionals should elucidate further limits to confidentiality that may apply beyond the therapeutic group, including threat of harm to self or others, report of ongoing or imminent child abuse, communicable diseases, risk of driving while impaired by alcohol or drugs, subpoena to court, peer-supervision, and so on. For example, professionals could say, "What we talk about here stays in this room. However, there are a few limits to confidentiality outside of the family you need to know about. If any of you talk about plans to hurt yourself then we need to go together to get some help for you. If you talk about plans to hurt someone else, we would need to talk with the police. If you talk about ongoing risk of child abuse, then we would need to report that to the Children's Protective Services."

When sessions with subunits of the family are completed, it is recommended that professionals take a moment to ask about session content to ensure that nothing considered confidential by clients is inadvertently discussed later on. To minimize this possibility, professionals could say, "We've talked about many things today. Is there anything that you said that you do not want your parents/siblings/family/children to know about?"

If some content is considered important to share with others in the family, professionals are encouraged to ask for permission: "You told me three things that you would change in your life if you could. Is it okay if I tell your parents about them?" Better yet, we could invite them to share the information themselves: "Would you be willing to tell your parents about the three things you would like to change in your life?"

Interviewing families can be ethically challenging. Professionals who are interested in working with children must be up to the task, since children are rarely interviewed in isolation from their parents. Even if professionals are working with children apart from their families, they must consider various factors such as when to work with minors without parental consent, risks and consequences of not working with the child, risk that parents will deny their child's participation if asked, the seriousness of children's problems, and relevant legal statutes (Corey et al., 1993).

CUSTODY EVALUATION

Many professionals who work with children will eventually become involved in custody and visitation disputes (Brodzinsky, 1993), as well as permanency planning including foster care, return to biological parents, or adoption (Wiltse, 1985). Custody and divorce proceedings can be challenging and complicated. For example, the College of Psychologists of British Columbia (1996) reported that half of the ethical complaints made during 1995 were against professionals involved in divorce and custody disputes. Some of these may have been spurious accusations of incompetence by parents who were displeased with the professional's findings or recommendations. However, a high percentage were found guilty of unprofessional conduct. Often, this was because they had not received proper training or supervision in custody evaluations; because they had a dual relationship with one of the parents (e.g., have been counseling the mother and child); or because they made statements about one parent based only on allegations made by the other and without having actually met with the subject parent.

The American Psychological Association provided some guidelines for evaluations in child custody disputes (APA, 1994). In its report, the association emphasized the psychological interests and well-being of children, with particular attention to evaluating parenting capacity, children's psychological and developmental needs, and the match between the two. Balancing children's rights with parental rights can be a delicate act and needs to be attempted in all custody evaluations (Elrod, 1996).

To alleviate the apparent problems of overinterpretation of results or misapplication of particular tests for the purposes of custody evaluation, Brodzinsky (1993) has proposed some alternate methods of assessment, including functional capacities of the parent (knowledge, understanding, beliefs, and abilities), standardized measures of the children's impressions of parenting skill, and observational assessment.

In the final analysis, custody evaluations must be carried out cautiously, with full consent of all parties, with advance understanding of the purpose and method of the evaluation, with reports reflecting only what can be validly interpreted from test results, and with inflammatory or unfounded statements entirely absent, (obvious though that last may seem). In the case of permanency planning, professionals must consider the psychological stress of children being removed from their homes, as well as the common problem of children drifting through placements in foster care (Wiltse, 1985). Fortunately, courts often consider many factors—including the children's wishes—when making decisions, so custody determinations rarely fall solely on the recommendations of any single professional.

CHILD ABUSE

Reporting suspected or known child abuse is required by law and by most professional ethical guidelines and codes of conduct, so there should be little discussion on this matter. Unfortunately, the vagaries of the real world present a range of dilemmas to professionals. The result is that professionals do not always choose to report suspected abuse immediately. Pope and Bajt (1988) reported that in a serious or agonizing instance, 21% of 60 psychologists refused to report child abuse in light of a client's well-being or a deeper value, with 73% saying they would repeat their behavior.

Beck and Ogloff (1995) found that in British Columbia, Canada, 12% of teachers admit to not having reported suspected abuse because of what they believed to be a lack of evidence, lack of confidence in child protective services, fear of negative consequences for the child or for the family, fear of harm to the therapeutic relationship, or fear of breaching confidential trust.

Other reasons for not reporting have been reported in the literature. Ost (1991) pointed out that in some cases, removal of children from their home and change in custody could be more damaging to children than the unsatisfactory home situation. Jackman Cram and Dobson (1993) suggested that:

1. some professionals dislike the policing role;

2. others could utilize professional judgments rather than making indiscriminate reports (considering that the majority of reports are not substantiated);

3. accusations could place parents under undue stress (even persecution) from the community, notably if children are apprehended during the investigation; and

4. in some cases where professionals have clients who report a one-time past incident, therapy could benefit clients in contrast to a punitive court system.

Although ethical dilemmas exist, the law is explicit. Consequently, Stadler (1989) advanced a decision tree for use with adults or with children (see also, Stadler, 1987). The process she outlined progresses from most to least client involvement and from least to most professional involvement. In the case of incest uncovered during family therapy, professionals are encouraged to consider existing laws, the needs of children, and the obligation to do no harm during the reporting process (Haverkamp & Daniluk, 1993; Lippitt, 1985).

Similar convictions were espoused by MacNair (1992), who advised professionals to communicate the limits of confidentiality in cases of child abuse from the outset of their interactions. Following this, MacNair suggested that a "firm but respectful affirmation of the law should allow moral, ethical, and professional beliefs to be congruent with their [professionals'] actions" (p. 134) by working cooperatively with child abuse reporting agencies on a macroecological level.

PSYCHOPHARMACOLOGY

Although prescribing privileges are currently limited to physicians and dentists, professionals should have a basic understanding regarding the potential influences of medication. Even though some professionals are not physicians, parents and others may expect them to be knowledgeable about medications and request opinions on pharmacological intervention. Professionals are often recruited to help evaluate the effectiveness of medication. Some professionals working in child welfare (e.g., social workers) may be asked to give permission for medication or to manage the medication of children in their care (Cordoba, Wilson, & Orten, 1983). As a result, Cordoba et al. have advised professionals to seek training in conditions requiring medication, follow-up, side effects, compliance, problems of drug combinations, as well as other relevant factors. Kratochwill (1994) also suggested that professionals seek additional training, and recommended that advanced training could potentially lead to prescription privileges for psychologists, an option that is currently being tested in military settings in the United States.

Although some professionals may want to disavow involvement in medication planning or monitoring, they will never be able to disregard entirely the impact of medication. If the effects of medication on children's performance during an interview is ignored, erroneous judgments and conclusions may be made. For example, MLZ witnessed children who reacted to stimulant medication by having severe tics, including facial grimacing. Once the medication had worn off, the tics were no longer evident. Had he not known about the medication, MLZ could easily have attributed the tics to other causes, including emotional or neurological antecedents.

When children are under the care of a physician and are receiving medication, professionals should know under what conditions they use the medication. Professionals need to ask parents whether children have taken medication before an interview and if this is a usual pattern. Of course there are instances where children pretend to take their medication, but instead dispose of it. Children are also given double doses of medication. If multiple medications are involved, professionals should inquire about how parents ensure that their children get the required medications at the required times.

Brown, Dingle, and Landau (1994) submitted that professionals have an ethical obligation to be involved in psychopharmaceutic interventions with children. They advised professionals to support the effectiveness of pharmacologic intervention through initial evaluation of behavior and condition; ongoing monitoring of behavior, cognition, and learning, as well as possible side effects; provision for informed consent and compliance; the use of adjunctive treatment; and ongoing research on drug effectiveness.

DeMers (1994) countered that professionals must consider carefully the ramifications of their involvement in the solicitation and delivery of medication to children. His concerns included the level of training and experience of the professional; legal issues surrounding competence, credentialing, malpractice, and liability related to informed consent, assessment, and treatment; confidentiality surrounding record-keeping and access; potential conflicts of interest in professional relationships; and welfare of the client, arguably the most important issue at stake.

In addition, the advocacy role of professionals is significant and vital. Far too often, medications are prescribed following quick diagnoses, potential risks and benefits are not discussed fully, and the effect of the medication is not effectively monitored. Controlled research on the effects of drugs on children is scarce (DuPaul & Kyle, 1995), with many recorded through the use of case studies rather than group investigations. As a result of the recency of pharmacologic intervention with children, the potential long-term repercussions of drug use is unknown and speculative at best. Professionals should be as informed as possible if they are to support the use of medication with children.

RESEARCH

Research involving children is important in all areas of the helping professions, yet the field of research resonates with ethical concerns that must be conscientiously addressed. In Chapter 6, we addressed some of the main ethical considerations relevant to research. Grodin and Glantz (1994) provided a detailed and thorough reference for conducting ethical research with children in a variety of settings and circumstances, offering discussions of vulnerability, risk, and consent to involvement. Koren (1993) offered a comprehensive review of issues in pediatric research. These recent volumes provide an excellent resource for investigators.

The same ethical concerns evident in other areas of professional functioning apply when conducting research. Thompson (1991) advised researchers to conduct a risk and benefit analysis and to make special consideration of children as participants due to their variable levels of vulnerability, extant individual differences, limited cognitive capacities, limited social power, and the potential conflict between their best interests, their parents' interests, and the state's interests. Goldberg (1993) suggested that any cost-benefit analysis should include an evaluation of psychological factors as well as physical factors.

Professionals have noted that children's ability to consent to research is largely underestimated and that even elementary school students are able to make the same decisions as adults, and that, certainly by age 14, consent is possible (Stanley, Sieber, & Melton, 1987; Weithorn & Shearer, 1994). In a series of studies with children aged 5 to 12 years, Abramovitch, Freedman, Thoden, and Nikolich (1991) concluded that children generally have the ability to understand what they are asked to do in psychological research and then assent to participation. However, there are a number of factors that make it difficult for them to do this freely, including knowing precisely how to withdraw from a study, feeling pressured to participate if parents had given consent, believing that there would be negative consequences for withdrawing, and not believing that their performance would remain confidential.

Investigators must gain informed consent, yet a review of 114 research studies involving children published in four leading journals (Range & Cotton, 1995) revealed that 68.5% of studies failed to specify assent (children's agreement), and 43% of them failed to specify permission (parent's agreement on behalf of their children). The authors recommended that researchers talk with others in order to identify potential ethical concerns that they may be blind to in their own research; document how they obtained assent and permission; train students in ethical considerations; sensitize themselves to issues of assent and permission; ensure that children are not coerced to participate; and allow children to withdraw.

Hoagwood (1994) reported on the National Institute of Mental Health certificate of confidentiality. This certificate provides a researcher immunity from having research records subpoenaed; its purpose is to protect participants in research on mental disorders. Hoagwood stated that the certificate is helpful in some situations, as long as relevant legal concerns (such as mandatory child abuse reporting) are considered and respected. Children and their parents should not be placed in a vulnerable or untenable position by research.

In addition to general ethical concerns in research, specific ethical concerns have been raised about conducting research with specific populations and in various settings including: developmental research with young children (Thompson, 1991); educational and psychosocial research (Koocher & Keith-Spiegel, 1994); refugee children (Rousseau, 1993); low-income minority children (Scott-Jones, 1994); at-risk and socially disadvantaged children (Fisher, 1994; Scarr, 1994); institutionalized children (Wells & Sametz, 1985); hospitalized children (Alderson, 1990); abused children (Kinard, 1985); children as witnesses (Goodman & Tobey, 1994; Westcott, 1994); counseling and individual therapy (Powell & Vacha-Haase, 1994); and family therapy (Jurich & Russell, 1985).

Professionals who conduct research with children should plan carefully, consider risks and benefits, consult with others, inform fully and respectfully both children and parents, and monitor effects and outcomes.

TRAINING

Finding solutions to ethical dilemmas will never be easy. Nevertheless, professionals who are sensitive to potential ethical concerns, and some of the relevant precedents, will be better prepared to recognize problems before they arise and to deal with them proactively. Training programs for developing professionals who plan to work within the counseling and human services field must offer training in ethics: Emerging professionals cannot be expected to know naturally how to act ethically and to respond to ethical dilemmas.

Peterson, Young, and Tillman (1990) reported that a personal and individual self-study approach may be used effectively. Sondheimer and Martucci (1992) differed by advancing a multistage professional practice model that helps students identify potential ethical conflicts and implement a process of ethical analysis while they forestall action before a thoughtful resolution. In addition, the authors emphasized the four areas of confidentiality, treatment refusal, treatment termination, and the crossover between individual and family therapies. Haverkamp (1995) suggested that students receive training in ethics and professional practice prior to and during work with clients, and outlined both a curriculum and a process for teaching ethics. Plante (1995) described a model for training clinical psychologists in ethical principles and issues through a seminar program for predoctoral and postdoctoral interns working in medical settings. Although models differ, so little has been written on the training of ethical professionals that it is premature to evaluate the effectiveness of such education. Future research certainly needs to address this shortfall.

Professionals who interview children encounter a range of ethical concerns and issues. In order to conduct interviews effectively and ethically, professionals must be familiar with, sensitive to, and educated about ethical concerns in addition to having a working knowledge of methods for their resolution. This chapter offers a broad overview pertaining to the ethical interviewing of children, including the significant areas of informed consent, confidentiality, assessment, family work, custody evaluation, child abuse, psychopharmacology, and research, as well as the effective training of new professionals.

Chapter 8

DIAGNOSTIC CLINICAL INTERVIEWS

The clinical interview is the cornerstone of professional diagnostic practice, particularly in the fields of psychiatry and psychology. This chapter reviews the use of interviewing in clinical diagnosis with children, including structured and semi-structured methods. Implications are made for direct interviewing with children, in contrast to the indirect interviewing of parents and others who work or live with the children. Finally, attention is rendered to the history-taking and mental status examination.

THE DEVELOPMENT OF THE CLINICAL METHOD

Perhaps more has been written about the clinical interview than any other type of interview conducted with children (e.g., Barker, 1990; Bierman, 1983; Bierman & Schwartz, 1986; Garbarino & Stott, 1992; Gardner, 1993; Ginsburg, 1997; Goldman, L'Engle Stein, & Guerry, 1983; Greenspan & Greenspan, 1991; Hughes, 1989; Hughes & Baker, 1990; Lukas, 1993; Yarrow, 1960).

Initially, the clinical interview consisted of an examination that typically took place in a professional clinic. Hence the name. The purpose of such an interview was usually to collect a history of the presenting problem to determine its origins and development. Determinations of both etiology and illness progression were usually framed in the theoretical notions of individual clinicians and were often presented in psychoanalytic terms.

Gradually, clinical interviews have evolved into diagnostic interviews with the use of diagnostic formulations to remove the accusatory stance and the stigma often associated with previous approaches to problem identification. Psychodynamic explanations have been replaced by more specific clinical formulations, particularly with the evolution of the diagnostic nosology used in the various editions of the *International Statistical Classification of Diseases and Related Health Problems* (*ICD-10*, 1992) and *The Diagnostic and Statistical Manual of Mental Disorders* (*DSM-IV*). Although these classification systems continue to rely on symptomatic phenomenology and clinical observation for their content, they are more frequently grounded in carefully researched and validated criteria for the development of formal diagnostic categories, rather than idiosyncratic presentations. With the introduction of *Professional Practice Parameters* (AACAP, 1997) by the American Psychiatric Association, decisions cannot be made without confirming evidence and the active participation of children in the diagnostic process.

CHILDREN AS INFORMANTS

Previously, research and clinical investigation of children was generally conducted using adults (e.g., parents, teachers, caregivers) as the primary and often sole sources of information. Such practices are now difficult to justify ethically. Examination of the social, psychological, and educational aspects of children's lives should involve careful first-hand exploration of their emotional, cognitive, and physiological experiences. Professionals should therefore not expect adults to understand what youngsters are experiencing, nor should professionals assume that they know what is going on in the minds or bodies of the children being interviewed. For example, when investigating pain in children, parents can report on behavioral changes in their children (e.g., crying, rubbing the painful area, inability to sleep, need for reassurance), but only children can report on what they are actually experiencing (e.g., location, intensity, form, duration).

Long-standing beliefs among medical professionals were that the neurological systems of newborns were not adequately developed for them to be able to experience pain as intensely as adults, that children had no memory for painful experiences, and that children recovered more quickly following surgery (Eland & Anderson, 1977). As a result, many operations—from routine circumcisions to open-heart surgery—were performed without anesthetic, and few or no analgesics were prescribed (and even fewer administered) following such surgeries (Russo, Lehn, & Berde, 1993).

If there had been a direct way of asking these infants and toddlers whether or not they felt pain, the results would have been affirmative and definite. It wasn't until researchers began to examine several areas of children's physiological and behavioral responses that they discovered infants do in fact feel pain. These areas include facial expressions (Izard, Huebner, Resser, McGiness, & Dougherty, 1980); heart rate acceleration and blood pressure elevation (Williamson & Williamson, 1983); and metabolic stress responses such as cathecholamines, cortisol, aldosterone and other corticosteroids, growth hormone, and glucagen (Anand & Aynsley-Green, 1985).

Besides the well-documented behavioral and physiological responses to pain, neurological pain pathways and neurochemical systems associated with the transmission and modulation of pain are now known to be well-developed before birth (Anand & Hickey, 1987).

Nevertheless, some medical professionals continue to underestimate the amount of pain experienced by children and routinely undermedicate following surgery (Beyer, DeGood, Ashley, & Russell, 1983; Lemaire, D'Herouville, Piquard-Gauvain, & Flamant, 1987). Aside from needless suffering, the undermedication of pain may have serious health consequences (e.g., sepsis, metabolic acidosis, and disseminated intravascular coagulation) and contribute to higher mortality rates, negative outcomes that have been documented in infants who have been underanaesthetized during open-heart surgeries (Anand & Hickey, 1992).

More recently, professionals have debunked the myths about children's inability to experience pain, their susceptibility to respiratory distress, and their potential addiction to narcotics, while calling for the ethical management of pain in children (Walco, Cassidy, & Schechter, 1994). Although physiological and behavioral indicators must be used as cues when working with infants and toddlers, research has suggested that by the age of 5, children are capable of verbally describing their pain across several dimensions (Ross & Ross, 1984; Russo, Lehn, & Berde, 1993). As more research is conducted, the ability to interview children developmentally should improve and allow professionals to use more direct methods of assessing and remediating pain and other childhood problems.

When professionals seek information regarding the inner lives of children, they must generally view children as their best available informants. As Flanery

(1990) said, "children's thoughts and feelings about themselves and those around them are crucial to scientific and clinical understanding and are best obtained from the child" (p. 58). Children's perceptions and opinions regarding themselves and others furnish important information not available anywhere else (Bierman & Schwartz, 1986). For example, although children have experienced parental separation and trauma for centuries, it wasn't until professionals conducted first-hand interviews with children that they were able to understand the potent and enduring effects of those major life events (e.g., Terr, 1983, 1990, 1994; Wallerstein, 1984, 1985, 1987).

Using these findings, professionals have developed methods of interviewing to support children who encounter violence (e.g., Pynoos & Eth, 1986), or sexual abuse (e.g., Hunter & Yuille, 1990). Evidence suggests that even young children are generally reliable reporters of their inner experiences and are capable of responding to direct questions about their life (Hodges, 1993), with their reliability typically improving with age (Hodges, 1994). In reviewing the use of self-reports in the assessment of depression, Kazdin (1990) stated that children can be accurate reporters of their own depressive symptomatology. Following a detailed review of structured interviews with children, Hodges (1993) concluded that children and adolescents are capable of responding to direct questions about their mental status and reported that children are accurate reporters about themselves, although these general findings are obviously relative to circumstances and individual differences.

CHILD VERSUS ADULT REPORTS

In the case of externalizing disorders—where children's behavior becomes a problem to others—referrals are frequently made by concerned parents, teachers, and caregivers. However, in the case of internalizing disorders—where problems usually affect the children more than others around them—the concern is often overlooked. For example, adult judgments of children's emotional reactions to divorce, especially negative states, have been found to be routinely underestimated in both intensity and breadth (Kurdek & Berg, 1987). Children who suffer may not have the metacognitive awareness to know that they have a problem, and even if they do recognize that their experience is unusual, they are rarely in a position to seek help unless their caregivers support them. As a result, internalizing disorders such as anxiety and depression are frequently not recognized or diagnosed until years after their onset.

Recent findings suggest that parents and teachers are good informants regarding their children's outer lives including behavior, habits, and difficulties, while the children are much better reporters of inner experiences such as thoughts and feelings (Edelbrock, Costello, Dulcan, Conover, & Kalas, 1986; LaGreca, 1990; Orvaschel, Ambrosini, & Rabinovich, 1993; Thompson, Merritt, Keith, Bennett Murphy, & Johndrow, 1993). Although children tend to be better reporters of internalized symptoms, their parents can still provide important observations and information, particularly if their children are young. Orvaschel et al. indicated that the reliability of parents' reporting is better for younger than for older children, most likely because they watch their younger children more carefully, spend more time with them, and rely less on language as a basis for communication. However, parental reports cannot be considered infallible, since research has found that inter-parental agreement on facts about children is not always strong (e.g., Berg & Fielding, 1979; Kazdin, French, Unis, & Esveldt-Dawson, 1983; Orvaschel et al., 1993).

In addition, when considering that children with mental health problems often come from families that are experiencing difficulty, parents can be expected to be less aware of potential problems, less able to respond to children's needs if they are recognized, and more apt to avoid disclosure. With the high incidence of mental disorders found across generations, it is also more likely that parents who experience mental disorders will have distorted impressions or be in mental states that interfere with their ability to appropriately and accurately describe their children's experiences. In some circumstances, children's reports about inner phenomena should be accorded more credibility than those of their caregivers and other adults around them.

One of the difficulties inherent in making childhood diagnoses is that a gold standard model of assessment or source of data does not exist. There is generally poor agreement between parents and children on reports of symptoms (e.g., Kashani & Orvaschel, 1990; Rapee, Barrett, Dadds, & Evans, 1994). Some professionals support the use of parent data as the gold standard source of information, while others support the use of children as the primary source. In the case of internalizing symptoms, many consider the individual as the most reliable reporter. With adults, this advisement is not even questioned; with children it often is, perhaps with valid reasons. Children cannot always be counted on to report internal behaviors or symptoms for several reasons:

- lack of self-awareness (e.g., emotions, ability to discriminate and name feelings);

- lack of vocabulary;

- embarrassment or a fear of being judged;

- the presence and influence of parents; and

- denial as a form of self-protection.

In a study of self-reports of anxiety symptoms in children, some diagnosed children were found to underreport symptoms of anxiety, possibly because of denial or the use of distracting coping strategies (Manassis, Tannock, Mendlowitz, Laslo, & Masellis, 1997).

Developmentally tailored open-ended interviews should reflect children's changing abilities. Competent professionals recognize that verbal skills and interpersonal orientation change as children develop, and that children process and conceptualize interpersonal and affective information in qualitatively distinct ways from adults and from each other at different ages (Bierman & Schwartz, 1986). These elements influence the effectiveness of various interview strategies and cannot be ignored. To be thorough, data is often collected from both children and parental or caregiver reports. These can take the form of informal clinical interviews, structured diagnostic interviews, or paper and pencil severity measures, but in some cases direct observations may be made of the child.

After reviewing the use of self-report instruments in medical settings (pain, anxiety, medical compliance), Dahlquist (1990) suggested that when working with children, the best instruments for obtaining the most unbiased information regarding experiences are open-ended interviews and questionnaires that can be reliably scored, while visual analog scales appear to be the best way to identify quantifiable changes in children's experiences. These methods all require the skilled application of interview techniques.

Sherak, Speier, and Cantwell (1994) evaluated the multiplicity of methods utilized in the identification of depression in children and adolescents. The methods of data collection used during diagnosis included: informal clinical interviews, structured and semi-structured diagnostic interviews, paper and pencil questionnaires, and direct behavioral observations. Professionals are more recently calling for the use of either child or parental reports when making diagnoses (e.g., Cantwell, Lewinsohn, Rohde, & Seeley, 1997; Kaufman, Birmaher, Brent, Rao, Flynn, Moreci, Williamson, and Ryan, 1997; Silverman & Eisen, 1992; Thompson et al., 1993), and more specifically for the integration and triangulation of results from multiple sources including questionnaires and interviews (AACAP, 1997; Bell-Dolan, Last, & Strauss, 1990; Kasius, Ferdinand, Van den Berg, & Verhulst, 1997), unless there is clear evidence and rationale that one informant is more reliable than another (Stone & Lemanek,

1990). Professionals cannot settle for collecting data from parents alone; it must be collected from children as well.

DIAGNOSTIC SYSTEMS

Accurate and useful diagnosis and classification have long been a concern in mental health research and clinical work. Some propose dimensional models (e.g., Achenbach, 1982; Lessing, Williams, & Gil, 1982), distinct diagnostic entities (e.g., *DSM-IV* and *ICD-10*), or multicelled models that take into account the interaction of genetics, psychological factors, and social factors (e.g., Cowan, 1988). Epidemiological studies have attempted to identify prevalence rates of various disorders, but have had variable success in this endeavor. A notable review of epidemiologic studies based on the *DSM* system was provided by Doll (1996). Some epidemiological studies have been conducted using symptom questionnaires (e.g., Boyle, Offord, Hofmann, et al., 1989; Boyle, Offord, Racine, et al., 1993; Links, Boyle, & Offord, 1989; Offord, Boyle, Racine, et al., 1992; Offord, Boyle, Szatmari, et al., 1987). Other epidemiological studies have been conducted using computer administered or individually administered standardized diagnostic interviews (e.g., Lewinsohn, Hops, Roberts, Seeley, & Andrews,1993; McGee et al., 1990; Reinherz, Giaconia, Lefkowitz, Pakiz, & Frost, 1993; Whitaker et al., 1989).

Prevalence estimates from these and other studies vary due to differences in methodology and diagnostic criteria utilized, as well as general problems associated with accurate identification of disorders. As a result, some disorders are overdiagnosed (false positives) while others remain underidentified (false negatives). Trained researchers tend to be more reliable than are practicing clinicians when using diagnostic classification systems, since clinicians tend to rely on idiosyncratic sources of data when making decisions, while decision-making procedures are often preplanned in research studies (Cantwell, 1996).

There are also problems in making differential diagnoses and identifying comorbid diagnoses, since critical decisions must be made about symptom severity when symptom presentations overlap syndromes, particularly when one diagnosis does not clearly override another. Although the *ICD-10* identifies some specific disorders that have comorbid presentations (e.g., Mixed Anxiety and Depressive Disorder), the *DSM-IV* encourages the use of multiple diagnoses. Issues of comorbidity are more frequently being considered in the literature (e.g., Alessi & Magen, 1988; Caron & Rutter, 1991; Nottelmann & Jensen, 1995).

STRUCTURED AND SEMI-STRUCTURED INTERVIEWS

Standardized interview schedules that involve sequences of questions presented in either a structured or semi-structured way (Gutterman, O'Brien, & Young, 1987), were developed in response to disenchantment with the poor interrater reliability of psychiatric diagnoses that were often determined by variable and inconsistent play interviews (Hodges & Cools, 1990) or second-hand parental reports.

Structured and semi-structured interviews were developed to organize and direct professionals in their diagnostic work. In some cases, these instruments were intended to allow paraprofessionals to collect data in large research projects, ostensibly to reduce the amount of expensive and time-consuming professional involvement in the diagnostic process. Examples of this type of interview include: the *Diagnostic Interview Schedule for Children* or *DISC* (Costello, Edelbrock, Dulcan, Kalas, & Klaric, 1984), and its three revisions, the *DISC-R* (Shaffer et al., 1988), the *DISC-2* (Fisher et al., 1991), and the most current version the *DISC-2.3* (Shaffer, Fisher, Dulcan, & Davies, 1996); the *Diagnostic Interview for Children and Adolescents* or *DICA* (Herjanic, Herjanic, Brown, & Wheatt, 1975), and its two revisions, the *DICA-R* (Reich, Welner, & Herjanic, 1988), and the most current version, the *DICA-R-DSM-IV* (Reich, 1997).

Although standardized interview schedules begin to address some of the problems inherent in the subjective expert model of diagnostic assessment, they have never been able to replace the knowledge developed by experienced professionals, and therefore contain a number of limitations. Hodges, Kline, Stern, Cytryn, and McKnew (1982) pointed out that standardized interviews do not follow "generally accepted principles for establishing rapport" (p. 174), and are formidable to children because of their length or their requirements for children to report detailed histories of symptoms and to make subtle discriminations between symptoms. Gutterman, O'Brien, and Young (1987) noted that some interviews are so structured that they do not allow investigators to adapt and change questions in order to increase attention span and level of comprehension in children. In general, highly structured interviews are unsuccessful with children (Orvaschel, Ambrosini, & Rabinovich, 1993) and can elicit inconsistent and confusing responses (Breslau, 1987).

Hodges and Cools (1990) added that lack of sensitivity to children's developmental processes (e.g., their knowledge of emotions and the self, their ability to compare self to others, and their comprehension of time and sequence) compromises some questions in standardized interviews. Hodges (1993) underscored the important balance between procedural rigor and clinical sensitivity when obtaining valid and meaningful information from children about themselves. It is unlikely that highly structured interviews will ever achieve this balance.

Semi-structured interview schedules have typically been more successful in accurately and reliably identifying childhood disorders than have been their more structured counterparts, but their success tends to be more highly dependent upon clinician skill and experience. Examples of this type of interview include the *Child Assessment Schedule* (Hodges, Kline, Fitch, McKnew, & Cytryn, 1981), the *Interview Schedule for Children* (Kovacs, 1983) and the *Child and Adolescent Psychiatric Assessment* (Angold, Cox, Prendergast, Rutter, & Simonoff, 1987).

Other semi-structured interviews have developed over time and often utilize screening questions that allow interviewers to skip out of diagnostic categories or to move on. An example of this development can be seen in the *Schedule for Affective Disorders and Schizophrenia,* which had four different versions prior to the current version, now known as the present and lifetime version (Kaufman et al., 1997).

PRACTICAL CONSIDERATIONS

Forming Diagnoses

Effective diagnostic interviewing involves more than simply checking off symptoms and behaviors from diagnostic categories. Professionals must be able to discriminate clinical levels of individual symptoms and disorders to ensure that behaviors that are actually within the normal range of development do not inadvertently contribute to a misdiagnosis. Forming a diagnosis involves the investigation of all possible explanations for behaviors and symptoms, including ensuring that symptoms cannot be accounted for by a medical condition, or the effects of medications, drugs, or alcohol. In addition, professionals must screen for all possible diagnoses so that important comorbid conditions are not missed.

Finally, a differential diagnosis must occur to determine those disorders which are primary, those which are secondary, and those which may be present but not at a clinically significant level (some symptoms but not enough to make a diagnosis). However, even if symptoms do not meet diagnostic criteria, diagnoses may be made using Not Otherwise Specified (NOS) categories, if symptoms cause a clinically significant level of impairment of life functioning (Rapoport & Ismond, 1996). These diagnostic decisions require advanced clinical skills that can not be replaced by computer-generated interviews or by even the best designed standardized instruments.

Unfortunately, what is supposed to occur in clinical interviews and what actually takes place are often two very different things. Professionals may experience boredom or an inflated sense of self-competence (e.g., "I knew that child had an eating disorder as soon as I set eyes on her!"). Of course, professionals want to generate possible hypotheses as soon as they first begin to collect information about children; however, professionals shouldn't bring premature foreclosure to their investigations simply because they are convinced that they have found the right answer. Experience should tell professionals that their initial hypotheses are not always correct, and that what they are seeing may be explained by something unanticipated.

Professionals can misdiagnose if they limit their areas of investigation, influence children and parental responses, or conveniently ignore information that doesn't fit with their hypotheses. In their thorough and scathing indictment of what they call "The Real World of Child Interrogations" in the field of child sexual abuse, Underwager and Wakefield (1990) described in great detail the many ways that interviews with children go awry; they did so using examples of actual interview dialogue with additional support from the research literature. The same indictment could easily apply to diagnostic and clinical interviewing.

Pitfalls of Interviewing Children About Their Symptoms

Professionals must consider the impact of language on children's self-reports during diagnostic interviews and must be prepared to use the youngsters' words for symptoms, thoughts, and behaviors. For example, when asked, "Do you worry?" children might answer "No." But if asked, "Do you get nervous?" or "Are you afraid?" they may make a positive endorsement. MLZ has found that children will often have difficulty describing feelings that may in fact be intense or debilitating.

For example, a 10 year-old boy who was found to have symptoms consistent with a diagnosis of dysthymia was unable in the interview to provide examples of times when he had felt sad, or even to recognize that he ever felt that way. In his case, sadness had become such an ingrained part of his existence that he was not able to discriminate it as a distinct emotion (a figure-ground problem). A similar case involved a child who had been severely depressed for several years. She was no longer able to remember a time when she had not felt sad and hopeless. Sometimes, children deny or dissociate from their feelings and will adamantly state that they feel fine, even when evidence points to the contrary. In some circumstances, usually in circumstances of severe abuse and deprivation, children have been taught to deny any expression of emotion. Sometimes, children will have an awareness of their feelings but will find it unacceptable to endorse certain negative emotions. For example, when asked about his feelings of anger, a 10-year-old boy stated unequivocally, "I never get angry." However, later on in the interview, he declared, "I get upset often. Like when I have homework . . . . I take my bag and throw it and I bang my bed." Although he refused to use the word "anger" to describe his feelings, he was willing to talk about "becoming upset" and the way that that affected him.

In situations where children's vocabulary for emotions is in doubt, professionals may want to invest some time in asking children to think of all the feelings that they have experienced. Sometimes, showing children photographs of people (from magazines and books) or line drawings of facial expressions can help to elicit their words for certain feelings. When trying to elicit reports of negative feelings, professionals are advised to say, "Most children experience negative emotions like anger. Tell me about some times when you may have felt angry."

When investigating problems, possible underlying causes of complaints can be explored. For example, if children have difficulty sleeping, the specific manifestations of this problem can be investigated (e.g., difficulty falling asleep, staying asleep, or waking up). The quality of sleep (e.g., restless, shallow, bedding churned up), fears, nightmares, night terrors, and sleepwalking can also be examined. Once the problem has been clarified, alternate explanations for the sleep problem (e.g., siblings bothering them, sexual abuse, loud parties by neighbors) can be pursued. MLZ once interviewed a boy who experienced difficulty concentrating and remaining awake during school. He lived in a two-bedroom apartment with his mother, grandmother, uncle, and two siblings. Since he was the eldest, he was required to sleep in the living room in a sleeping bag, which meant he had to wait until the adults went to bed before he could fall sleep.

History-Taking During the Clinical Interview

Conducting an assessment and making a successful diagnosis require a thorough and detailed history-taking, particularly when working with children. Methods of history-taking typically involve the use of questionnaires and interviews. When collecting information to assist in making a diagnosis, multiple informants should be used including parents, guardians, caregivers, and the child's self-reports. Much significant information will not be gleaned unless informants are asked highly specific questions. The following list provides an overview of key areas within which to seek information.

Child's Personal History

- Biological (Genetic, Prenatal, Perinatal, Postpartum, & Neonatal)

- Medical and Health

- Temperament and Attachment

- Developmental (Cognitive, Speech/Language, Fine & Gross Motor, Social and Emotional, Sleeping, Eating, Toileting, and Self-Help Skills)

- Abuse (Physical, Sexual, Emotional, Neglect)

- Childcare (Daycare, Babysitter, Nanny)

- School and Academic

- Professional, Agency, Criminal, or Legal Involvement

- Relevant Treatment (Therapy, Medication)

Family History

- Custody and Care (Adopted, Blended, Gay/Lesbian, Single Parent, Grandparent, Extended)

- Parenting Styles and Practices

- Cultural Background (Mixed or Uni-Ethnic, Immigration Status, Family Ties)

- Social (Education, Occupation, Socioeconomic Status, Movement or Transitions)

- Religious/Spiritual Affiliations (Traditional, Nontraditional, Cult, Personal-Individual)

- Exceptional Physical or Psychological Circumstances (Victim of Crime, War, or Natural Disaster, Witness to Violence or Crime, Accident, Family Death or Loss)

- Birth Order and Sibling Relationships

- Mother's Prenatal State (Drug and Alcohol, Smoking, Medications, Mental Disorder, High Blood Pressure, Other Medical Conditions)

- Medical and Mental Health History of Other Family Members

- General Circumstances (Couple Relationship, Past Abuse, Emotional Tone)

Present Situation Including Status and Stressors

- Symptoms and Presenting Problem

- Living Arrangements (Who, Where, When)

- School and Educational

- Health and Medical

- Financial and Occupational

- Family

- Friends and Peers

- Other Support Systems

- Mental Status

- Broader Systemic Involvement (Social Service, Children's Aide, Community Agency, Mental Health, Medical, Church, Lay Counselors, Support Groups)

Adapted from Seymour, Torssonen, & Zwiers, 1996. Used by permission.

Many detailed guidelines are available when obtaining historical data and during careful observation (e.g., AACAP, 1997; Billings & Stoeckle, 1989; Gardner, 1993; Holmes, 1988).

Mental Status Examination

The child mental status examination emerged as an attempt to organize the evaluation of children's mental functioning (Goodman & Sours, 1994). These authors described the mental status examination as an evaluation of current psychiatric and broad neurological functioning during the diagnostic process. They advised that it should accompany the collection of a developmental history and history of social/family functioning in the context of the presenting problem. Their proposed schema for the mental status examination of children included a broad neurological screen (sensory, motor, reflex, and nerve function) and a general assessment of functioning including:

1. Size and General Appearance

2. Motility Level

3. Coordination and Motor Skills

4. Speech and Language

5. Cognitive Functioning (Intelligence, Memory)

6. Modes of Thinking and Perception (Self-Esteem, Odd or Unusual Perceptions)

7. Emotional Reactions

8. Manner of Relating

9. Fantasies and Dreams

10. Character of Play

Although their model contained many psychodynamic references that may seem out of place today, Goodman and Sours (1994) offered a developmentally based framework for assessment of current functioning and provided a host of specific questions to help professionals inquire about personal knowledge, self-image and interests/hobbies; home, school, and social interactions; wishes, dreams, ambitions, fears and anxieties; understanding of the presenting concern; and attitude toward the interview.

Benham (as cited in AACAP, 1997) has proposed a preliminary model for an infant and toddler mental status examination. Observationally based, this model includes the appraisal of:

1. Appearance

2. Reaction to the Situation

3. Self-Regulation

4. Motor Function

5. Speech and Language

6. Thought

7. Affect and Mood

8. Play

9. Broad Cognitive Functioning

10. Social Relatedness

This chapter addressed the use of the clinical interview in professional diagnostic practice, including structured, semi-structured, and unstructured methods. Available literature on child and adult sources of data has been reviewed, including support for specific sources in various circumstances. The emerging consensus is that information should be collected from as many sources as possible (adult and child) using a range of methods (questionnaires, interviews) in order that the information may be amalgamated and triangulated. Finally, several models for the process of history-taking and evaluation of mental status in children were presented.

EPILOGUE

The intention of this book was to synthesize, consolidate, and contribute to the literature regarding child-focused interviews. Despite the number of professionals who work with children, the critical elements that compromise the interview process have received little attention. It can be assumed, therefore, that without guiding principles and recommendations, professionals merely attempt to modify adult-oriented formats to fit children or expect children to adjust to adult-oriented interview formats. Upon closer examination, however, transitioning and adapting to a child-focused context is not as straightforward as one might expect. The inability or reluctance of children to articulate and/or express their apprehensions, fears, or discomfort for example, underscores an important difference between children and adults. Consequently, in order for interviews to be productive and rewarding for children, professionals must ensure that the interview setting and agenda is appropriate for their young clients.

Despite the well-intended efforts of professionals to meet the needs of children, important distinctions must be drawn between adult-focused and child-focused interviews for obvious reasons. In our experience, minimal attention is given to these distinctions and as a result, both professionals and children experience frustration and inadvertently contribute to poor outcome. By appreciating the unique needs of children, the circumstances surrounding child-focused interviews, and the necessary knowledge and skills to conduct effective interviews, professionals can increase their awareness and sensitivity when interacting with children.

It is our sincere hope that this book has provided professionals with clarification, insight, and new ideas to advance the interview process and research with children.

References

Abramovitch, R., Freedman, J. L., Thoden, K., & Nikolich, C. (1991). Children's capacity to consent to participation in psychological research: Empirical findings. *Child Development, 62*(5),1100–1109.

Achenbach, T. M. (1982). *Developmental psychopathology* (2nd ed.). New York: Wiley.

Ackroyd, S., & Hughes, J. (1992). *Data collection in context* (2nd ed.). Essex, England: Longman.

Alberta Education, Special Education Services. (1986). *Review of issues in intelligence test use in Alberta schools.* Edmonton, Alberta: Author.

Alderson, P. (1990). *Children's consent to surgery.* Philadelphia: Open University.

Alderson, P. (1993). *Children's consent to surgery.* Philadelphia: Open University.

Alessi, N. E., & Magen, J. (1988). Comorbidity of other psychiatric disturbances in depressed, psychiatrically hospitalized children. *American Journal of Psychiatry, 145*(12), 1582–1584.

Amato, P. R., & Ochiltree, G. (1987). Interviewing children about their families: A note on data quality. *Journal of Marriage and the Family, 49*(3), 669–675.

American Academy of Child and Adolescent Psychiatry. (1997). Supplement. *Journal of the American Academy of Child and Adolescent Psychiatry, 36*(10).

American Academy of Child and Adolescent Psychiatry. (1997). Special section on ethical issues with children. *Journal of the American Academy of Child and Adolescent Psychiatry, 31*(3), 393–414.

American Psychological Association. (1985). *Standards for educational and psychological testing.* Washington, DC: Author.

American Psychological Association. (1986). *Guidelines for computer–based tests and interpretations.* Washington, DC: Author.

American Psychological Association. (1988). *Code of fair testing practices in education.* Washington, DC: Author.

American Psychological Association. (1994). Guidelines for child custody evaluations. *American Psychologist, 49*(7), 677–680.

Amundson, J., Stewart, K., & Valentine, L. (1993). Temptations of power and certainty. *Journal of Marital and Family Therapy, 19*(2), 111–132.

Anand, K. J. S., & Aynsley-Green, A. (1985). Metabolic and endocrine effects of surgical ligation of patent ductus arteriosus in the human preterm neonate: Are there implications for further improvement of postoperative outcome? *Modern Problems in Pediatrics, 23,* 143–157.

Anand, K. J. S., & Hickey, P. R. (1987). Pain and its effects in the human neonate and fetus. *New England Journal of Medicine, 317*(21), 1321–1329.

Anand, K. J. S., & Hickey, P. R. (1992). Halothane-morphine compared with high–dose sufentanil for anesthesia and postoperative analgesia in neonatal cardiac surgery. *New England Journal of Medicine, 326*(1), 1–9.

Angold, A., Cox, A., Prendergast, M., Rutter, M., & Simonoff, E. (1987). *The child and adolescent psychiatric assessment (CAPA).* Unpublished manuscript.

Armstrong, M. P. (1993). Ethics of research in children: A parent's perspective. In G. Koren (Ed.), *Textbook of ethics in pediatric research* (pp. 271–280). Malabar, FL: Krieger.

Astington, J. W. (1993). *The child's discovery of the mind.* Cambridge, MA: Harvard University.

Bagnato, S. J., & Neisworth, J. T. (1994). A national study of the social and treatment "invalidity" of intelligence testing for early intervention. *School Psychology Quarterly, 9*(2), 81–102.

Barenboim, C. (1981). The development of person perception in childhood and adolescence: From behavioral comparisons to psychological constructs to psychological comparisons. *Child Development, 52*(1), 129–144.

Barker, P. (1990). *Clinical interviews with children and adolescents.* New York: Norton.

Barnett, B. (1987). School psychology and children's rights. *School Psychology International, 8*(1), 1–10.

Basch, M. (1982). Behavioral and psychodynamic psychotherapies: Mutually exclusive or reinforcing? In P. L. Wachtel (Ed.), *Resistance: Psychodymanic and behavioral approaches* (pp. 187–203). New York: Plenum.

Baylis, F., & McBurney, C. (1993). *In the case of children: Paediatric ethics in a Canadian context.* Toronto, Ontario: The Hospital for Sick Children.

Beck, K. A., & Ogloff, R. P. (1995). Child abuse reporting in British Columbia: Psychologists' knowledge of and compliance with the reporting law. *Professional Psychology: Research and Practice, 26*(3), 245–251.

Becker, C. (1986). Interviewing in human science research. *Methods, 1,* 101–124.

Beekman, T. (1983). Human science as a dialogue with children. *Phenomenology + Pedagogy, 1*(1), 36–44.

Bell, C. J. (1986). Children as organ donors: Legal rights and ethical issues. *Health and Social Work, 11*(4), 291–300.

Bell–Dolan, D. J., Last, C. G., & Strauss, C. C. (1990). Symptoms of anxiety disorders in normal children. *Journal of the American Academy of Child and Adolescent Psychiatry, 29*(5), 759–765.

Bell–Dolan, D. J., & Wessler, A. E. (1994). Ethical administration of sociometric measures: Procedures in use and suggestions for improvement. *Professional Psychology: Research and Practice, 25*(1), 23–32.

Berg, B. L. (1989). A dramaturgical look at interviewing. In B. L. Berg (Ed.), *Qualitative research methods* (pp. 13–49). Boston: Allyn & Bacon.

Berg, I., & Fielding, D. (1979). An interview with a child to assess psychiatric disturbance: A note on its reliability and validity. *Journal of Abnormal Child Psychology, 7*(1), 83–89.

Bernard, J., & Goodyear, R. (1992). *Fundamentals of clinical supervision.* Boston: Allyn & Bacon.

Bernstein, B. E. (1982). Ignorance of the law is no excuse. In L. L' Abate & J. C. Hansen (Eds.), *Values, ethics, legalities and the family therapist. The family therapy collections* (pp. 87–102). Rockville, MD: Aspen.

Beyer, J. E., DeGood, D. E., Ashley, L. C., & Russell, G. A., (1983). Patterns of postoperative analgesic use with adults and children following cardiac surgery. *Pain, 17*(1), 71–81.

Bierman, K. L. (1983). Cognitive development and clinical interviews with children. In B. B. Lahey & A. E. Kazdin (Eds.), *Advances in clinical child psychology* (pp. 217–250). New York: Plenum.

Bierman, K. L., & Schwartz, L. A. (1986). Clinical child interviews: Approaches and developmental considerations. *Journal of Child and Adolescent Psychotherapy, 3*(4), 267–278.

Billings, J. A., & Stoeckle, J. D. (1989). *The clinical encounter: A guide to the medical interview and case presentation.* Chicago: Year Book Medical.

Bjorklund, D., & Muir, J. (1988). Children's development of free recall memory: Remembering on their own. *Annals of Child Development, 5*(4) 79–123.

Boggs, S. R., & Eyberg, S. A. (1990). Interview techniques and establishing rapport. In A. M. La Greca (Ed.), *Through the eyes of the child: Obtaining self–reports from children and adolescents* (pp. 85–108). Boston: Allyn & Bacon.

Bohannon III, J. N., & Symons, V. L. (1992). Flashbulb memories: Confidence, consistency, and quantity. In E. Winograd & U. Neisser (Eds.), *Affect and accuracy in recall: Studies of "flashbulb" memories* (pp. 65–91). New York: Cambridge University Press.

Boyd, G. A. (1976). *Developmental processes in the child's acquisition of syntax: Linguistics in the elementary school.* Itasca, IL: Peacock.

Boyle, M. H., Offord, D. R., Hofmann, H. G., Catlin, G. P., Byles, J. A., Cadman, D. T., Crawford, J. W., Links, P. S., Rae–Grant, N. I., & Szatmari, P. (1989). Ontario child health study: I. Methodology. *Archives of General Psychiatry, 44*(9), 826–831.

Boyle, M. H., Offord, D., Racine, Y., Fleming, J. E., Szatmari, P., & Sanford, M. (1993). Evaluation of the revised Ontario child health study scales. *Journal of Child Psychology and Psychiatry and Allied Disciplines, 34*(2), 189–213.

Bracken, B. A. (1987). Limitations of preschool instruments and standards for minimal levels of technical adequacy. *Journal of Psychoeducational Assessment, 5*(4), 313–326.

Bracken, B. A. (1994). Advocating for effective preschool assessment practices: A comment on Bagnato and Neisworth. *School Psychology Quarterly, 9*(2), 103–112.

Breslau, N. (1987). Inquiring about the bizarre: False positives in diagnostic interview schedule for children (DISC) ascertainment of obsessions, compulsions, and psychotic symptoms. *Journal of the American Academy of Child and Adolescent Psychiatry, 26*(5), 639–644.

Bretherton, I., Fritz, J., Zahn–Waxler, C., & Ridgeway, D. (1986). Learning to talk about emotions: A functionalist perspective. *Child Development, 57*(3), 529–548.

Brewer, T., & Faitak, M. T. (1989). Ethical guidelines for the inpatient psychiatric care of children. *Professional Psychology: Research and Practice, 20*(3), 142–147.

Briggs, C. L. (1984). Learning to ask: Native metacommunicative competence and the incompetence of fieldworkers. *Language in Society, 13*(1), 1–28.

Briggs, C. L. (1986). *Learning how to ask: A sociolinguistic appraisal of the role of the interview in social science research.* Cambridge, UK: Cambridge University Press.

Briggs, C. L. (1992). Mazes of meaning: How a child and a culture create each other. In W. A. Corsaro & P. J. Miller (Eds.), *New directions for child development: Interpretive approaches to children's socialization* (pp. 25–49). San Francisco: Jossey–Bass.

Brodzinsky, D. M. (1993). On the use and misuse of psychological testing in child custody evaluations. *Professional Psychology: Research and Practice, 24*(2), 213–219.

Broughton, J. (1978). Development of concepts of self, mind, reality, and knowledge. In W. Damon (Ed.), *Social cognition: New directions for child development, 1* (pp. 75–100). San Francisco: Jossey–Bass.

Brown, R. T., Dingle, A., & Landau, S. (1994). Overview of psychopharmacology in children and adolescents. *School Psychology Quarterly, 9*(1), 4–25.

Browning, P. C., & Hatch, J. A. (1995). Qualitative research in early childhood settings: A review. In J. A. Hatch (Ed.), *Qualitative research in early childhood settings* (pp. 99–114). Westport, CT: Praeger.

Bruner, J. S. (1977). Early social interaction and language acquisition. In H. R. Schaffer (Ed.), *Studies in mother–infant interaction* (pp. 271–289). London: Academic.

Bruner, J. S. (1990). *Acts of meaning.* Cambridge, MA: Harvard University Press.

Bussey, K. (1990, August). Adult influence on children's eyewitness reporting. In S. Ceci (Chair), *Do children lie? Narrowing the uncertainties.* Symposium conducted at the American Psychology and Law Society Biennial Meeting, Williamsburg, Virginia.

Campbell, B. A. (1981). Race–of–interviewer effects among southern adolescents. *Public Opinion Quarterly, 45*(2), 231–244.

Canadian Psychological Association. (1987). *Guidelines for educational and psychological testing.* Ottawa, Ontario: Author.

Canadian Psychological Association. (1991). *Canadian code of ethics for psychologists revised.* Ottawa, Ontario: Author.

Canadian Psychological Association. (1993). Ethical issues [special issue]. *Canadian Psychology, 34*(3).

Cantwell, D. P. (1996). Classification of child and adolescent psychopathology. *Journal of Child Psychology and Psychiatry and Allied Disciplines, 37*(1), 3–12.

Cantwell, D. P., Lewinsohn, P. M., Rohde, P., & Seeley, J. R. (1997). Correspondence between adolescent report and parent report of psychiatric diagnostic data. *Journal of the American Academy of Child and Adolescent Psychiatry, 36*(5), 610–619.

Carey, S. (1978). The child as world learner. In M. Halle, J. Bresman, & G. A. Miller (Eds.), *Linguistic theory and psychological reality* (pp. 264–293). Cambridge, MA: MIT Press.

Carey, S. (1985). *Conceptual change in childhood.* Cambridge, MA: MIT Press.

Caron, C., & Rutter, M. (1991). Comorbidity in child psychopathology: Concepts, issues and research strategies. *Journal of Child Psychology and Psychiatry and Allied Disciplines, 32*(7), 1063–1080.

Carroll, M. A., Schneider, H. G., & Wesley, G. R. (1985). *Ethics in the practice of psychology.* Englewood Cliffs, NJ: Prentice–Hall.

Cecchin, G., Lane, G., & Ray, W. (1992). *Irreverence: A strategy for therapists survival.* New York: Karnac Books.

Cecchin, G., Lane, G., & Ray, W. (1993). From strategizing to non–intervention: Toward irreverence in systemic practice. *Journal of Marital and Family Therapy, 19*(2), 125–136.

Ceci, S. J., & Crotteau Huffman, M. L. (1997). How suggestible are preschool children? Cognitive and social factors. *Journal of the Academy of Child and Adolescent Psychiatry, 36*(7), 948–958.

Ceci, S. J., Toglia, M. P., & Ross, D. F. (1987). *Children's eyewitness memory.* New York: Springer–Verlag.

Clement, D. B., Zartler, A. S., & Mulick, J. A. (1983). Ethical considerations for school psychologists planning for special needs children. *School Psychology Review, 12*(3), 131–143.

Cochran, L. R. (1980). Client evaluation in psychotherapy: The role of contrast and alignment. *Journal of Psychiatric Treatment and Evaluation, 2*(1), 135–146.

Colaizzi, P. (1978). Psychological research as the phenomenologist views it. In R. Valle & M. King (Eds.), *Existential–phenomenological alternatives for psychology* (pp. 48–67). London: Oxford University Press.

Cole, C. B., & Loftus, E. F. (1987). The memory of children. In M. Ceci, M. Toglia, & D. Ross (Eds.), *Children's eyewitness memory* (pp. 178–208). New York: Springer.

Coles, R. (1986). *The moral life of children.* Boston: Houghton Mifflin.

Coles, R. (1990). *The spiritual life of children.* Boston: Houghton Mifflin.

College of Psychologists of British Columbia. (1985). *Ethical standards of psychologists.* Vancouver, BC: Author.

College of Psychologists of British Columbia. (1996). *Chronicle, 6.* Vancouver, BC: Author.

Coloroso, B. (1987). *Discipline: Winning at teaching* (rev. ed.). Littleton, CO; Kids Are Worth It.

Coloroso, B. (1994). *Kids are worth it! Giving your child the gift of inner discipline.* Toronto, Ontario: Somerville House.

Copeland, W., Birmingham, C., De La Cruz, E., & Lewin, B. (1993). The reflective practitioner in teaching: Toward a research agenda. *Teaching and Teacher Education, 9*(4), 347–359.

Cordoba, O. A., Wilson, W., & Orten, J. D. (1983). Psychotropic medications for children. *Social Work, 28*(6), 448–453.

Corey, G., Corey, M., & Callahan, P. (1993). *Issues and ethics in the helping professions* (4th ed.). Pacific Grove, CA: Brooks/Cole.

Corey, G., Corey, M., & Callahan, P. (1998). *Issues and ethics in the helping professions* (5th ed.). Pacific Grove, CA: Brooks/Cole.

Costello, A. J., Edelbrock, L. S., Dulcan, M. K., Kalas, R., & Klaric, S. H. (1984). *Report on the NIMH diagnostic interview schedule for children (DISC).* Washington, DC: National Institute of Mental Health.

Cowan, P. A. (1988). Developmental psychopathology: A nine–cell map of the territory. In F. D. Nannis & P. A. Cowan (eds.), *Developmental psychopathology and its treatment: New directions for child development (No. 39*; pp. 5–29). San Francisco: Jossey–Bass.

Coyne, J., Wortman, C., & Lehman, D. (1988). The other side of support: Emotional overinvolvement and miscarried helping. In B. H. Gottlieb (Ed.), *Marshalling social support* (pp. 305–330). Thousand Oaks, CA: Sage.

Crowhurst, B., & Dobson, K. S. (1993). Informed consent: Legal issues and applications to clinical practice. *Canadian Psychology, 34*(3), 329–346.

Crum, T. F. (1987). *The magic of conflict.* New York: Simon & Schuster.

Dahlquist, L. M. (1990). Obtaining child reports in health care settings. In A. M. La Greca (Ed.), *Through the eyes of the child: Obtaining self–reports from children and adolescents* (pp. 395–439). Boston: Allyn & Bacon.

Damon, W. (1977). *The social world of the child.* San Francisco: Jossey–Bass.

Damon, W. (1983). *Social and personality development: Infancy through adolescence.* New York: Norton.

Damon, W., & Hart, D. (1982). The development of self–understanding from infancy through adolescence. *Child Development, 53*(4), 841–864.

DeMers, S. T. (1994). Legal and ethical issues in school psychologists' participation in psychopharmacological interventions with children. *School Psychology Quarterly, 9*(1), 41–52.

Dewey, J. (1933). *How we think.* Chicago: Regnery.

Diamond, C. T. P. (1991). *Teacher education as transformation: A psychological perspective.* Bristol, PA: Open University.

Dickson, W. P. (1981). *Children's oral communication skills.* New York: Academic.

Dinkmeyer, D., & Dreikurs, R. (1963). *Encouraging children to learn: The encouragement process.* Englewood Cliffs, NJ: Prentice–Hall.

Doll, B. (1996). Prevalance of psychiatric disorders in children and youth: An agenda for advocacy by school psychology. *School Psychology Quarterly, 11*(1), 20–47.

Donaldson, M. (1978). *Children's minds.* Edinburgh, Scotland: Fontana.

Dreikurs, R. (1968). *Psychology in the classroom: A manual for teachers* (2nd ed.). New York: Harper & Row.

Dreikurs, R. (1972). *Coping with children's misbehavior: A parent's guide.* New York: Hawthorn.

Dreikurs, R., Grunwald, B. B., & Pepper, F. C. (1971). *Maintaining sanity in the classroom: Illustrated teaching techniques.* New York: Harper & Row.

Dreikurs, R., & Soltz, V. (1964). *Children: The challenge.* New York: Hawthorn/ Dutton.

Dunn, J., Bretherton, I., & Munn, P. (1987). Conversations about feeling states between mothers and their young children. *Developmental Psychology, 23*(1), 132–139.

Dunn, J., & Kendrick, C. (1982). *Siblings: Love, envy and understanding.* Cambridge, MA: Harvard University Press.

Dunne, J. E. (Ed.). (1997). 1997 supplement to the *Journal of the American Academy of Child and Adolescent Psychiatry. Journal of the American Academy of Child and Adolescent Psychiatry, 36*(10).

DuPaul, G. J., & Kyle, K. E. (1995). Pediatric pharmacology and psychopharmacology. In M. C. Roberts (Ed.), *Handbook of pediatric psychology* (pp. 741–758). New York: Guilford.

Dupont, H. (1994). *Emotional development, theory and applications: A neo–Piagetian perspective.* Westport, CT: Praeger.

Dyson, S. (1986). Professionals, mentally handicapped children, and confidential files. *Disability, Handicap and Society, 1*(1), 73–87.

Eckman, P. (Ed.). (1989). *Why kids lie: How parents can encourage truthfulness.* New York: Penguin.

Edelbrock, C. S., Costello, A. J., Dulcan, M. K., Conover, N. C., & Kalas, R. (1986). Parent–child agreement on child psychiatric symptoms assessed via structured interview. *Journal of Child Psychology and Psychiatry and Allied Disciplines, 27*(2), 181–190.

Egan, G. (1994). *The skilled helper: A problem–management approach to helping* (5th ed.). Pacific Grove, CA: Brooks/Cole.

Eland, J. M., & Anderson, J. E. (1977). The experience of pain in children. In A. Jacx (Ed.), *Pain: A sourcebook for nurses and other professionals* (pp. 453–473). Boston: Little, Brown.

Elrod, L. D. (1996). *Child custody: Practice and procedure.* Deerfield, IL: Clark, Boardman, Callaghan.

Erickson, E. (1963). *Childhood and society.* New York: Norton.

Feeney, S., Christensen, D., & Moravcik, E. (1983). *Who am I in the lives of children? An introduction to teaching young children* (2nd ed.). Columbus, OH: Merrill.

Feldman, C. F. (1992). The new theory of theory of mind. *Human Development, 35*(2), 107–117.

Fisher, C. B. (1994). Reporting and referring research participants: Ethical challenges for investigators studying children and youth. *Ethics and Behavior, 4*(2), 87–95.

Fisher, P., Shaffer, D., Piacentini, J., Lapkin, J., Wicks, J., & Rojas, M. (1991). *Completion of revisions of the NIMH diagnostic interview schedule for children (DISC–2).* Washington, DC: National Institute of Mental Health.

Fivush, R. (1993). Developmental perspectives on autobiographical recall. In G. S. Goodman & B. L. Bottoms (Eds.), *Child victims, child witnesses: Understanding and improving testimony* (pp. 1–24). New York: Guilford.

Fivush, R., & Hamond, N. R. (1990). Autobiographical memory across the preschool years. In R. Fivush & J. A. Hudson (Eds.), *Knowing and remembering in young children* (pp. 223–248). Cambridge, UK: Cambridge University Press.

Fivush, R., Hamond, N. R., Harsch, N., Singer, N., & Wolf, A. (1991). Content and consistency in early autobiographical recall. *Discourse Processes, 14*(3), 373–388.

Flanery R. C. (1990). Methodological and psychometric considerations in child reports. In A. M. La Greca (Ed.), *Through the eyes of the child: Obtaining self–reports from children and adolescents* (pp. 57–82). Boston: Allyn & Bacon.

Flin, R., & Boon, J. (1989). The child witness in court. In H. Blagg, J. A. Hughes, & C. Wattam (Eds.), *Child sexual abuse: Listening, hearing and validating the experiences of children* (pp. 122–137). London: Longman.

Fogelman, E, & Hogman, F. (1994). A follow–up study: Child survivors of the Nazi holocaust reflect on being interviewed. In J. S. Kestenberg & E. Fogelman (Eds.), *Children during the Nazi reign: Psychological perspective on the interview process* (pp. 73–80). Westport, CT: Praeger.

Fontana, A., & Frey, J. H. (1994). Interviewing: The art of science. In N. Denin & Y. Lincoln (Eds.), *Handbook of qualitative research* (pp. 361–375). Thousand Oaks, CA: Sage.

Foreman, M. (1996). Access to psychological test scores: *Chronicle, 6.* Vancouver, BC: College of Psychologists.

Garbarino, J., & Stott, F. M. (1992). *What children can tell us: Eliciting, interpreting, and evaluating critical information from children.* San Francisco: Jossey–Bass.

Gardner, R. A. (1971). *Therapeutic communication with children: The mutual storytelling technique.* New York: Science House.

Gardner, R. A. (1993). *Child psychotherapy: The initial screening and the intensive diagnostic evaluation.* Northvale, NJ: Aronson.

Geiselman, R. E., Saywitz, K. J., & Bornstein, G. K. (1993). Effects of cognitive questioning techniques on children's recall performance. In G. S. Goodman & B. L. Bottoms (Eds.), *Child victims, child witnesses: Understanding and improving testimony* (pp. 71–93). New York: Guilford.

Gilligan, C. (1982). *In a different voice.* Cambridge, MA: Harvard University Press.

Ginsburg, H. P. (1997). *Entering the child's mind: The clinical interview in psychological research and practice.* Cambridge, UK: Cambridge University Press.

Glasgow, D. (1989). Play-based investigative assessment of children who may have been sexually abused. In H. Blagg, J. A. Hughes, & C. Wattam (Eds.), *Child sexual abuse: Listening, hearing and validating the experiences of children* (pp. 138–151). London: Longman.

Glasser, W. (1969). *Schools without failure.* New York: Harper & Row.

Glasser, W. (1986). *Control theory in the classroom.* New York: Harper & Row.

Glasser, W. (1990). *The quality school: Managing students without coercion.* New York: Harper & Row.

Glenn, C. M. (1980). Ethical issues in the practice of child psychotherapy. *Professional Psychotherapy, 11*(4), 613–619.

Goldberg, S. (1993). Some costs and benefits of psychological research in pediatric settings. In G. Koren (Ed.), *Textbook of ethics in pediatric research* (pp. 63–73). Malabar, FL: Krieger.

Goldman, J., L'Engle Stein, C., & Guerry, S. (1983). *Psychological methods of child assessment.* New York: Brunner/Mazel.

Goodman, G. S., & Reed, R. (1986). Age differences in eyewitness testimony. *Law and Human Behavior, 10*(4), 317–322.

Goodman, G. S., Rudy, L., Bottoms, B. L., & Aman, C. (1990). Children's concerns and memory: Ecological issues in the study of children's eye-witness testimony. In R. Fivush & J. A. Hudson (Eds.), *Knowing and remembering in young children* (pp. 249–284). New York: Cambridge University Press.

Goodman, G. S., & Tobey, A. E. (1994). Ethical issues in child witness research. *Child Abuse and Neglect, 18*(3), 290–293.

Goodman, J. D., & Sours, J. A. (1994). *The child mental status examination.* Northvale, NJ: Aronson.

Goodman, R. (1997). The strengths and difficulties questionnaire: A research note. *Journal of Child Psychology and Psychiatry and Allied Disciplines, 38*(5), 581–586.

Goodwin, J, Sahd, D, & Rada, T. (1982). False accusations and false denials of incest: Clinical myths and clinical realities. In J. Goodwin (Ed.), *Sexual abuse: Incest victims and their families* (pp. 17–26). London: John Wright.

Graham, S., & Weiner, B. (1991). Testing judgments about attribution-emotion-action linkages: A lifespan approach. *Social Cognition, 9*(3), 254–276.

Graue, M. E., & Walsh, D. J. (1995). Children in context: Interpreting the here and now of children's lives. In J. A. Hatch (Ed.), *Qualitative research in early childhood settings* (pp. 135–154). Westport, CT: Praeger.

Greenspan, S. I., & Greenspan, N. T. (1991). *The clinical interview of the child* (2nd ed.). Washington, DC: American Psychiatric Association.

Grodin, M. A., & Glantz, L. H. (Eds.). (1994). *Children as research subjects: Science, ethics, and law.* New York: Oxford University Press.

Gustafson, K. E., McNamara, J. R., & Jensen, J. A. (1994). Parents' informed consent decisions regarding psychotherapy for their children: Consideration of therapeutic risks and benefits. *Professional Psychology: Research and Practice, 25*(1), 16–22.

Gutterman, E. M., O'Brien, M. D., & Young, J. G. (1987). Structured diagnostic interviews for children and adolescents: Current status and future directions. *Journal of the American Academy of Child and Adolescent Psychiatry, 26*(5), 621–630.

Halliday, L. (1986). *Sexual abuse: Interviewing techniques for police and other professionals.* Campbell River, BC: Ptarmigan.

Hammond, M., Howarth, J., & Keat, R. (1991). *Understanding phenomenology.* Malden, MA: Blackwell.

Hamond, N. R., & Fivush, R. (1991). Memories of Mickey Mouse: Young children recount their trip to Disneyworld. *Cognitive Development, 6*(4), 433–448.

Hansen, J., Stevic, R., & Warner, R. (1977). *Counseling: Theory and practice* (2nd ed.). Boston: Allyn & Bacon.

Harris, P. L. (1989). *Children and emotion: The development of psychological understanding.* New York: Basil Blackwell.

Harter, S. (1986). Cognitive-developmental processes in the integration of concepts about emotions and the self. *Social Cognition, 4*(2), 119–151.

Harter, S., & Whitesell, N. R., (1989). Developmental changes in children's understanding of single, multiple, and blended emotion concepts. In C. Saarni & P. L. Harris (Eds.), *Children's understanding of emotion* (pp. 81–116). Cambridge, UK: Cambridge University Press.

Hatch, J. A. (1990). Young children as informants in classroom studies. *Early Childhood Research Quarterly, 5*(2), 251–264.

Hatch, J. A. (1995). Studying childhood as a cultural intervention: A rationale and framework. In J. A. Hatch (Ed.), *Qualitative research in early childhood settings* (pp. 117–133). Westport, CT: Praeger.

Haugaard, J. J., & Crosby, C. (1989). *Children's definitions of the truth and their competency as witnesses in legal proceedings.* Paper presented at the Southeastern Psychological Association Conference, Washington, DC.

Haverkamp, B. E. (1995). Teaching ethics: Linking abstract principles to actual practice. In W. E. Schulz (Ed.), *Counselling ethics casebook* (pp. 166–170). Ottawa, Ontario: Canadian Guidance and Counselling Association.

Haverkamp, B. E., & Daniluk, J. C. (1993). Child sexual abuse: Ethical issues for the family therapist. *Family Relations, 42*(2), 134–139.

Hazel, N. (1995). Elicitation techniques with young people. *Social Research Update, 12*. Available on–line: http://www.soc.surrey.ac.uk/sru/SRU12.html

Heckhausen, J. (1988). Becoming aware of one's competence in the second year: Developmental progression within the mother–child dyad. *Journal of Behavioral Development, 11*(3), 305–326.

Hendrix, D. H. (1991). Ethics and intrafamily confidentiality in counseling with children. *Journal of Mental Health Counseling, 13*(3), 323–333.

Henson–Matthews, C., & Marshal, L. (1988). Self–monitoring and intake interviewer's therapeutic orientations. *Professional Psychology: Research and Practice, 19*(4), 433–435.

Hepworth, D. H., & Larsen, J. A. (1993). *Direct social work practice: Theory and skills* (4th ed.). Pacific Grove, CA: Brooks/Cole.

Herjanic, B., Herjanic, M., Brown, F., & Wheatt, T. (1975). Are children reliable reporters? *Journal of Abnormal Child Psychology, 3*(1), 41–48.

Hesson, K., Bakal, L., & Dobson, K. S. (1993). Legal and ethical issues concerning children's rights of consent. *Canadian Psychology, 34*(3), 317–328.

Hoagwood, K. (1994). The certificate of confidentiality at the national institute of mental health: Discretionary considerations in its applicability in research on child and adolescent mental disorders. *Ethics and Behavior, 4*(2), 123–131.

Hodges, K. (1993). Interviewing. In T. Ollendick & M. Hersen (Eds.), *Handbook of child and adolescent assessment* (pp. 65–81). Boston: Allyn & Bacon.

Hodges, K. (1994). Debate and argument: Reply to David Shaffer: Structured interviews for assessing children. *Journal of Child Psychology and Psychiatry and Allied Disciplines, 35*(4), 785–787.

Hodges, K., & Cools, J. N. (1990). Structured diagnostic interviews. In A. M. La Greca (Ed.), *Through the eyes of the child: Obtaining self–reports from children and adolescents* (pp. 109–149). Boston: Allyn & Bacon.

Hodges, K., Kline, J., Fitch, P., McKnew, D., & Cytryn, L. (1981). The child assessment schedules: A diagnostic interview for research and clinical use. *Catalog of Selected Documents in Psychology, 11,* 56.

Hodges, K., Kline, J., Stern, L., Cytryn, L., & McKnew, D. (1982). The development of a child assessment interview for research and clinical use. *Journal of Abnormal Child Psychology, 10*(2), 173–189.

Holmes, J. M. (1988). History and observations. In R. G. Rudel, J. M. Holmes, & J. R. Pardes (Eds.), *Assessment of developmental learning disorders* (pp. 144–165). New York: Basic Books.

Hudson, J. A., & Fivush, R. (1987). *As time goes by: Sixth graders remember a kindergarten experience.* Emery Cognition Project Report #13. Atlanta: Emery University.

Huey, W. C., & Remley Jr., T. P. (1988). *Ethical and legal issues in school counseling.* Alexandria, VA: American School Counselor Association.

Hughes, J. N. (1989). The child interview. *School Psychology Review, 18*(2), 247–259.

Hughes, J. N., & Baker, D. B. (1990). *The clinical child interview.* New York: Guilford.

Hunter, R., & Yuille, J. C. (1990). A coordinated approach to interviewing in child sexual abuse investigations. *Canada's Mental Health, 38*(2/3), 14–8.

Huxley, E. (1982). *The flame trees of Thica: Memories of an African childhood.* London: Chatto & Windus.

Izard, C. E., Huebner, R. R., Resser, D., McGiness, G. C., & Dougherty, L. M. (1980). The infant's ability to produce discrete emotional expressions. *Developmental Psychology, 16*(2), 132–140.

Jackman Cram, S., & Dobson, K. S. (1993). Confidentiality: Ethical and legal aspects for Canadian psychologists. *Canadian Psychology, 34*(3), 347–363.

Jennings, K. D. (1993, March). *Developmental changes in toddlers' social orientation and affect during mastery play.* Paper presented at the biennial meeting of the Society for Research in Child Development, New Orleans.

Johnson, H. C., Cournoyer, D. E., & Bond, B. M. (1995). Professional ethics as consumers: How well are we doing? *Families in Society: The Journal of Contemporary Human Services, 76*(7), 408–421.

Johnson, M. K., & Foley, M. A. (1984). Differentiating fact from fantasy: The reliability of children's memory. *Journal of Social Issues, 40*(2), 33–50.

Joint Advisory Committee. (1993). *Principles for fair student assessment practices for education in Canada.* Edmonton, Alberta: Centre for Research in Applied Measurement and Evaluation.

Jones, D. P. H. (1992). *Interviewing the sexually abused child: Investigation of suspected abuse.* London: Gaskell.

Jurich, A., & Russell, C. S. (1985). The conflict between the ethics of therapy and outcome research in family therapy. In L. L. Anderson (Vol. Ed.), R. F. Levant (Consulting Ed.), & J. Hansen (Series Ed.), *Integrating research and clinical practice. The family therapy collections* (pp. 90–97). Rockville, MD: Aspen.

Kagan, J. (1984). *The nature of the child.* New York, NY: Basic Books.

Kahn, C. (1994). Interviewing: The crossroad between research and therapy. In J. S. Kestenberg & E. Fogelman (Eds.), *Children during the Nazi reign: Psychological perspective on the interview process* (pp. 91–108). Westport, CT: Praeger.

Kanfer, R., Eyberg, S. M., & Krahn, G. L. (1983). Interviewing strategies in child assessment. In C. E. Walker & M. C. Roberts (Eds.), *Handbook of clinical child psychology* (pp. 95–108). New York: Wiley.

Kashani, J. H., & Orvaschel, H. A. (1990). A community study of anxiety in children and adolescents. *American Journal of Psychiatry, 147*(3), 313–318.

Kasius, M. C., Ferdinand, R. F., Van den Berg, H., & Verhulst, F. C. (1997). Associations between different diagnostic approaches for child and adolescent psychopathology. *Journal of Child Psychology and Psychiatry and Allied Disciplines, 38*(6), 625–632.

Kauffman, J. M. (1984). *Saving children in the age of big brother: Moral and ethical issues in the identification of deviance.* Paper presented at the Midwest Symposium for Leadership in Behavior Disorders, Kansas City, MO.

Kaufman, J., Birmaher, B., Brent, D., Rao, U., Flynn, C., Moreci, P., Williamson, D., & Ryan, N. (1997). Schedule for affective disorders and schizophrenia for school-age children—present and lifetime version (K–SADS–PL): Initial reliability and validity data. *Journal of the American Academy of Child and Adolescent Psychiatry, 36*(7), 980–988.

Kazdin, A. E. (1990). Assessment of childhood depression. In A. M. La Greca (Ed.), *Through the eyes of the child: Obtaining self-reports from children and adolescents* (pp. 189–233). Boston: Allyn & Bacon.

Kazdin, A. E., French, N. H., Unis, A. S., & Esveldt-Dawson, K. (1983). Assessment of childhood depression: Correspondence of child and parent ratings. *Journal of the American Academy of Child Psychiatry, 22*(1), 157–164.

Kinard, E. M. (1985). Ethical issues in research with abused children. *Child Abuse and Neglect, 9*(3), 301–311.

King, M., & Yuille, J. (1987). Suggestibility and the child witness. In M. Ceci, M. Toglia, & D. Ross (Eds.), *Children's eyewitness memory* (pp. 24–35). New York: Springer.

Kitayama, S., Markus, H. R., & Matsumoto, H. (1995). Culture, self, and emotion: A cultural perspective on "self–conscious" emotions. In J. P. Tagney & K. W. Fischer (Eds.), *Self-conscious emotions: The psychology of shame, guilt, embarrassment, and pride* (pp. 439–464). New York: Guilford.

Kohlberg, L. (1969). Stage and sequence: The cognitive–developmental approach to socialization. In D. A. Goslin (Ed.), *Handbook of socialization theory and research*. Chicago: Rand McNally.

Koocher, G. P. (1993). Ethical issues in the psychological assessment of children. In H. Orvaschel, P. Ambrosini, & H. Rabinovich (Eds.), *Handbook of child and adolescent assessment* (pp. 51–61). Boston: Allyn & Bacon.

Koocher, G. P., & Keith–Spiegel, P. (1994). Scientific issues in psychosocial and educational research with children. In M. A. Grodin & L. H. Glantz (Eds.), *Children as research subjects: Science, ethics, and law* (pp. 47–80). New York: Oxford University Press.

Koocher, G. P., & Keith–Spiegel, P. C. (1990). *Children, ethics, and the law: Professional issues and cases*. Lincoln, NB: University of Nebraska Press.

Koren, G. (Ed.). (1993). *Textbook of ethics in pediatric research*. Malabar, FL: Krieger.

Kovacs, M. (1983). *The interview schedule for children (ISC): Interrater and parent–child agreement*. Unpublished manuscript.

Kratochwill, T. R. (1994). Psychopharmacology for children and adolescents: Commentary on current issues and future challenges. *School Psychology Quarterly, 9*(1), 53–59.

Kurdek, L. A., & Berg, B. (1987). Children's beliefs about parental divorce scale: Characteristics and concurrent validity. *Journal of Consulting and Clinical Psychology, 55,* 712–718.

Kurpius, D., Baker, R., & Thomas, I. (1977). *Supervision of applied training: A comparative review*. Westport, CT: Greenwood Press.

Kvale, S. (1979). The qualitative research interview: A phenomenological and a hermeneutical mode of understanding. *Journal of Phenomenological Psychology, 14*(2), 171–196.

La Greca, A. M. (1983). Interviewing and behavioral observations. In C. E. Walker & M. C. Roberts (Eds.), *Handbook of clinical child psychology* (pp. 109–131). New York: Wiley.

La Greca, A. M. (1990). Issues and perspectives on the child assessment process. In A. M. La Greca (Ed.), *Through the eyes of the child: Obtaining self-reports from children and adolescents* (pp. 3–17). Boston: Allyn & Bacon.

Langer, D. H. (1985). Child psychiatry and the law: Children's legal rights as research subjects. *Journal of the American Academy of Child Psychiatry, 24*(5), 653–662.

Leary, J. B., & Boscardin, M. L. (1992). Ethics and efficacy of verbal testing of nonverbal children: A case study. *Remedial and Special Education, 13*(4), 52–61.

Lefrancois, G. R. (1990). *The lifespan* (3rd ed.). Belmont, CA: Wadsworth.

Lemaire, F., D'Herouville, A., Piquard-Gauvain, A., & Flamant, F. (1987, August). *Painful procedures in children: Pain evaluation by the child himself.* Paper presented at the World Congress on Pain, Hamburg, Germany.

Lepore, S. J., & Sesco, B. (1994). Distorting children's reports and interpretations of events through suggestion. *Journal of Applied Psychology, 79*(1), 108–120.

Lessing, E. E., Williams, V., & Gil, E. (1982). A cluster-analytically derived typology: Feasible alternative to clinical diagnostic classification of children? *Journal of Abnormal Child Psychology, 10*(4), 451–482.

Levine, M., Anderson, E., Ferretti, L., & Steinberg, K. (1993). Legal and ethical issues affecting clinical child psychology. In T. H. Ollendick & R. J. Prinz (Eds.), *Advances in clinical child psychology* (*Vol. 15,* pp. 81–120). New York: Plenum.

Lewinsohn, P. M., Hops, H., Roberts, R. E., Seeley, J. R., & Andrews, J. A. (1993). Adolescent psychopathology: I. Prevalance and incidence of depression and other DSM–III–R disorders in high school students. *Journal of Abnormal Psychology, 102*(1), 133–144.

Lewis, J. (1991). *Swimming upstream: Teaching and learning psychotherapy in a biological era.* New York: Brunner/Mazel.

Lewis, M. (1981). Comments on some ethical, legal, and clinical issues affecting consent in treatment, organ transplants, and research in children. *Journal of the American Academy of Child and Adolescent Psychiatry, 20*(3), 581–596.

Lewis, M., & Brooks-Gunn, J. (1979). *Social cognition and the acquisition of self.* New York: Plenum.

Lewis, M., Sullivan, M., Stanger, C., & Weiss, M. (1989). Self development and self-conscious emotions. *Child Development, 60*(1), 146–156.

Lindsay, G. (1991). Psychologists and ethical behavior. *Educational and Child Psychology, 8*(4), 33–42.

Links, P. S., Boyle, M. H., & Offord, D. R. (1989). The prevalance of emotional disorder in children. *Journal of Nervous and Mental Disease, 177*(2), 85–91.

Lippitt, D. N. (1985). The ethical task in family therapy. *Family Therapy, 12*(3), 297–301.

Lishman, J. (1994). *Communication in social work.* London: Macmillan.

Livesley, W. J., & Bromley, D. (1973). *Person perception in childhood and adolescence.* London: Wiley.

Loftus, E. F., & Davies, G. M. (1984). Distortions in the memory of children. *Journal of Social Issues, 40*(2), 51–67.

Looff, D. H. (1976). *Getting to know the troubled child.* Knoxville: University of Tennessee Press.

Lukas, S. (1993). *Where to start and what to ask: An assessment handbook.* New York: Norton.

Luthar, S., Burach, J., Cicchetti, D., & Weisz, J. (Eds.). (1997). *Developmental psychopathology: Focus on adjustment, risk and disorder.* New York: Cambridge University Press.

MacNair, R. R. (1992). Ethical dilemmas of child abuse reporting: Implications for mental health counselors. *Journal of Mental Health Counseling, 14*(2), 127–136.

Manassis, K., Tannock, R., Mendlowitz, S., Laslo, D., & Masellis, M. (1997). Distinguishing axiety disorders psychometrically. *Journal of the American Academy of Child and Adolescent Psychiatry, 36*(12), 1645.

Marin, B. V., Holmes, D. L., Guth, M., & Kovac, P. (1979). The potential of children as eyewitnesses. *Law and Human Behavior, 3*(4), 295–305.

Marshall, R. J. (1972).The treatment of resistances in psychotherapy of children and adolescents. *Psychotherapy: Theory, Research, and Practice, 9*(2), 143–148.

Marton, F. (1981). Phenomenography: Describing conceptions of the world around us. *Instructional Science, 10*(2), 177–200.

Matarazzo, J. (1990). Psychological assessment versus psychological testing: Validation from Binet to the school, clinic, and courtroom. *American Psychologist, 45*(9), 999–1017.

Matthews, G. (1983). Philosophical thinking in young children. *Phenomenology + Pedagogy, 1*(1), 18–28.

McCartney, J. J., & Beauchamp, T. L. (1981). Ethical issues in pediatric treatment and research. *Journal of Pediatric Psychology, 6*(2), 131–143.

McGee, R., Feehan, M., Williams, S., Partridge, F., Silva, P. A., & Kelly, J. (1990). DSM-III disorders in a large sample of adolscents. *Journal of the American Academy of Child and Adolescent Psychiatry, 29*(4), 611–619.

McNamee, G. D. (1989). Language development. In J. Garbarino, F. M. Stott, & faculty of the Erikson Institute (Eds.), *What children can tell us* (pp. 67–91). San Francisco: Jossey Bass.

Melton, G. B. (1987). Children, politics, and morality: The ethics of child advocacy. *Journal of Clinical Child Psychology, 16*(4), 357–367.

Melton, G., & Thompson, R. (1987). Getting out of a rut: Detours to less traveled paths in child–witness research. In S. Ceci, M. Toglia, & D. Ross (Eds.), *Children's eyewitness memory* (pp. 209–229). New York: Springer-Verlag.

Merrell, K. W. (1994). *Assessment of behavioral, social, and emotional problems: Direct and objective methods for use with children and adolescents.* White Plains, NY: Longman.

Miller, P. H., & Aloise, P. A. (1989). Young children's understanding of the psychological causes of behavior: A review. *Child Development, 60*(2), 257–285.

Mishler, E. (1986). *Research interviewing: Context and narrative.* Cambridge, MA: Harvard University Press.

Mishne, J. M. (1992). Ethical assessment and moral reasoning in child therapy. *Child and Adolescent Social Work Journal, 9*(1), 3–19.

Mitchell, G. (1995). Reflection: The key to breaking with tradition. *Nursing Science Quarterly, 8,* 57.

Morgan, M. (1995). *How to interview sexual abuse victims: Including the use of anatomical dolls.* Thousand Oaks, CA: Sage.

Morrison, H. L. (1986). The forensic evaluation and treatment of children: Ethics and values. *Bulletin of the American Academy of Psychiatry and the Law, 14*(4), 353–359.

Morrison, J. K., Layton, B., & Newman, J. (1982). Ethical conflict in clinical decision making: A challenge for family therapists. In L. L'Abate & J. C. Hansen (Eds.), *Values, ethics, legalities and the family therapist: The family therapy collections* (pp. 75–85). Rockville, MD: Aspen.

Morrissette, P. (1989). Benevolent restraining: A strategy for interrupting vicious cycles in residential care. *Journal of Strategic and Systemic Therapies, 8*(1), 31–35.

Morrissette, P. (1996a). Beginning family therapist and client system conflict: Analysis and reparation. *Journal of Family Psychotherapy, 7*(1), 1–13.

Morrissette, P. (1996b). Engagement strategies with reluctant homeless young people. *Psychotherapy, 29*(3), 447–451.

Moston, S. (1987). The suggestibility of children in interview studies. *First Language, 7*(2), 67–78.

Munby, H., & Russel, T. (1989). Educating the reflective teacher: An essay review of two books by Donald Schon. *Journal of Curriculum Studies, 21*(1), 71–80.

Neisser, U., & Harsch, N. (1992). Phantom flashbulbs: False recollections of hearing the news about Challenger. In E. Winograd & U. Neisser (Eds.), *Affect and accuracy in recall: Studies of "flashbulb" memories* (pp. 9–31). New York: Cambridge University Press.

Neisworth, J. T., & Bagnato, S. J. (1992). The case against intelligence testing in early intervention. *Topics in Early Childhood Special Education, 12*(1), 1–20.

Nelson, K., & Ross, G. (1980). The generalities and specifics of long–term memory in infants and young children. In M. Perlmutter (Ed.), *Children's memory: New directions for child development* (No. 10, pp. 87–101). San Francisco: Jossey–Bass.

Nottelmann, E. D., & Jensen, P. S. (1995). Comorbidity of disorders in children and adolescents. In T. H. Ollendick & R. J. Prinz (Eds.) *Advances in clinical child psychology* (pp. 109–155). New York: Plenum.

Offord, D. R., Boyle, M. H., Racine, Y. A., Fleming, J. E., Cadman, D. T., Munroe Blum, H., Byrne, C., Links, P. S., Lipman, E. L., MacMillan, H. L., Rae-Grant, N. I., Sanford, M. N., Szatmari, P., Thomas, H., & Woodward, C. A. (1992). Outcome, prognosis, and risk in a longitudinal follow-up study. *Journal of the American Academy of Child and Adolescent Psychiatry, 31*(5), 916–923.

Offord, D. R., Boyle, M. H., Szatmari, P., Rae-Grant, N. I., Links, P. S., Cadman, D. T., Byles, J. A., Crawford, J. W., Munroe Blum, H., Byrne, C., Thomas, H., & Woodward, C. A. (1987). Ontario child health study: II. Six-month prevalence of disorder and rates of service utilization. *Archives of General Psychiatry, 44*(9), 832–836.

Orvaschel, H., Ambrosini, P., & Rabinovich, H. (1993). Diagnostic issues in child assessment. In T. Ollendick & M. Hersen (Eds.), *Handbook of child and adolescent assessment* (pp. 26–40). Boston: Allyn & Bacon.

O'Shea, M., & Jessee, E. (1982). Ethical, value, and professional conflicts in systems therapy. In L. L'Abate & J. C. Hansen (Eds.), *Values, ethics, legalities and the family therapist: The family therapy collections* (pp. 1–21). Rockville. MD: Aspen.

Ost, D. (1991). Bioethics and paediatrics. In M. M. Burgess & B. E. Woodrow (Eds.), *Contemporary issues in paediatric ethics* (pp. 1–15). Lampeter, Wales: Edwin Mellen.

Paley, V. G. (1984). *Boys & girls: Superheroes in the doll corner.* Chicago: University of Chicago Press.

Paley, V. G. (1988). *Bad guys don't have birthdays: Fantasy play at four.* Chicago: University of Chicago Press.

Paley, V. G. (1990). *The boy who would be a helicopter: The uses of storytelling in the classroom.* Cambridge, MA: Harvard University Press.

Palfrey, C. F. (1972). Piaget's questions to young children. *Educational Review, 24*(2), 122–131.

Parker, W. C. (1984). Interviewing children: Problems and promise. *Journal of Negro Education, 53*(1), 18–28.

Pedersen, P. (1995). *The five stages of culture shock: Critical incidents around the world.* Westport, CT: Greenwood.

Pence, D., & Wilson, C. (1994). *Team investigation of child sexual abuse: The uneasy alliance.* Thousand Oaks, CA: Sage.

Perner, J. (1991). *Understanding the representational mind.* Cambridge, MA: Bradford/MIT.

Perry, N. W., & Wrightsman, L. S. (1991). *The child witness: Legal issues and dilemmas.* Thousand Oaks, CA: Sage.

Peterson, R. W., Young, S. E., & Tillman, J. S. (1990). Applied ethics: Educating professional, child and youth workers in competent caring through self apprenticeship training. *Child and Youth Services, 13*(2), 219–234.

Phelan, T. W. (1994). *1–2–3 magic: Effective discipline for children 2–12.* Glen Ellyn, IL. Child Management.

Piaget, J. (1926). *The language and thought of the child.* New York: Harcourt, Brace.

Piaget, J. (1929). *The child's conception of the world.* London: Routledge & Kegan Paul.

Piaget, J. (1930). *The child's conception of physical causality.* London: Routledge & Kegan Paul.

Piaget, J. (1959). *The language and thought of the child.* London: Routledge.

Pillemer, D. B. (1992). Preschool children's memories of personal circumstances: The fire alarm study. In E. Winograd & U. Neisser (Eds.), *Affect and accuracy in recall: Studies of "flashbulb" memories* (pp. 121–137). New York: Cambridge University Press.

Pipe, M. E., Gee, S., & Wilson, C. (1993). Cues, props, and context: Do they facilitate children's event reports? In G. S. Goodman & B. L. Bottoms (Eds.), *Child victims, child witnesses: Understanding and improving testimony* (pp. 25–45). New York: Guilford.

Plante, T. G. (1995). Training child clinical predoctoral interns and postdoctoral fellows in ethics and professional issues: An experimental model. *Professional Psychology: Research and Practice, 26*(6), 616–619.

Pope, K. S., & Bajt, T. R. (1988). When laws and values conflict: A dilemma for psychologists. *American Psychologist, 43*(10), 828–829.

Powell, M. P., & Vacha–Haase, T. (1994). Issues related to research with children: What counseling psychologists need to know. *The Counseling Psychologist, 22*(3), 444–453.

Pramling, I. (1983). The child's conception of learning. *Goteborg Studies in Educational Sciences, 46.* Goteborg, Sweden: ACTA Universitatis Gothoburgensis

Pramling, I. (1986). The origin of the child's idea of learning through practice. *European Journal of Psychology of Education, 1*(3), 31–46.

Pramling, I. (1988). Developing children's thinking about their own learning. *British Journal of Educational Psychology, 58*(3), 266–278.

Pramling, I. (1990). *Learning to learn: A study of Swedish preschool children.* New York: Springer-Verlag.

Purvis, K. L., & Tannock, R. (1997). Language abilities in children with attention deficit hyperactivity disorder, reading disabilities, and normal controls. *Journal of Abnormal Child Psychology, 25*(2), 133–144.

Pynoos, R. S., & Eth, S. (1986). Witness to violence: The child interview. *Journal of the American Academy of Child and Adolescent Psychiatry, 25*(3), 306–319.

Rae, W. A., Worchel, F. F., & Brunnquell, D. (1995). Ethical and legal issues in pediatric psychology. In M. C. Roberts (Ed.), *Handbook of pediatric psychology* (pp. 19–36). New York: Guilford.

Range, L. M., & Cotton, C. R. (1995). Reports of assent and permission in research with children: Illustrations and suggestions. *Ethics and Behavior,* *5*(1), 49–66.

Rapee, R. M., Barret, P. M., Dadds, M. R., & Evans, L. (1994). Reliability of the DSM-III-R childhood anxiety disorders using structured interviews of interrater and parent-child agreement. *Journal of the American Academy of Child and Adolescent Psychiatry, 33*(7), 984–992.

Rapoport, J. L., & Ismond, D. R. (1996). *DSM-IV training guide for diagnosis of childhood disorders.* New York: Brunner/Mazel.

Redl, F. (1966). *When we deal with children.* New York: Free Press.

Redl, F., & Wineman, D. (1951). *Children who hate: The disorganization and breakdown of behavior controls.* New York: Free Press.

Redl, F., & Wineman, D. (1952). *Controls from within: Techniques for the treatment of the aggressive child.* New York: Free Press.

Reich, W. (1997). *Diagnostic interview for children and adolescents—revised DSM-IV version.* Toronto, Ontario: Multi–Health Systems.

Reich, W., Welner, Z., & Herjanic, B. (1988). *Diagnostic interview for children and adolescents—revised (DICA–R).* Toronto, Ontario: Multi–Health Systems.

Reinherz, H. Z., Giaconia, R. M., Lefkowitz, E. S., Pakiz, B., & Frost, A. K. (1993). Prevalence of psychiatric disorders in a community population of older adolescents. *Journal of the American Academy of Child and Adolescent Psychiatry, 32*(2), 369–377.

Reisberg, D., & Heuer, F. (1992). Remembering the details of emotional events. In E. Winograd & U. Neisser (Eds.), *Affect and accuracy in recall: Studies of "flashbulb" memories* (pp. 162–190). New York: Cambridge University Press.

Reynolds, W. M. (1993). Self-report methodology. In T. Ollendick & M. Hersen (Eds.), *Handbook of child and adolescent assessment* (pp. 98–123). Boston: Allyn & Bacon.

Rich, J. (1968). *Interviewing children and adolescents.* New York: St. Martin's.

Rolf, J., Masten, A. S., Cicchetti, D., Nuechterlein, K. H., & Weintraub, S. (Eds.). (1990). *Risk and protective factors in the development of psychopathology.* New York: Cambridge University Press.

Ross, D. M., & Ross, S. A. (1984). The importance of type of question, psychological climate and subject set in interviewing children about pain. *Pain, 19*(1), 71–79.

Roth, L., Meisel, A., & Lidz, C. (1977). Tests of competency to consent to treatment. *American Journal of Psychiatry, 134*(3), 279–284.

Rousseau, C. (1993). The place of the unexpressed: Ethic and methodology for research with refugee children. *Canada's Mental Health, 41*(4), 12–16.

Russo, D. C., Lehn, B. M., & Berde, C. B. (1993). Pain. In T. Ollendick & M. Hersen (Eds.), *Handbook of child and adolescent assessment* (pp. 413–438). Boston: Allyn & Bacon.

Sattler, J. M. (1992). *Assessment of children* (3rd rev.). San Diego: Jerome M. Sattler.

Saywitz, K. (1990). The child as witness: Experimental and clinical considerations. In A. M. La Greca (Ed.), *Through the eyes of the child: Obtaining self-reports from children and adolescents* (pp. 329–367). Boston: Allyn & Bacon.

Saywitz, K. J., & Snyder, L. (1993) Improving children's testimony with preparation. In G. S. Goodman & B. L. Bottoms (Eds.), *Child victims, child witnesses: Understanding and improving testimony* (pp. 117–146). New York: Guilford.

Scarr, S. (1994). Ethical problems in research on risky behaviors and risky populations. *Ethics and Behavior, 4*(2), 147–155.

Schaufeli, W., Maslach, C., & Marek, T. (Eds.). (1993). *Professional burnout: Recent developments in theory and research.* Washington, DC: Taylor and Francis.

Schon, D. (1983). *The reflective practitioner: How professionals think in action.* New York: Basic Books.

Schon, D. A. (1987). *Educating the reflective practitioner.* San Francisco: Jossey-Bass.

Schwartz, A. R., & Schwanenflugel, P. J. (1989). Eyewitness testimony of children and the school psychologist. *School Psychology Review, 18*(2), 235–246.

Scott-Jones, D. (1994). Ethical issues in reporting and referring in research with low-income minority children. *Ethics and Behavior, 4*(2), 97–108.

Seymour, D., Torssonen, C., & Zwiers, M. (1996). *Child and family history checklist.* Unpublished manuscript.

Shaffer, D., Fisher, P., Dulcan, M. K., & Davies, M. (1996). The NIMH diagnostic interview schedule for children (DISC2.3): Description, acceptability, prevalences, and performance in the MECA study. *Journal of the American Academy of Child and Adolescent Psychiatry, 35*(7), 865–877.

Shaffer, D., Schwab-Stone, M., Fisher, P., Davies, M., Piacentini, J., & Gioia, P. (1988). *Results of a field trial and proposals for a new instrument (DISC–R).* Washington, DC: National Institute of Mental Health.

Shapiro, S., & Reiff, J. (1993). A framework for reflective inquiry on practice: Beyond intuition and experience. *Psychological Reports, 73,* 1379–1394.

Sherak, D. L., Speier, P. L., & Cantwell, D. P. (1994). Classification and diagnostic criteria. In W. M. Reynolds & H. M. Johnston (Eds.), *Handbook of depression in children and adolescents.* New York: Plenum.

Siegal, M. (1991). *Knowing children: Experiments in conversation and cognition.* Mahwah, NJ: Lawrence Erlbaum.

Silverman, W. K., & Eisen, A. R. (1992). Age differences in the reliability of parent and child reports of child anxious symptomatology using a structured interview. *Journal of the American Academy of Child and Adolescent Psychiatry, 31*(1), 117–124.

Smiley, P., & Huttenlocher, J. (1989). Young children's acquisition of emotion concepts. In C. Saarni & P. L. Harris (Eds.), *Children's understanding of emotion* (pp. 27–49). New York: Cambridge University Press.

Sondheimer, A., & Martucci, L. C. (1992). An approach to teaching ethics in child and adolescent psychiatry. *Journal of the American Academy of Child and Adolescent Psychiatry, 31*(3), 415–422.

Stadler, H. A. (1987). *Child abuse reporting: A strategy for acting on ethical responsibilities.* Videotape script, Office of Extended Programs, University of Missouri, Kansas City.

Stadler, H. A. (1989). Balancing ethical responsibilities: Reporting child abuse and neglect. *The Counseling Psychologist, 17*(1), 102–110.

Stanley, B., Sieber, J. E., & Melton, G. B. (1987). Empirical studies of ethical issues in research: A research agenda. *American Psychologist, 42*(7), 735–741.

Steward, M. S., Bussey, K., Goodman, G. S., & Saywitz, K. J. (1993). Implications of developmental research for interviewing children. *Child Abuse and Neglect, 17*(1), 25–38.

Stipek, D. (1995). The development of pride and shame in toddlers. In J. P. Tagney & K. W. Fischer (Eds.), *Self-conscious emotions: The psychology of shame, guilt, embarrassment, and pride* (pp. 237–252). New York: Guilford.

Stipek, D., Recchia, S., & McClintic, S. (1992). Self-evaluation in young children. *Monographs of the Society for Research in Child development, 57*(1, Serial No. 226).

Stone, W. L., & Lemanek, K. L. (1990). Developmental issues in children's self-reports. In A. M. La Greca (Ed.), *Through the eyes of the child: Obtaining self-reports from children and adolescents* (pp. 18–56). Boston: Allyn & Bacon.

Svensson, L., & Theman, J. (May, 1983). *The relation between categories of description and an interview protocol in a case of phenomenographic research.* Paper presented at the Annual Human Science Research Conference. Pittsburg, PA.

Swanson, H. L., & Watson, B. L. (1989). *Educational and psychological assessment of exceptional children* (2nd ed.). Columbus, OH: Merrill.

Tannock, R., & Schachar, R. (1996). Executive dysfunction as an underlying mechanism of behavior and language problems in attention deficit hyperactivity disorder. In J. H. Beitchman, N. J. Cohen, M. M. Konstantareas, & R. Tannock (Eds.), *Language, learning, and behavior disorders* (pp. 128–155). New York: Cambridge University Press.

Taylor, M. G., & Purfall, P. B. (1987, April). *A developmental analysis of directional terms frontwards, backwards, and sideways.* Paper presented at the meeting of the Society for Research in Child Development, Baltimore.

Terr, L. (1983). Chowchilla revisited: The effects of psychic trauma four years after a school bus kidnapping. *American Journal of Psychiatry, 140*(12), 1543–1550.

Terr, L. (1990). *Too scared to cry: How trauma affects children ... and ultimately us all.* New York: Basic Books.

Terr, L. (1994). *Unchained memories: True stories of traumatic memories, lost and found.* New York: Basic Books.

Terwogt, M. M., & Olthof, T. (1989). Motion, empathy, and experience. In C. Saarni & P. L. Harris (Eds.), *Children's understanding of emotion* (pp. 209–237). New York: Cambridge University Press.

Teyber, E. (1992). *Interpersonal process in psychotherapy: A guide for clinical training* (2nd ed.). Pacific Grove, CA: Brooks/Cole.

Thompson, R. A. (1991). Vulnerability in research: A developmental perspective on research risk. In S. Chess & M. E. Hertzig (Eds.), *Annual progress in child psychiatry and child development* (pp. 119–143). New York: Bruner/Mazel.

Thompson, R. J., Merritt, K. A., Keith, B. R., Bennett Murphy, L., & Johndrow, D. A. (1993). Mother-child agreement on the child assessment schedule with nonreferred children: A research report. *Journal of Child Psychology and Psychiatry and Allied Disciplines, 34*(5), 813–820.

Todd, C., & Perlmutter, M. (1980). Reality recalled by preschool children. In M. Perlmutter (Ed.), *Children's memory: New directions in child development* (pp. 69–85). San Francisco: Jossey-Bass.

Tranel, D. (1994). The release of psychological data to nonexperts: Ethical and legal considerations. *Professional Psychology: Research and Practice, 25*(1), 33–38.

Treischman, A. E., Whittaker, J. K., & Brendtro, L. K. (1969). *The other 23 hours: Child-care work with emotionally disturbed children in a therapeutic milieu.* New York: Aldine De Gruyter.

Underwager, R., & Wakefield, H. (1990). *The real world of child interrogations.* Springfield, IL: Charles C. Thomas.

Walco, G. A., Cassidy, R. C., & Schechter, N. L. (1994). Pain, hurt, and harm: The ethics of pain control in infants and children. *New England Journal of Medicine, 33*(8), 541–544.

Wall, M., Amendt, H., Kleckner, T., & Bryant, R. (1989). Therapeutic compliments: Setting the stage for successful therapy. *Journal of Marital and Family Therapy, 15*(2), 159–167.

Wallerstein, J. S. (1984). Children of divorce: The psychological tasks of the child. *Annual Progress in Child Psychiatry and Child Development* (pp. 263–280).

Wallerstein, J. S. (1985). Children of divorce: Preliminary report of a ten-year follow-up of older children and adolescents. *Journal of the American Academy of Child Psychiatry, 24*(5), 545–553.

Wallerstein, J. S. (1987). Children of divorce: Report of a ten-year follow-up of early latency-age children. *American Journal of Orthopsychiatry, 57*(2), 199–221.

Warren, A. R., & Swartwood, J. N. (1992). Developmental issues in flashbulb memory research: Children recall the Challenger event. In E. Winograd & U. Neisser (Eds.), *Affect and accuracy in recall: Studies of "flashbulb" memories* (pp. 95–120). New York: Cambridge University Press.

Watkins, S. A. (1989). Confidentiality and privileged communications: Legal dilemma for family therapists. *Social Work, 34*(2), 133–136.

Weber, S. J. (1986). The nature of interviewing. *Phenomenology + Pedagogy, 4*(2), 65– 72.

Weeks, M. F., & Moore, P. (1981). Ethnicity-of-interviewer effects on ethnic respondents. *Public Opinion Quarterly, 45*(2), 245–249.

Weithorn, L. A., & Schearer, D. G. (1994). Children's involvement in research participation decisions: Psychological considerations. In M. A. Grodin & L. H. Glantz (Eds.), *Children as research subjects: Science, ethics, and law* (pp. 133–179). New York: Oxford University Press.

Wellman, H. M. (1990). *The child's theory of mind.* Cambridge, MA: MIT Press.

Wellman, H. M., & Hickling, A. K. (1993). Understanding pretense as pretense. In P. L. Harris & R. D. Kavanaugh (Eds.), *Young children's understanding of pretense: Monographs of the Society for Research in Child Development, 58*(1, Serial No. 231), 103–107.

Wells, J. (1989). Powerplays: Considerations in communicating with children. In H. Blagg, J. A. Hughes, & C. Wattam (Eds.), *Child sexual abuse: Listening, hearing and validating the experiences of children* (pp. 44–58). London: Longman.

Wells, K., & Sametz, L. (1985). Involvement of institutionalized children in social science research: Some issues and proposed guidelines. *Journal of Clinical Child Psychology, 14*(3), 245–251.

Westcott, H. L. (1994). On sensitivity and ethical issues in child witness research. *Child Abuse and Neglect, 18*(3), 287–290.

Whitaker, A., Johnson, J., Shaffer, D., Rapoport, J. L., Kalikow, K., Walsh, B. T., Davies, M., Braiman, S., & Dolinsky, A. (1989). Uncommon troubles in young people: Prevalence estimates of selected psychiatric disorders in a nonreferred adolescent population. *Archives of General Psychiatry, 47*(5), 487–496.

White, S. (1990). The investigatory interview with suspected victims of child sexual abuse. In A. M. La Greca (Ed.), *Through the eyes of the child: Obtaining self-reports from children and adolescents* (pp. 368–394). Boston: Allyn & Bacon.

Williams, A. (1995). *Visual and active supervision: Roles focus technique.* New York: Norton.

Williamson, P. S., & Williamson, M. L. (1983). Physiologic stress reduction by a local anaesthetic during newborn circumcision. *Pediatrics, 71*(1), 36–40.

Wilson, T. D. (1985). Strangers to ourselves: The origins and accuracy of beliefs about one's own mental states. In J. H. Harvey & G. Weary (Eds.), *Attributions: Basic issues and applications* (pp. 9–36). Orlando, FL: Academic Press.

Wiltse, K. T. (1985). Ethical issues in permanency planning. *Children and Youth Services Review, 7*(2/3), 259–266.

Winograd, T. (1980). What does it mean to understand language? *Cognitive Science, 4*(3), 209–241.

Wood, H., & Wood, D. (1983). Questioning the preschool child. *Educational Review, 35*(2), 149–162.

World Health Organization. (1992). *International statistical classification of diseases and related health problems: Volume 1* (10th ed.). Geneva, Switzerland: Author.

Yarrow, L. J. (1960). Interviewing children. In P. J. Mussen (Ed.), *Handbook of research methods in child development* (pp. 561–602). New York: Wiley.

Yonemura, M. (1974). Learning what children know. *Childhood Education, 51*(2), 64–67.

Yuille, J. C., Hunter, R., Joffe, R., & Zaparniuk, J. (1993). Interviewing children in sexual abuse cases. In G. S. Goodman & B. L. Bottoms (Eds.), *Child victims, child witnesses: Understanding and improving testimony* (pp. 95–115). New York: Guilford.

Zilbach, J. (1986). *Young children in family therapy.* New York: Brunner/Mazel.

Zilversmit, C. (1990). Family treatment with families with young children. *Families in Society, 71*(4), 211–219.

Zingaro, J.C. (1983). Confidentiality: To tell or not to tell. *Elementary School Guidance and Counseling, 17*(4), 261–267.

Index

ABOUT THE AUTHORS

Michael L. Zwiers, M.Ed. is a doctoral candidate at the University of British Columbia and has almost two decades of experience working with children and youth as a teacher, therapist, assessor, consultant, and researcher. He has worked with children and youth in schools, clinics, group homes, and community settings.

Mr. Zwiers has been an adult educator since 1983 and has taught as a University Sessional Instructor for both undergraduate and graduate courses.

He has presented internationally on conducting effective interviews with children. Mr. Zwiers works in the Child and Adolescent Family Service (Mental Health Services) at Markham-Stouffville Hospital and contracts with the Psychiatry Department at the Hospital for Sick Children in Toronto, Canada.

Patrick J. Morrissette, Ph.D., NCC., LCPC is Assistant Professor, Department of Counseling and Human Services, Montana State University at Billings. Dr. Morrissette is a Clinical Member and Approved Supervisor with the American Association for Marriage and Family Therapy, an Approved Clinical Supervisor with the National Board for Certified Counselors, and a Licensed Clinical Professional Counselor in the State of Montana.

Over the past 20 years, Dr. Morrissette has worked, supervised, and consulted in a variety of inpatient and outpatient child/adolescent treatment centers in both Canada and the United States. He has published widely in national and international counseling and family therapy journals on issues critical to educators and practitioners and serves on the editorial boards of several journals.

Dr. Morrissette currently resides in Billings, Montana with his wife, Debbie, and their three children, Matthew, Alana, and Samuel.